# Edith Craig
## and
# The Theatres
## of Art

# RELATED TITLES FROM BLOOMSBURY METHUEN DRAMA

*British Musical Theatre since 1950*
by Robert Gordon, Olaf Jubin and Millie Taylor
ISBN 978-1-4725-8436-6

*British Theatre and Performance 1900–1950*
by Rebecca D'Monte
ISBN 978-1-4081-6565-2

*Craig On Theatre*
by Edward Gordon Craig, edited by J. Michael Walton
ISBN 978-0-4134-7220-5

*A Cultural History of Theatre*
edited by Christoper B. Balme and Tracy C. Davis
ISBN 978-1-4725-8584-4

*The Methuen Drama Book of Suffrage Plays: How the Vote Was Won, Lady Geraldine's Speech, Pot and Kettle, Miss Appleyard's Awakening, Her Vote, The Mother's Meeting, The Anti-Suffragist or The Other Side, Tradition*
edited by Naomi Paxton
ISBN 978-1-4081-7658-0

*The Sixth Sense of the Avant-Garde: Dance, Kinaesthesia and the Arts in Revolutionary Russia*
Irina Sirotkina and Roger Smith
ISBN 978-1-3500-1431-2

*Verse Drama in England, 1900–2015*
Irene Morra
ISBN 978-1-4725-8013-9

# Edith Craig
# and
# The Theatres
# of Art

## KATHARINE COCKIN

Bloomsbury Methuen Drama
An imprint of Bloomsbury Publishing Plc

B L O O M S B U R Y
LONDON · OXFORD · NEW YORK · NEW DELHI · SYDNEY

**Bloomsbury Methuen Drama**

An imprint of Bloomsbury Publishing Plc
Imprint previously known as Methuen Drama

| 50 Bedford Square | 1385 Broadway |
| London | New York |
| WC1B 3DP | NY 10018 |
| UK | USA |

www.bloomsbury.com

**BLOOMSBURY, METHUEN DRAMA and the Diana logo are trademarks of
Bloomsbury Publishing Plc**

First published 2017

**British Library Cataloguing-in-Publication Data**
A catalogue record for this book is available from the British Library.

ISBN: HB: 978-1-4725-7062-8
PB: 978-1-4725-7061-1
ePDF: 978-1-4725-7064-2
ePub: 978-1-4725-7063-5

**Library of Congress Cataloging-in-Publication Data**
A catalog record for this book is available from the Library of Congress.

Typeset by Newgen Knowledge Works (P) Ltd., Chennai, India.
Printed and bound in Great Britain

*For Michael Lumsden*

# CONTENTS

# ILLUSTRATIONS

# LIST OF ABBREVIATIONS

AFL        Actresses' Franchise League
BDL        British Drama League
*CLET*     *The Collected Letters of Ellen Terry*
GBS        George Bernard Shaw
HI         Henry Irving
IWW        Industrial Workers of the World
LAT        Leeds Art Theatre
MSFG       Masses' Stage and Film Guild
NFRA       National Food Reform Association
NUWSS      National Union of Women's Suffrage Societies
OUDS       Oxford University Dramatic Society
PPAR       Pioneer Players Annual Reports
SSAR       Stage Society Annual Reports
*STC*      *Shaw-Terry Correspondence*
V&A        Victoria and Albert Museum, London
WFL        Women's Freedom League
WI         Women's Institute
WSPU       Women's Social and Political Union

## Archival sources

ET- and EC- prefixes    National Trust's Ellen Terry and Edith
                        Craig Archive
THM 384 prefixes        Ellen Terry collection, Theatre Collection,
                        V&A, London
VJH prefix              Vera Holme collection, Women's Library,
                        LSE London

# ACKNOWLEDGEMENTS

I am grateful to many institutions and individuals who have supported my research in different ways, beginning with the University of Hull and colleagues in the Department of English who facilitated my research leave in 2014–15. I am grateful for the financial support of the following funding bodies: the AHRC for a Small Grant in the Performing Arts (2004), Resource Enhancement (2006) and Follow-on funding (2015); and the British Academy for Small Grants (2005, 2008) for the *Collected Letters of Ellen Terry* project. St John's College, Oxford awarded a Visiting Scholarship (2014) which enabled me to consult the John Johnson Collection. I am also grateful for the assistance of staff and resources at the Bodleian Library, Oxford; British Library; Victoria and Albert Museum Theatre Collection, Blythe Road, Olympia, London; the Women's Library at the LSE, London; Yorkshire Film Archive; York City Archives; the Folger Shakespeare Library, Washington DC, United States; the Special Collections at the Morris Library, University of Delaware, United States; Mark Samuels Lasner Collection at the University of Delaware, United States.

Some material for chapters was presented at conferences and so I would particularly like to thank the organizers and audiences, including: International Federation for Theatre Research, Warwick, 2014; British Association of Modernist Studies, London, 2014; Exotic Bodies, University of Oxford, 2014; International Women's Day event, Department of Philosophy, University of Durham, 2015 and the Who is Gordon Craig? event at the Gordon Craig Theatre, Stevenage, 2016. I was honoured in 2010 to be invited by Equity to give a talk at the Theatre Arts Club, London, to their members on Edith Craig, the LGBT History Month figure. I am grateful for the invitation to contribute to the LGBT History Month pre-launch in 2014 in Birmingham, where I gave a short presentation on the passionate and political activities of the world-famous lesbian composer Dame Ethel Smyth (who features here in Chapter Four).

The publisher's readers provided excellent advice and suggestions and I am indebted to them, and to other colleagues who kindly read and commented on one or more chapters: Professor Nicholas Allen, Professor Susan Bassnett, Dr Catherine Clay, Professor Laura Doan, Professor J. Ellen Gainor, Professor Alex Goody, Dr Stewart Mottram and Professor Jeff Wallace. The end result is, of course, my responsibility. I am grateful also to Mark Dudgeon, Senior Commissioning Editor and Emily Hockley at Bloomsbury Methuen Drama for their support of the project and to Claire Cooper, Ellen Conlon and Kalyani who worked on the production of the book.

This book benefitted greatly from the permission to quote from unpublished material and reproduce photographic illustrations. For this valuable addition to the book, I would like to thank the following: Alexander Murray for permission to quote from the correspondence of Professor Gilbert Murray; Brian Read for permission to quote from the correspondence of Arthur Symons; The Society of Authors for permission to quote from the correspondence of George Bernard Shaw; the executors of the Edward Gordon Craig Estate for permission to quote from Gordon Craig's letter; the estate of Sir William Rothenstein/Bridgman Images for permission to quote from a letter from Sir William Rothenstein to Edith Craig; Higham Associates for permission to quote from the letters of Dame Ethel Smyth and to reproduce the trumpet score for 'The March of the Women' sent in a letter to Edith Craig owned by the National Trust in the Ellen Terry and Edith Craig Archive, held at the British Library, London; the V&A for permission to reproduce two photographs of Edith Craig in the Ellen Terry collection THM 384 held at the V&A Theatre Collection, London; and, last but not least, The National Trust for permission to quote from their archival holdings and to reproduce photographs of Edith Craig in the National Trust's Ellen Terry and Edith Craig Archive, held at Smallhythe Place, Tenterden, Kent, and to Susannah Mayor at Smallhythe Place for her assistance.

My research on Edith Craig over the years has led me to meet many researchers and theatre practitioners. I am grateful to Richard Foulkes, Professor Emeritus, University of Leicester and Professor Susan Bassnett, University of Warwick for their advice and support and, for encouragement on my research on George Bernard Shaw and the Terry family, to Leonard Conolly, Professor Emeritus, University, Canada and Honorary Fellow, Robinson College, Cambridge. I was very fortunate to have been granted interviews

# A NOTE ON
# SOURCES AND MORE
# DRAMATIC LIVES

*Edith Craig and the Theatres of Art* is a new biographical study. As a sequel to *Edith Craig: Dramatic Lives* (1998), it reassesses Craig's work in the theatre as an actor, costumier and director in light of new archival research. *Edith Craig (1869–1947): Dramatic Lives* (1998) was published in Cassell's Sexual Politics list, bringing her life story as a lesbian hidden from history out of the long shadows of her more famous mother, the Shakespearean actor, Ellen Terry (1847–1928),[1] and her brother, Edward Gordon Craig (1872–1966). His innovative scene designs and new theories for prioritizing the director's vision over the author's words and the actor's interpretation have an unquestionable place in theatre history.[2] In *Lesbian Lives: Identity and Auto/biography in the Twentieth Century* (1999), Nicky Hallett argued that *Edith Craig: Dramatic Lives* (1998) was a ground-breaking lesbian biography in its treatment of Craig and her female partners, the author Christopher St John (1871–1960) and artist Tony Atwood (1866–1962)[3]: 'It presents a lesbian Life and lives which extend in application beyond the specific to the particularly, and historically, generalised' (Hallett 1999: 66).[4] It emulated the kind of biography described by Liz Stanley as 'a self refracted through others' (Stanley 1991: 215) and established the case for Craig's inclusion in the landscape of theatre history, showing, as Graham Saunders has noted, 'Edy Craig's role as theatrical innovator, but also to test the parameters of the theatrical canon' (Saunders 2011: 825).[5] Edith Craig and her theatre society, the Pioneer Players, are mentioned briefly in Alan Sinfield's *Out on Stage: Lesbian and Gay Theatre* (1999). The consideration of Edith Craig's work in the theatre sets in chain a seismic shift in perspective and from this new faultline emerge others who played their hitherto unacknowledged parts in the developments of British theatre.

## Edith Craig in the archives

Since 1998 several major archives relating to Edith Craig have become available to researchers. This book draws on the National Trust's Ellen Terry and Edith Craig archive of over 20,000 documents, one of the most significant theatre archives in the United Kingdom and now described in the AHRC Ellen Terry and Edith Craig Database (2006–08) project.[6] *The Collected Letters of Ellen Terry* (8 vols; 2010–) draws on over 3,000 letters held in repositories in the United Kingdom and United States, including the Stephen Coleridge correspondence at the Garrick Club. The many new insights into Ellen Terry's life, work and family relationships including her relationship with her daughter, provided by these letters, therefore inform the following account up to Terry's death in 1928.

The Ellen Terry collection, acquired by the Victoria & Albert Museum, London in 2010, includes hundreds of letters and documents relating to Ellen Terry's family and numerous documents relating specifically to Edith Craig.[7] The private papers of Vera Holme (1881–1969), deposited in 2006, with the Women's Library, include correspondence relating to Craig and her two partners, Atwood and St John.[8] Craig dictated her memoirs to Holme and these were recently published (Rachlin 2011).

## Out of her mother's shadows: Restaging Edith Craig

Edith Craig has featured peripherally in various exhibitions and plays focusing on Ellen Terry.[9] Her influence has been felt in the number of theatrical productions that explore the relevance today of women's suffrage and have restaged plays formerly directed by Edith Craig. In 2011, to mark the centenary of Edith Craig's founding of the Pioneer Players theatre society, two plays were produced.

A new play entitled *Suffragette* was written and performed by Hull College students, with a scene in which Edith Craig is shown in rehearsal, directing the performers in *A Pageant of Great Women* by Cicely Hamilton (1872–1952). This was followed by a new production of *A Pageant of Great Women* directed by Anna Birch,[10] and in 2014 a reading was staged of Edith Craig's historic revival of a tenth-century play by Hrotsvit, said to be the first female dramatist.[11]

For modern audiences and readers, the association of Edith Craig with women's suffrage is perhaps becoming stronger than that with her famous family members. However, the range and depth of her contribution to theatre history has yet to be fully acknowledged and it is hoped that this book will set further discussions in motion towards that general goal. This book also aims to promote the remembering and acknowledging of Edith Craig's achievements and more widely to expose some of the processes of being hidden from history – the reforgetting and casual overlooking – that regrettably continues to shape contemporary culture.

# CHAPTER ONE

# Introduction: Edith Craig retrospectives

Edith Craig's role as a significant theatre director in twentieth-century British theatre is gradually being acknowledged. The reassessment here, based on extensive new archival research, establishes that Edith Craig's prolific theatre work constitutes a developing and coherent project. Unlike that of her brother, Edward Gordon Craig, Edith Craig's approach to theatrical production was grounded in a theatre practice drawing together and equally valuing all elements, including the actor and the performance space. Nina Auerbach has said that Craig 'made a style out of obscuring herself' (1987: 366) but Craig's attention was always rather on the theatrical production than on herself. She made an art out of resourcefulness, creatively responding to and transforming whatever material she found. Hers was an aesthetic influenced by her training at the Lyceum Theatre, London led by actor-manager Henry Irving (1838–1905) and her work for the nationalist theatres of social reform, the independent theatres demanding liberation from censorship, and the revolutionary political theatres of British women's suffrage and socialism.

Edith Craig's many art theatres, designated by the title of this book, were founded at a time when debates about the relationship between art and the theatre became a matter of national interest. They informed the British government's report on the role of the arts in education (1921) and responded to the democratization of the arts in the age of a mass market. When the arts became a contested site where the 'highbrow' designated a despised elitism and the 'middlebrow' was disparaged as vulgar,[1] Edith Craig promoted amateur theatre nationwide. Craig's role in the British Drama League from 1919 was to set the fires of inspiration for the Little Theatre movement in a community and then move on,[2] beginning in London's suburb of Hampstead and then in Leeds, a principal city in Yorkshire, when it had already become established as the centre of modernism in the North of England.

Edith Craig's was a humanist theatre with a vision of a new, regenerated society after the devastation of the First World War. In returning to the roots of theatre in the church, she tapped into powerful institutional forces at the heart of a conservative Englishness. However, in the interwar period she was also engaging with the democratizing impulses of the cultural strands of the Independent Labour Party.[3] She was evasive when pressed to talk about her work, but revealed a holistic approach to the ebb and flow of life, art and theatre. Her theatres of art were diverse; open and small-scale, they tended towards the anti-commercial. International financial crises and the tide of popular cinema inevitably shortened the life of the independent theatres in this period. It was not until 1946 that British government subsidy was available from the Arts Council and 1963 when the National Theatre in London was founded.

In the role of what is now known as the theatre 'director', Edith Craig was collaborative and creative. Her productions were the result of collective endeavour; they were driven by her single, coherent vision as 'producer' and shaped by her deliberate anonymity in that role. Craig's attitude frustrated her political peers in the women's suffrage movement. Rather than a feminized behavioural trait of self-effacement, it becomes apparent as a coherent and aesthetic position, intelligible in the context of a holistic approach to art and politics. In some ways it was akin to the anarchist position on leadership, and in others it harked back to the anonymity of medieval craftwork. It was also influenced by the British bureaucratic culture of interwar reconstruction. Edith Craig's work in the theatre is also reconsidered in the following chapters in relation to that of her brother, Edward Gordon Craig, with whom she collaborated as well as antagonized; they worked apart and along parallel lines.

Since Edith Craig eschewed fame and publicity for herself and was reluctant to write about her theatrework or methodology, she inadvertently contributed to the greater efficiency of rendering herself hidden from history.[4] Diffidence and self-consciousness were aspects of her personality, developing from her own family circumstances, as the eldest child, the only daughter and first illegitimate child of a famous theatrical performer. The more her mother and brother sought attention, the more Edith Craig sought a role in the background. As a lesbian and a friend of the author Radclyffe Hall (1880–1943), Craig lived through the homophobic storm created by the publication of Hall's novel, *The Well of Loneliness* (1928) and its trial for obscenity.[5] With these difficulties in mind, the researcher needs to embark on an active harvesting of available sources. In this alchemical process – panning for gold in the more obscure official records, in the anecdotes and passing references in autobiographies of her contemporaries and their private correspondence – more aspects of Edith Craig start to rematerialize. Unlike the most thoroughly forgotten or obscured life, Edith Craig was very famous during her lifetime, although usually designated as the daughter of a famous mother. Her theatrical productions were always reviewed nationally and some internationally. Much of her work had the effect of a catalyst; it was associated with a short-term political campaign or aesthetic movement. For this reason, a return to the records of her contemporaries has provided new insights into how her name came to be omitted or her full contribution was downplayed.

Valuable published accounts of Edith Craig's work as a theatre director and costume designer are provided by her contemporaries, notably Norman MacDermott (1890–1977) director and founder of the Everyman Theatre, Hampstead and E. Martin Browne (1900–80), director and leading authority on religious drama. Craig's advocates and supporters included Charles F. Smith at the Leeds Art Theatre (LAT) and Leeds Civic Playhouse,[6] and Margaret Webster (1905–72). Webster's parents, actors May Whitty and Ben Webster, had toured with Ellen Terry and the family lived in a flat in the same building as Edith Craig at 31 Bedford Street, Covent Garden. Margaret Webster's earliest memory was being put on stage with Ellen Terry and she had great respect for Edith Craig. Writing at a time when she had acquired a reputation for courageous frankness,[7] Webster exposed the impact on Edith Craig's reputation of the family conflicts at work in the published versions of Ellen Terry's life which were largely influenced by the extensive writings of Edward Gordon Craig:

> As a result, the Terry-Craig biographies concentrate on him. The references to [Edith Craig] are scanty and misleading; some are openly hostile. She could arouse bitter antagonisms and never suffered fools with even a semblance of gladness. (Webster 1969: 280)

The impact of this family conflict has been long lasting; it served to marginalize Edith Craig's contributions to theatre history to the same extent that her brother had acquired a solid place in it.[8] Webster described the siblings in dialectical terms, as polar opposites:

> She and her much more famous brother Gordon – 'Teddy' – had many things in common. But he was essentially an artist of the imagination, she a craftsman in practice. She wrote nothing about herself; he never stopped. (Webster 1969: 280)

Webster contrasts aesthetic modes and behaviours: art and craft, imagination and practice, voluble self-representation and silence. In a rare insight into the legacy of theatrical direction, Webster recounts how gestures and techniques were transmitted when no manifestoes or guidebooks were recorded for posterity. This form of pedagogy – based on observation and learnt by means of a practical, corporeal, sensuous experience rather than an objective, logical theorized approach – is especially relevant for reassessing Edith Craig's impact on other theatre practitioners, as Webster recalls:

> I know now that I have done many things because of what I watched her do – set a light, angle a rostrum, drape a cloak, compose a picture on the stage; my eyes and hand learned these things. She made me understand what craft meant in the theatre. She knew everybody's job, from the author's to the usher's. From all she executed workmanship, to all she accorded value. Her shows were frequently a battle, but it was always an exciting one. (Webster 1969: 280)

This kind of ingrained routine becomes a physical memory some-how automatic and hard to define. The terminology of 'craft' and 'workmanship' have their roots in the medieval period and shape the anti-commercial, slow working of the Arts and Crafts movement.

These influences inform the anonymity characterizing Craig's aesthetic. Like the potter's thumb mark on the handle of a clay vessel, Craig's style was recognizable in other ways than the attribution of a name and its accompanying ego.

*Edith Craig and the Theatres of Art* is a new biography focusing on Craig's work in the theatre in various roles but primarily as a director. In its engagement with new discoveries in the archive, it will interest an academic researchers but it is also aimed at a general readership and hence contextual information has been provided where necessary for this purpose. Whereas *Edith Craig: Dramatic Lives* kaleidoscopically involved Christopher St John and Tony Atwood,[9] this book tends more towards placing a spotlight on Edith Craig. The time is right to do so in order to reinforce Craig's place in theatre history and raise further questions about the networks and associations she worked within.

Chapter One begins with a reflection on Edith Craig's career at a critical point, when she was interviewed in a newspaper in 1923. It explores the various ways in which her contemporaries tried to describe her unusual and creative powers and considers the influences which shaped her sense of self in and out of the theatre. Even as a child she seems to have been the responsible adult in an extraordinary theatrical family. Chapter Two examines Edith Craig's formative years, her education and musical training in Germany and her training in the theatre as an actor and costumier. Chapter Three explores Craig's continuing interest in the masque and the pageant forms in the period during which she developed her costume design work and turned towards stage direction. Following her collaboration with Edward Gordon Craig at the Imperial Theatre, Craig became briefly involved in a theatre society called The Masquers (1903), assisted in some way with her mother's stage jubilee event in 1906 and, during her mother's tour of North America in 1907, she publicly identified herself as a producer and stage director. It was in this role that Craig became known and respected in the British women's suffrage movement, and it is a reassessment of the breadth of Craig's political activism and her collaborations which concerns Chapter Four.

After the intensively active period of directing women's suffrage productions, Edith Craig founded the Pioneer Players (1911–25), a new theatre society based in London with a reputation for the production of the 'play of ideas'.[10] Chapter Five concerns new insights into the Pioneer Players' relationship with George Bernard Shaw, James Joyce and Susan Glaspell and traces some points of comparison between Edith Craig's work with the Pioneer Players and Edward Gordon Craig's interests at the time. Chapter Six establishes that Edith Craig was not only an influential figure in the interwar promotion of nativity plays but also a significant national leader in the promotion of amateur theatre as a humanizing force at a time when the British government was scrutinizing the place of drama and English literature in education. Chapter Seven reconsiders Craig's prolific work in the decade from 1919 until her mother's death in 1928, situating her leadership in the Little Theatre movement in the context of interwar modernism and 'middlebrow' theatre. Craig organized Little Theatres in the London suburbs and in the north of England where she became one of the key figures in the modernist circle in Leeds. She gained recognition with her appointment to a prestigious lectureship and developed a reputation for organizing historical pageants. With reference to Craig's unpublished notes on theatrical production and the impact her work had on Virginia Woolf, Chapter Eight briefly considers Edith Craig's legacy as a theatre director whose approach in both art and politics was focused on action, collectivism and the present moment.

Edith Craig eschewed the egocentrism and self-promotion which would have driven her to write for posterity. Instead she committed a great deal of energy to construct a memorial to her mother which took a number of different forms – the Barn Theatre, a memorial museum, the transatlantic promotion of her mother's lectures on Shakespeare – and in so doing her own contributions to theatre history threatened to recede into the corners of her unpublished archive. This biography shows that Craig's legacy was nevertheless handed on in training others, in acting as a role model, a mentor and an inspiration. In order to do this, it begins at a point when, in mid-career, Craig was expected to conform to expectations and record her own ideas and theories. This chapter will therefore provide a survey of her career and an exploration of the attitude that she and her colleagues had towards retrospectives, official accounts and acknowledgements in order to introduce the complex circumstances in which Craig's work has been overlooked.

# Edith Craig retrospectives: A life in theatre and opposition to theory

In 1923 when Edith Craig was interviewed about her prolific work as a theatre practitioner over the past fifty years, she was asked why she had never written about it. A brief summary will give a sense of the incredulity of the interviewer and indicate some of the fascinating productions to be explored in the forthcoming chapters. Craig had been the women's suffrage movement's principal director of plays and even street processions. Her directorial achievements included productions of plays by internationally renowned authors, from France, Holland, Spain, Italy, Russia, America and Japan. To the vibrant Anglo-Russian cultural dialogue in the pre-revolutionary modernist period, she contributed productions of plays by Anton Chekhov, Nikolai Evreinov and Leonid Andreyev. Her directorial credits included a number of plays from America, notably those by Charlotte Perkins Gilman, Susan Glaspell, Eugene O'Neill and Upton Sinclair.[11] Craig not only acted in several plays by George Bernard Shaw but also directed *Mrs Warren's Profession, The Inca of Perusalem* and the highly challenging *Back to Methuselah*. Craig was at the forefront of the interwar Little Theatre movement. She directed for the Everyman Theatre (1920–21). In 1920s, Leeds had become a vibrant cultural centre for modernism, with the Leeds Art Club at its heart and it was at the LAT that Edith Craig was welcomed as Art Director from 1922 to 1924. Edith Craig's production in 1923 of a dramatization of Joseph Conrad's *The Secret Agent* was very well received by the author, who sent a message by telegram to LAT, thanking 'the players for their production of his play and wished them success in their project' (EC-G1367). For the LAT, Edith Craig directed the famous 1922 production of *The Boatswain's Mate*, an operetta by Dame Ethel Smyth, in which Smyth sang the part of the missing cello. In 1925 for the Renaissance Theatre society, Craig directed the first modern production of John Webster's *The White Devil*. As well as politically focused plays, dramatizations of novels, operetta and revivals of medieval and early modern drama, Craig played a part in the production of Jewish drama in Britain, directing for the Pioneer Players Michael Sherbrooke's performance of a monologue by Sholom Alecheim, and for the Leeds Civic Playhouse, *The Dybbuk* by S. Ansky.[12]

In this context, there was ample evidence to make Craig's reply to the *Yorkshire Post* journalist on 12 March 1923 highly persuasive: 'the theatre is too much a part of my life for me to theorise about it' (EC-G174). She was too busy staging and reviving the work of some of the most influential writers of the age to divert attention to writing about what she did. She also implied that theorization would require a distance or removal from the production whereas her priority was on action and to be at the centre of theatre practice.

The interviewer was probably inviting Edith Craig to compare herself with her brother, Edward Gordon Craig, who had become internationally famous for his theories and theatre designs. He was interested in a creative vision for the whole production and to this end he invented a system of moveable screens to transform the acting space. In reconceptualizing performance, he also dehumanized the performer as one of many elements under the control of the director. By 1923 he had published and revised *The Art of the Theatre* (1905, 1911), edited his own journal, *The Mask*, and designed for Konstantin Stanislavski's revolutionary production of *Hamlet* for the Moscow Art Theatre (1912). Gordon Craig made no reference to his sister in his publications; her achievements as a director were still developing but at that time were nevertheless nationally known in relation to the women's suffrage movement which he despised. The siblings shared much of the revolutionary thinking which has hitherto been attributed solely to Edward. This concerned the role of the director or 'stage manager' of the future, as someone in control of all aspects of the production, knowledgeable in all elements from interpretation of the playscript to lighting and costume and stage design. Craig's achievements feature only as ghostly allusions in her brother's magazine, *The Mask* (1908–29), as will be seen in Chapter 5. George Bernard Shaw succinctly formulated the conundrum posed by the Terry children's impact on the world in terms of the inverse proportion of fame to productivity that defined them:

> Gordon Craig had made himself the most famous producer [director] in Europe by dint of never producing anything, while Edith Craig remains the most obscure by dint of producing everything. (quoted in Auerbach 1987: 367–8)

Shaw refrained from passing judgement on the siblings' talents. Harold Nicholson's view was that Edward Gordon Craig had become many other things including famous but that Edith Craig had, by contrast, remained herself (Nicholson 1950: 15). In Nicholson's analysis, fame fundamentally altered Gordon Craig.

Edith Craig's theatre work was always characterized as art. On reflection it was idiosyncratic, eclectic, risk-taking, scholarly, innovative and pragmatic. Anyone regularly following her career would have been struck by her intense activity. She directed many individual productions of great quality and depth but, for a variety of reasons, there was insufficient scope to build on them. To a certain extent the principal reasons – economic and institutional – were related to the funding of theatre activities in Britain in this period when drama competed with film and music hall or variety theatres and before any government funding of any regional or national theatre. In 1917, four years after Edward Gordon Craig had founded the Arena Goldoni in Florence, Edith Craig explored opportunities to set up a drama school with Rosina Filippi.[13] She was in search of a theatre of her own or at least a reliable salary that would enable her to develop as a director.

Her work had a high visual impact, lingering provocatively in the memory. The drama critic William Archer (1856–1924), who had been so critical of Henry Irving at the Lyceum Theatre, had only the most emphatic praise for Edith Craig's scene designs. After her Pioneer Players' production of Paul Claudel's *The Tidings Brought to Mary* in 1917, Archer wrote to her personally because his review of her production had been edited apparently without his approval, omitting some aspects of his appraisal: 'I thought the cave scene one of the most ingenious and beautiful things I had ever seen on the stage' (11 June 1917; EC-3.008). Virginia Woolf recalled Edith Craig had transformed one theatrical enterprise, from an unpromising and chaotic rehearsal fraught with human frailty and technical problems into a visually striking scene of beauty: 'Then we went into the theatre, & there was the light on, the group significant [...] gold tissue, something stimulating & unreal' (Woolf 1978: 174).

Dramatists as well as critics praised Edith Craig's treatment of their work. Sheila Kaye-Smith (1887–1956), regional novelist, was equally impressed by Edith Craig's 'conscientiousness' as a director to her wishes as the author of *The Child Born at the Plough*, when she directed it at the Barn Theatre:

Most authors complain that the producer ignores them, twisting and mangling so heartlessly that in the end they hardly recognize their own work. I have heard this said by experienced playwrights, whose work probably had no deficiencies on technical grounds. But Edy consulted me on every change she made, and a general authorization from me to do anything she liked failed to move her from this integrity. (Kaye-Smith 1949: 129)

Edith Craig's style was, in this respect, collaborative and attentive to the author and the actors. It was very different from Edward Gordon Craig's liberation of the playscript for free interpretation by the director and his preference for marionettes over live actors.[14]

## Edith Craig, the magician

After her death on 27 March 1947, Edith Craig was eulogized by her contemporaries in appropriately wide-ranging accounts that did justice to her achievements as a polymath. Harold Nicholson described in *The Spectator* the 'stereoscopic perspective' provided by the seventeen essays collected by Eleanor Adlard in *Edy: Recollections of Edith Craig* (1949).[15] Craig is presented as a stalwart; magnanimous and patient, untroubled by ego although unswervingly driven by her directorial goal. Such 'recollections' provide a valuable insight into Craig's attitude and values. They also drew their terms widely and metaphorically to describe her method of working; ordinary language could not quite capture it. Her contribution to the theatre as an art form demanded a new vision and opened up new possibilities. For May Whitty, Craig was 'the magician' with influential powers to enlist friends and acquaintances as 'djinns' on her projects.[16]

Metaphors of electricity and magnetism were used by the French dramatist Saint-Georges de Bouhélier (1876–1947) to describe Edith Craig's powerful command of a production and the strange rapport that she, like other great theatre producers, achieved (de Bouhélier 1949: 62–3).[17] De Bouhélier places Craig firmly in the context of a modernist practice, engaging with the unconscious in her staging which brought about a change in the atmosphere in creating character in performance. He remarked on the subtlety of interpretation she brought about in her 1920 London staging of his play *The Children's Carnival*. De Bouhélier described Craig's profound genius ['un génie profond']: 'Le style d'Edith Craig rejoignait le mien, et avec une intensité hallucinatoire' [Edith Craig's style complemented mine and achieved a visual and emotional effect that transformed the senses] (de Bouhélier 1949: 63–4).

The magical activities recalled by May Whitty took place at The Farm, Ellen Terry's house in Tenterden, Kent, now named Smallhythe Place and at Priest's House, next door where Edith Craig lived during her later years with Christopher St John and Tony Atwood. Vita Sackville-West records the dynamism and creative conflicts at work in their interactions:

> They talk. It is enchanting talk; it ranges widely; it isn't always consecutive; it starts too many hares too quickly to follow up; they argue; they quarrel; they interrupt; it is impossible to have any sequence of conversation. Yet how stimulating it is! And how friendly! How lively! What live wires they all are; what a sense of life one gets from them. (Sackville-West 1949: 124)

Eleanor Adlard recalled that Edith Craig had endeavoured to collect and preserve for posterity documents and artefacts related to her mother, describing the house in terms of a site of pilgrimage:

> Edy's last achievement was making her mother's Tudor shrine, for it is not merely a place containing a catalogued list of interesting relics. She had the satisfaction of knowing that its future was safe in the hands of the National Trust and that her years of toil and work had not been in vain. (Adlard 1949: 151)

The half-timbered house has attracted archaeologists and historians interested in its life story before Terry owned it. They have traced it back to the time when it was a public building in one of the country's most important medieval ship-building centres where some of the most famous warships were built in periods of international war and trade for Henry IV, Henry V and Henry VIII. At this time the River Rother reached further inland on the Romney marsh, explaining the name of the Isle of Oxney. Ancient ships' timber nails are still part of the fabric of the door of the church neighbouring Priest's House, where Edith Craig lived with Christopher St John and Tony Atwood; a previous occupant was Sir Richard Brigandyne, clerk of ships for Henry VIII and supervisor of the construction of the *Mary Rose*.[18] The floorboards of Ellen Terry's house have warped and shifted over time so much that a walk along the upper floor produces the uncanny effect of being onboard a ship. On a foggy day, a sideways glance out of the windows can give the effect of being at sea as the land disappears from view.

Edith Craig herself was named after the rocky island off the west coast of Scotland, Ailsa Craig; it associated her automatically with an archipelagic perspective that may, in its unorthodoxy, give the impression that Craig preferred to occupy the margins, where an oppositional force may gather its troops. Vita Sackville-West recalled the women of Smallhythe place as 'a gypsy encampment', in metaphorical terms drawn from the subcultural and dissident.[19] Her reading of Craig's household is ambivalent; there is something attractive and highly valued about the difference which this community of women represents to her:

> It was not wholly unlike that, the encampment at Smallhythe. It really seemed likely to drift away at any moment on the tide which some centuries ago had come right up to the bottom of the garden. Were not the black beams of the Priest's House themselves the timbers of broken ships? Was it a place in a fairy story? It certainly had the quality which makes things and places both more real and more unreal. Whenever you went there, you wondered whether you were living in the world you normally knew, or had walked through into a world more poetical, a world more romantic, a world where values were different. (Adlard 1949: 118–19)

The representation of Priest's House as a ship draws on local history but it also wrenches the place and its inhabitants out of history. The alternative values flourishing in Craig's household made it attractive and alien, something to be cherished and immortalized because it threatened to be as elusive as a ship on the high seas. At home and at work in the theatre, Craig became inseparably associated with heterotopias.[20]

# A very theatrical family

Edith Craig and her brother were born into a theatrical family and immersed in a world of the arts from the outset. They did not know their theatrical grandparents, however, until Terry's marriage in 1877 to the actor Charles Wardell (1839–85), which brought respectability to the household and smoothed the way for family reconciliation. Edith Craig shared her brother's idea, that he in turn had developed in different ways from their father, the architect and designer, Edward Godwin (1833–86) and from their surrogate father, the actor-manager Henry Irving: that the theatre was the temple of art, indebted to the appropriate design of its acting space as much as to the reverence with which those involved held the enterprise. She had a respect for this endeavour, being influenced both by the Arts and Crafts aesthetic of beauty and utility and the historical authenticity in costume design inherited from Charles Kean (1811–68), who had given Ellen Terry her first break on the stage in *The Winter's Tale* in 1856. These influences combined to provide Edith Craig with a ready grasp of how to use available resources imaginatively in order to achieve her artistic goal.

As a doer rather than theorizer, Craig emulated her mother (who urged her children always to work hard). If Craig had been planning her career she may have paused and reflected more, gathering her energies and trying to consolidate her efforts. However, theatre work was driven by a sense of urgency in dealing with the precarious arrangements that led to its realization on stage for the pleasure of the audience. Public performances in theatres in England and Wales from 1737 to 1968 required official approval in the form of a licence from the Lord Chamberlain's office. Theatre companies were businesses but the theatre societies operated by means of membership subscriptions and borrowed venues for one-off experimental productions. Their private performances for members circumvented the Lord Chamberlain's licensing authority. Edith Craig had extensive experience in both the commercial theatres and the theatre societies with their restricted budgets. She directed many unlicensed plays designed to challenge stage censorship. She worked as a performer, costumier and director at a time when theatre was not subsidized, employees did not have the benefit of sick pay or pensions, women were not equal citizens in the law and the new medium of film was starting to steal a march on the stage. The notion of a 'theatre of your own' seemed to be an elusive and foolhardy dream. Ellen Terry had already expressed reservations about 'the Syndicate game' (28 January 1900; *CLET* 4: 1073).[21] As George Bernard Shaw explained to Craig's mother in 1900, it was no time to go into theatre management (9 February 1900; letter CXXL *STC*) and in 1904 'that the day of the manager with his or her single theatre has passed by; and that now it is the syndicate with fifty theatres that controls the business of the English and American world' (9 September 1904; letter CCLXV *STC*). In 1903, against Shaw's advice, Terry had launched herself and her hard-earned savings into theatre management at the Imperial Theatre for the sake of her children's careers.

## 'The spear-carriers' revenge'

Edward Gordon Craig, by contrast, would not compromise on the execution of his designs or the quality of materials; he would not tolerate the frailty of the human resources on whom (in the absence of marionettes) he was obliged to rely. This did not endear him to other actors. The actor Ben Webster recalled the 'spear-carriers' revenge' when he received prods and shoves from extras (also known as 'supers' or supernumaries) on stage who had mistaken him for Edward Gordon Craig (Cockin 1998a: 36). In *On the Art of the Theatre* (1911) he theorized the shortcomings and failures of his own productions as evidence to support his argument. It was in these practical aspects of the realization of his ideas that, on several occasions, a planned production stalled and some promising relationships with collaborators soured. His sister had the insight and skills necessary to implement an imaginative interpretation whereas in these matters he both relied on others, including her, and lacked the personal qualities to gain their trust and develop sufficient rapport necessary to sustain the collaboration. Gordon Craig seems to have produced the designs for costumes but then handed the task over to his sister because she knew what he wanted. Edith Craig's imaginative, interpretative and practical skills could be relied upon in the realization of his work. For the production of Laurence Housman's *Bethlehem*, according to Christopher Innes, 'the costumes and props were far more elaborate than any Craig (helped by his sister, Edy) had designed before' (Innes 1998: 76). Some of the annotated notes for lighting and stage direction on the promptbook for Laurence Housman's *Bethlehem* reproduced in Christopher Innes's book may be attributable to Edith Craig (Innes 1998: 75). As I will argue in Chapter three, Edith Craig was in a position to contribute to lighting and staging as well as costume. The siblings' scenographic experiments, theories and practice met and diverged; they relied on mutual support or points of leverage. However, Edith Craig is rarely mentioned in critical studies of her brother. It is time to prompt that debate.

## Reflections on family values and 'the Priest's House life'

Some of the new questions that emerge about Edith Craig relate to the papery and visceral stuff of biographical data – the who, what, where, when – as new findings emerge from newly deposited or trawled archives and give rise to new interpretations. New branches on the official family tree have had to be grafted. Michael Holroyd (2008) uncovered more of the offspring of Edward Gordon Craig. My research revealed that Edith Craig was the adoptive mother of Robinetta or Ruby Chelta.[22] However, Edith Craig's relationships with Christopher St John and Tony Atwood were as significantly defining and emotionally sustaining as any on a family tree and they are therefore central to any account of her life. It is noteworthy that familial terminology is used by Sheila Kaye-Smith in her description of Craig's household: 'The family at Priest's House always gave me the impression of activity to the point of urgency. There was always something being done and done quickly, and done to the complete absorption of the faculties of those present' (Kaye-Smith 1949: 127). The characteristic features attributed to Craig's household by those who visited were life enhancing and magical; the artistic debates and creative fervour were inspiring. In their adoption of the 'simple life' in rural Kent, these revolutionary women of Smallhythe Place signified at once an oppositional cultural practice and a leading contribution to the institutions of theatre, literature and interwar Englishness.[23] George Bernard Shaw wrote to Christopher St John after Craig's death: 'You ought to write a history of that ménâge à trois. It was unique in my experience' (quoted in St John 1949: 32). The account given by Vita Sackville-West, entitled 'Triptych', borrows its title from religious iconography, emphasizing both the unity of the three women and their other-worldliness:

> Yet they are all one. Edy, and Tony, and Christopher, and the hedgehog, and Shakespeare – they are all one. They are all poetry, in this dark panelled room with the flower-piece glowing against the wall. They are so rare and unusual an experience that we can well believe that next time we come to Smallhythe we may find that Edy, Christopher and Tony have departed on a voyage where we cannot follow them. (Sackville-West 1949: 124)

Sackville-West provides a well-informed and intimate picture, emphasizing the compatibility and complementarity that the three women achieved: 'This is the remarkable thing about them: all three of them are still persons on their own. Strong personalities, living at such close quarters for so many years, yet none of them has been extinguished by the other' (Adlard 1949: 122). Sackville-West fails to mention the disruption she caused, unhinging that 'triptych' with her brief affair with St John. Sackville-West's portrait of Craig in a private letter is somewhat different, describing her as 'the most tearing old Lesbian – not unlike your friend Radclyffe Hall – but without any charms for me, I hasten to add' (Quoted in Glendinning 1984: 250–1). Sackville-West's published essay provides an intimate portrait of the relationships shared by these three women for decades at Priest's House and the embeddedness of life and work in what Sackville-West defines as 'the Priest's House life' (Sackville-West 1949: 123). This depiction by one of Craig's contemporaries raises questions about the relevance of Joy Melville's suggestion that Edith Craig was 'possibly bisexual' on the basis of Craig's apparent contemplation of marriage to the musician Martin Shaw (1875–1938) (Melville 2006: 183).[24]

## A passing phase

There seems to be little evidence of heterosexual encounters closeted away in Craig's life story. Associations with only three men have featured in the surviving third-hand accounts by her contemporaries and published after the deaths of Craig and her female partners (Webster 1969; Steen 1962). As a younger woman, Craig seems to have attracted interest from two other men: Sydney Valentine (1865–1919), Lyceum Theatre company actor and trade unionist; and the American artist Joe Evans (1857–98), who was also devoted to her mother. In the National Trust's Edith Craig archive, only one letter survives from Sydney Valentine, dated 1918 and relating to the whereabouts of one of Henry Irving's theatrical costumes (EC-Z3, 735) and one letter from Martin Shaw to Ellen Terry dated 1903 relating to costumes (ET-Z1, 451). Some thirty-seven letters from Joe Evans to Edith Craig (1888–96) and one telegram from Craig to Evans (1896) have survived in the Edith Craig archive, giving news of travels, friends and plans to meet.[25] Evans was noted for his landscape painting and was described in obituaries as a lifelong invalid. In his letters he refers briefly to gifts exchanged with Craig which seem to be of a personal nature: his birthday present to her of Tiffany glass in 1894; her presents to him of a bookplate designed by her brother, and a little picture with clover leaves in 1895. However, in 1890 there was a business transaction, as he acknowledged receipt of a considerable sum of £50 from her for photographs of his artwork. Many of his letters provide detailed, often beautifully illustrated accounts of plays he has seen, including the Lyceum production of *Macbeth*. There is only one letter in the Edith Craig archive from Ellen Terry which refers to Joe Evans. Written in 1899, the year that Edith Craig set up house with Christopher St John and a year after Joe Evans died, the letter from Terry to an American family friend, Satty Fairchild,[26] confessed that Terry missed him (ET-Z2, 195). In 1906 it is revealed that Terry had at some point given a historically significant gift to Evans. Loyall Farragut (son of Admiral David G. Farragut) wrote to Terry suggesting that Lord Nelson's magnifying glass, which she had given to Joe Evans, should be given to the Nelson collection (ET-Z1, 171).[27] In the New York Players Club archive, thirty-five letters from Ellen Terry to Joe Evans have come to light, some of which have been subject to redaction. Irregular pieces have been cut out of the paper so as to obliterate certain words and phrases. One of these, sent from Terry to Evans from the Lyceum Theatre tour company's transatlantic sea voyage, is signed with the injunction to tear it up but closes with 'Edy's love & mine – Nell!' (6 September [1895?]; *CLET* 3: 658).[28] Perhaps Ellen Terry was over-zealously courting Evans on behalf of her daughter. Any relationship, such that there was, between Evans and Craig seems to have been dissolved in 1896.

It was on the Lyceum Tour in 1896 apparently that Edith Craig 'fell deeply and passionately in love with Sydney Valentine, who was married' (Webster 1969: 175). Valentine was an actor in the Lyceum Theatre company and the account of this incident (but no mention of Martin Shaw or Joe Evans) is given by Margaret Webster, May Whitty's daughter, to whom both Edith Craig and her mother confided about the situation. Webster records that Terry 'crushed the incipient romance [... and] threatened to send Edy home to England at once. [...] Edy remained in the company and did as she was told. No one ever spoke of the episode again' (Webster 1969: 176). Although there is limited information about these encounters, there is extensive evidence of her lifelong attachments to her beloved Chris and Tony and the 'Priest's House life'.

## The sensible child

The designation of illegitimacy is relevant for both of Ellen Terry's children. Their lives were affected by their legal status and association with their mother's marriage, their relationships both with their parents and stepfathers and with each other, and it impinged on how they presented themselves and were received in society.[29] Edward Godwin had gone to the lengths of trying to kidnap one of his children, choosing his daughter rather than his son (Craig 1968: 47–8). After Terry's death, Craig's strained relationship with her stepfather, the American actor James Carew (1876–1938) who was twenty-nine years younger than Ellen Terry, and with her brother Edward Gordon Craig have been noted.

The education of Terry's children followed the fortunes of her career. They were taught at home and then at Mrs Cole's school in London. Gordon Craig went on to Bradfield College and Edith Craig was sent to the home of Mrs Cole's sister Elizabeth Malleson (1828–1916), leader of the movement for nursing reform, women's education and enfranchisement (Cockin 1998: 21). Malleson's daughters also had a hand in Craig's education and Mabel acted as her companion in Germany. As older children, Edith Craig and Edward Gordon Craig were both sent to Germany, providing them with opportunities for linguistic as well as cultural talents while transporting them away from the likelihood of awkward questions from their English peers about parentage and social class. Gordon Craig's schooling was disrupted much to his mother's consternation and he was effectively expelled from Heidelberg College in 1888 apparently for misconduct. *Ellen Terry's Memoirs* (1933) notes: 'a punishment for an escapade, which owing to its innocent character, his mother thought far too severe' (Craig and St John 1933: 192). Exactly what happened in the night time bicycle ride is not clear. On behalf of Ellen Terry, her legal adviser and mentor, Stephen Coleridge, endeavoured to cover up the incident. Ellen Terry's other child was also, like herself, a creature of the night. According to an anecdote in Edith Craig's memoirs, Craig apparently disguised herself in male attire as a student for nocturnal jaunts in Heidelberg (Rachlin 2011: 66). Although, unlike her brother, she escaped detection, she was subsequently reported by her companion Mabel Malleson and her Heidelberg days were also brought to an end.

The risk of scandal loomed over the children's lives whether or not they were directly aware of it. As adults, any awareness they had of the shadow of scandal and a sense of shame may have led to the development of different strategies: complete avoidance or recategorization, dismissing it with other vulgar or banal conventions. A self-destructiveness hung onto Gordon Craig's coat tails. He performed in motley a burdened masculinity in search of power and mastery to rival that of his absent father and win the love of his 'little Nelly who was [his] mother' (Gordon Craig 1931: vii). Edith Craig responded creatively to her mother's pioneering model of self-invention but rejected any capitulation to a docile and maternal femininity even on stage.

Questions of upbringing also arise when considering the absence of parents and the impact on children. The fact that Terry's children both experienced long-distance postal parenting provides evidence today of the kinds of advice they received. Overall, Terry's interventions seem to have been more controlling and detailed in the case of her son. By contrast, Edith Craig was generally trusted to use her own judgement. The mother's dominance during the family's six-year exile in the countryside is made clear in Ellen Terry's autobiography (1908). There she rewrites their life stories in retrospective, fairy-tale mode, introducing them as if in a faux Greek myth they had sprung from a prosaic cabbage patch.

Terry was deeply affected by the unavoidable separation from her children during her intermittent absences on theatrical tour. This was mitigated by her faith in Elizabeth Rumball (1823–1913) who acted in her stead as carer while Terry maintained a protective and intensive correspondence with her children.[30] This is particularly relentless and revealing in relation to Terry's son. As the designated Sensible Child, Edith seems to have been trusted to early independence. At the age of nine, as one of Ellen Terry's letters reveals, Edith Craig was travelling alone by train (*CLET* 1: 39). It is not clear by what class of ticket Edith Craig travelled and whether it afforded her any automatic guardianship on board, in the station and for her onward journey.

## 'Brains and Brawn': Mother's other lovers and *Marriage as a Trade* (1909)

The letters from Henry Irving to Ellen Terry deposited at the V&A in 2010 now seem to confirm the degree of intimacy between the Lyceum stars about which critics have hitherto speculated. George Bernard Shaw had enumerated Terry's lovers in the preface to the Shaw-Terry Correspondence:

> All this has to be grasped before the lay reader can understand how Ellen Terry could be a woman of very exceptional virtue without having the smallest respect for the law. She did not care enough about it to have even a prejudice against it. If the man of her choice was free, she married him. If the marriage was not a success, she left him. She had many enduring friendships, some transient fancies, and five domestic partnerships of which two were not legalized, though they would have been if the English marriage law had been decently reasonable. (*STC*, xvii)

It is timely to turn Shaw's gaze away from Ellen Terry and to consider what impact this may have had on Edith Craig and her brother. What kind of experience was it for Edith Craig as the daughter of the woman, internationally adored and circumscribed by an uncertain and ambiguous position in society, whom Oscar Wilde named 'Our Lady of the Lyceum' (Robertson 1931: 149). Terry was treated inconsistently in the extreme; feted by many, she was also shunned by others. A Mrs Yarnall, probably from the influential philanthropist family of Philadelphia, had entertained Terry on one North American tour only to ostracize her later (*CLET* 1: 187; 3: 551; 4: 1066). However, the American minister Reverend Henry Ward Beecher (1813–87), an abolitionist and supporter of women's suffrage, usually found actors were anathema but he made an exception for Ellen Terry and Henry Irving when they visited the United States in 1883.

To what extent was Stephen Coleridge or even George Bernard Shaw himself to be counted as a possible extra in Shaw's list of Terry's five 'domestic partnerships'? Their involvement with her exceeded the category of 'transient fancies'. New insights have emerged from the Stephen Coleridge correspondence held at the Garrick Club. Coleridge was the 'man of brains' on whom Terry relied for advice consistently up to the point when she married Carew and he took over the management of her finances. This had an impact on her children and especially Edith Craig. Coleridge was prepared to be explicit for the record about his disapproval of Terry's children's selfish dependence on their ever indulgent mother.

The separation of her parents must have had a profound impact on the child Edith Craig but she also faced the adult experience of a first and then a second stepfather, one of whom was younger than her own younger brother. In 1881 Terry enlisted the help of Stephen Coleridge to deal with the significant problem that her second husband, Charles Wardell, had become for her. As Mrs Ellen Wardell, she dispensed the new surname to her children along with the respectability that it seemed to afford them. However it seems that Mr Wardell's behaviour became abusive. The Coleridge correspondence indicates that on Ellen Terry's behalf Coleridge not only paid Wardell but also Wardell's relatives to keep away from her. To what extent this action and Wardell's behaviour was known to the children and what effect either this knowledge or indeed the secrecy surrounding it may have had on them is not clear. Violence and jealousy were mentioned in *Ellen Terry's Memoirs* (1933) in a long account of 'Ellen Terry's Second Marriage' given by the editors. The following extract is particularly revealing:

> No doubt one of her motives then for deciding to marry was a desire, in her children's interest, to regularize her position. Yet it

is conceivable that she was strongly attracted by Charles Wardell. All through her life the man of brains competed for her affections with the man of brawn. But this man of brawn, although a good fellow in some ways – he had a genuine affection for his wife's children, who for a time bore his name – had a violent and jealous temper which Ellen Terry eventually found intolerable. (Craig and St John 1933: 116–17)

Wardell was a veteran of the Crimean war and a professional soldier before he turned to the stage and met Ellen Terry, becoming her 'man of brawn' and a patriarchal influence on her children from 1877 during their impressionable early years. Edith Craig was eight when Wardell became her stepfather and Gordon Craig was five years old. It is to be hoped that the children did not read the article by Olive Weston in the *Philadelphia Press* (12 May 1889) which went into some details about Terry's relationships, exposing the family to gossip and reputational damage.[31]

Terry separated from Wardell in 1881 and he died in 1885. The Terry children as young adults were once again without an official patriarch at home but they were not short of surrogates; indeed, father figures proliferated, in the form of Henry Irving, Stephen Coleridge and Bram Stoker.[32] The experience of having an official stepfather was to be repeated in their adult years. In 1907 news of Terry's marriage to James Carew, the American actor on tour with her in George Bernard Shaw's *Captain Brassbound's Conversion*, dropped like a bombshell on everyone when the newly married couple returned from America. The extent to which Edith Craig objected is revealed in Terry's letters to others and in letters from Terry to Craig when the tension became too much to tolerate. As much as she loved her daughter, she felt she had a right to some respect for her own decisions (c. 1908; *CLET 5*: 1550). Such an assertion of a woman's independence and self-determination, as this marriage seemed to symbolize, should perhaps have been received more warmly by Edith Craig who was elsewhere committing herself to the campaign for women's enfranchisement. It is not clear to what extent was Edith Craig's response a personal dislike of Carew or whether it amounted to a jealous desire of not wanting to share her mother with anyone. She must have known him quite well since she had acted with him on tour. She may have regarded her mother's marriage to Carew in more complex terms. Ellen Terry performed the role of a Womanly Woman dependent on marriage very persuasively and now she seemed to be continuing it off-stage, a little too excessively. Only a few years afterwards, Edith Craig's collaborator in women's suffrage warfare Cicely Hamilton had published *Marriage as a Trade* (1909) in which she argued:

> If it be granted that marriage is, as I have called it, essentially a trade on the part of the woman – the exchange of her person for the means of subsistence – it is legitimate to inquire into the position of the worker in the matrimonial with the position of the worker in any other market. (Hamilton 1909: 36)

Ironically Terry had achieved the means of independence as a theatre worker, and her third marriage in 1907, distinctly optional rather than compulsory, brought her mostly hardship instead of the financial security she desired to enable her to retire. Her third marriage was effectively over when, in 1911, she was publicly associated with the 'freewoman' (instead of the 'bondswoman' or 'Womanly Woman') by the editorial in the first issue of the radical newspaper *The Freewoman*.[33] It is unlikely that anyone at the newspaper would have known that she was very much burdened by family responsibilities as the official breadwinner for an ever-extending cast of dependants.

In 1910 life changed for Edith Craig. It was a turning point in modern times, according to Virginia Woolf: the year of the first post-impressionist exhibition at the Grafton Galleries, London and the end of the Edwardian era with the death of Edward VII. For Edith Craig it was the year of heightened suffrage militancy and dominated by a gruelling schedule of nationwide productions of the popular women's suffrage play, *A Pageant of Great Women* (1910), written by Craig's indomitable collaborator Cicely Hamilton. Craig also had some personal difficulties that would have affected her confidence and presentation in public. Mentioned only briefly in a couple of letters from her mother, Craig's dental problems are likely to have had some impact on her and provide a new way of considering some of the fleeting records of her public persona. In publicity photographs, Craig has a sombre expression and reference is made in a newspaper interview to Craig's reputation for 'laughing self-effacement' (*The Vote*, 1910); her reticence naturally drew her to the occupation of the shadows and margins.

## Edith Craig's art theatre

The Pioneer Players theatre society was founded by Edith Craig in May 1911 in London and played a significant role in the promotion of new drama, the training of actors, the campaign against stage censorship and for women's suffrage, the development of political theatre and the engagement with the new art theatre internationally during the First World War.

Gradually the Pioneer Players and Edith Craig are beginning to feature in critical studies of this period, although the form of organization adopted by the Pioneer Players is often wrongly designated as a 'company'. In setting up as a subscription society, the Pioneer Players was funded by its membership and drew its actors as required from them for each production, honouring them with a reduced fee. With this form of organization it was designed to produce only a small number of annual productions for an audience of its membership and was therefore not engaging with the commercial context of public performances for a profit. The purpose of such organizations was defined in terms of experimentation and a limited lifespan. Contradictions arose when the desire for experimentation coincided with a desire for recognition and investment that would lead inevitably either to the radical transformation or the dissolution of the organization.

When I interviewed the actor Athene Seyler (1889–1990) in 1989, she recalled clearly that the Pioneer Players, for whom she had acted in their inaugural 1911 production, was 'more political' than the much larger Stage Society. As time went by the Stage Society was more ready to compromise on innovation than the Pioneer Players were when circumstances prevailed. As discussed in Chapter Six, there is evidence that the Pioneer Players theatre society was in material ways benefitting from the war years and that there were specific reasons why Edith Craig was not prominent in the attempts to keep the society going in 1920 when it was effectively taken over by the British Drama League. It seems that, rather than desperate-at-all-costs to ensure that the Pioneer Players continued, Craig had already moved her sights towards the larger national federation and was aiming for more ambitious projects and recognition elsewhere. At the same time, her mother's financial crisis was reaching a peak and some facing-up to the realities of living within one's means had become overdue. In addition, the demise of the Pioneer Players coincided with the association of some of its membership with scandal, as will be seen in Chapter Six. The extent to which this troubled Edith Craig is not clear but, given her own family history, she may have been loath to associate herself with perceptions of vulgarity or sexual impropriety from the perspective of good taste if not also the retention of a good reputation in the context of future theatrical business. Unlike her brother, who employed a business manager, Edith Craig relied on the informal advice of friends, such as the redoubtable Irene Cooper Willis.[34]

## The collector

Much research has been done on performance and the visual field, the commercial aspects of theatre and the use of photography. In these contexts, some of the archival materials that concern Edith Craig warrant further consideration, particularly what tends to be classified as ephemera, and a reconceptualization of her collection, beyond its utility, in terms of a modernist project in bricolage.[35] A large collection of cuttings and clippings, at first glance chaotic detritus, constituted Craig's extensive collection of research materials to assist her in costume and stage design. The process of their collection is recalled and interpreted by Eleanor Adlard:

> I see Edy cutting out endless scraps and pictures for her scrapbooks and evolving valuable reference books on diverse subjects from what looked like a magpie's hoard; again, Edy arranging costume pictures for her plays and pageants with every detail noted. 'I always make it a rule to make people wearing costumes wear the right underclothes as far as I can, anyhow stays and petticoats', she wrote me once. All this explains how and why she co-ordinated details in such a satisfying way. Everything looked right when she produced a play, nothing was too insignificant to be neglected, even to the right colour of a telephone used in a French play. (Adlard 1949: 150)

Like Gabrielle Enthoven (1868–1950), whose vast archive is the foundation of the V&A's theatre collection, Edith Craig was collecting in a context for a purpose, not for profit or to feed a personal

context of the increased interest in the history and culture of the First World War, my re-examination of the Pioneer Players' wartime work established that the organization became especially known for its internationalism and also for its production of Russian plays (Cockin 2015). The extent to which this affected the reputation of Craig and the Pioneer Players appears to have been crucial. As discussed in further detail in Chapter Five, as an art theatre the Pioneer Players' international outlook was at the cutting edge but in relation to their association with the dancer and exotic bodies they moved into dangerous territory as drugs and scandal emerged at a time of great uncertainty, just as the war ended.

The significance of Edith Craig's introduction of international theatre in translation to Britain and her work with authors, translators and performers needs to be reassessed. Roberta Gandolfi has analysed Craig's direction of three plays by Paul Claudel for the Pioneer Players (1915–19) in the context of 'the vast and scattered archipelago of art theatres' which were aware of each other, creating 'de facto an international circuit for experimental contemporary dramaturgy' (Gandolfi 2011: 108). Craig was seriously engaging in global theatre at a time when racist and xenophobic discourses ranged from banal trivialization and parody to active persecution. In 1925 Craig cast Rose Quong (b.1879), an Australian performer with Chinese heritage, in the role of Zanche in her production of Webster's *The White Devil* and of Florence Bell's *The Fog on the Moor*.[39] Angela Woollacott has argued that Quong achieved success in her career as a performer in England once she promoted a Chinese identity and that Edith Craig was one of those instrumental in Quong's promotion in British theatre (2011: 28). Yoko Chiba has established that it was Edith Craig who directed *Kanawa* (1917) and *The Toils of Yoshitomo* (1922) in Britain, the two plays by Torahiko Kori (1890–1924), who was described as 'Japan's first international writer' who 'bridg[ed] the gap between the theatres of East and West in the early twentieth century' (Chiba 1996: 431–2).

## Edith Craig's pioneering modernism

Edith Craig's commitment to Russian experimental theatre was demonstrated by the lengths she went to in staging *The Theatre of the Soul* by Nikolai Evreinov in 1915 and 1916. Although the first production of *The Theatre of the Soul* had been at the Crooked Mirror Theatre in Moscow on 14 October 1912, Edith Craig's 1915 London production of a play by Evreinov predated that by Jacques Copeau (1879–1949) in Paris and Luigi Pirandello (1867–1936) in Rome (Cockin 1994: 145–6). Russia was one of the centres of modernist ferment and the international transmission of these influences is currently the focus of much new research, interdisciplinary in approach and attentive to the interplay of literary, performance and visual cultures.[40]

The apparently sporadic and sluggish engagement of theatre in Britain with the experiments associated with modernism internationally has been a dominant narrative in literary studies. This has been questioned by Penny Farfan (2004) and others, in a wave of reassessments of modernist studies exploring wider historical periods, geographical locations and cultural forms that gave rise to the 'new modernism' (Mao and Walkowitz 2008). Farfan's study focuses on an unusual selection of performers and authors (Isadora Duncan, Djuna Barnes, Ellen Terry, Edith Craig and Virginia Woolf) whose aesthetic modes of performance suggest some shared concerns and innovative approaches to gender and performance. In this context, Craig's appearance as the French artist Rosa Bonheur (1822–99) in *A Pageant of Great Women* is considered briefly. Global modernisms and those which address interdisciplinarity, in art, music and dance, and new work on Russia are especially relevant for an understanding of Edith Craig's pioneering productions of Evreinov's *The Theatre of the Soul*.[41]

Some insights can be gleaned into Craig's thoughts about production from the production notes and prompt copies that have survived. In 1937 she directed a dramatization of Emily Bronte's *Wuthering Heights* by John Davison at the Little Theatre, London. The floor plan is annotated with an intriguing note: 'Question constantly arises whether you can pull down a structure so solid & complete – every detail of it being harmonious – & use the stones to build a play. Like the house built out of the stones of Fountain's [*sic*] Abbey. The stones are almost ludicrously massive for domestic architecture' (EC-N1). The architectural metaphors for adaptation of a novel for the stage are reminiscent of her father's insights into design, applying a detailed knowledge of buildings to the creation of other workable and aesthetically pleasing structures.

A widespread reassessment of theatre histories with the 'new modernist' studies and interdisciplinary transnational perspectives is timely. In *British Avant Garde Theatre* (2012), Claire Warden focuses on the Workers' Theatre Movement and three other groups of the 1930s, briefly mentioning the relevance of the earlier experimental work carried out by the Pioneer Players (Warden 2012: 19). The emphasis placed in Warden's account on the use of a platform or elevated stage is of specific interest here as it provides an opportunity to trace the genealogy of some of these staging techniques back to the women's suffrage productions and specifically to the directorial work of Edith Craig. Craig's production of Upton Sinclair's *Singing Jailbirds* in 1930 at the Apollo Theatre, London, for the Independent Labour Party's Masses' Stage and Film Guild, provides a clear link in personnel between the women's suffrage theatre and Theatres of the Left through its director, Edith Craig (Cockin 1998: 159–60).

The last production of the Pioneer Players is remarkable for various reasons, not least for its presentation to a London audience in 1925 of the work of the American dramatist Susan Glaspell, one of the leaders of the Provincetown Players, Massachusetts (1915–23). Glaspell's *The Verge* is a sensational expressionist play about a female botanist, obsessed with her experiments in creating new species of plant, the 'Breath of Life'. Rather than seeing Claire Archer as a female Victor Frankenstein, the critics were predisposed to focus on the association of women with madness.[42] This would have been an undesirable topic for Edith Craig at this time just as her mother was declining in health. But the sensational aspects would have been most fascinating to Sybil Thorndike (1882–1976) who appeared in José Levy's Grand Guignol in the 1920s. Thorndike had begged Craig to revive the Pioneer Players in order to stage *The Verge*. Correspondence reveals Craig's plans to stage the play at Kew Gardens in what would have been a highly innovative use of space.[43]

Edith Craig's involvement in transatlantic theatrical exchanges was not new. She had toured the United States with the Lyceum Theatre in the days of her apprenticeship as an actor. In 1912 as a director she had brought to London *Three Women*, one of the two plays by Charlotte Perkins Gilman published in her journal *The Forerunner*. Gilman is more widely known as the author of the short story entitled *The Yellow Wallpaper* (1892). She was a prolific writer who also experimented with drama. Craig's production of

Gilman's *Three Women* revised the ending, making it more ambiguous and thought-provoking about the difficulties of change and the intergenerational impact of women's liberation. The emphasis therefore fell on the process of decision-making when a young woman seeks advice from two older women on the marriage proposal she has received and how this might affect her career as a kindergarten teacher (Cockin 2000: 80, 82). The play's exploration of the potential paths taken by different women, especially choices between marriage and motherhood or a career, would have been familiar to a women's suffrage audience. They would also have had an extra resonance for Edith Craig, whose mother took such radical steps to cohabit outside marriage and in later life chose to marry a man who was younger than her children.

In 1919 Craig also directed *Trifles*, a play by Susan Glaspell that has become one of the most renowned plays in the history of women's writing. Elaine Showalter's history of American women writers (2009) takes the title of Susan Glaspell's later, related, short story 'A Jury of Her Peers' for its title and as a starting point for her investigation into the basis for the literary canon. Glaspell based these stories on the trial of Margaret Hossack for the murder of her husband on 2 December 1900 about which Glaspell reported in the *Desmoines News*. In adapting the elements of the story, Glaspell emphasized the abusive circumstances under which the woman lived and created female characters whose observations of the crime scene in the farmhouse lead to clues about a possible motive. The play highlighted the significance of gender as a lens and the question about how the law can achieve justice especially in a system in which the composition of the jury excluded women. Glaspell's Provincetown Players' production of *Trifles* was staged on 8 August 1916 and her short story 'A Jury of Her Peers' was published in *Everyweek*, 5 March 1917.[44] Only three years later, in 1919, Edith Craig's London production of *Trifles* for the Pioneer Players demonstrated the vitality of the transatlantic relationship of American women's writing and the transnational outlook that Edith Craig was taking as a director, in her selection of drama, casting and exploration of performance styles.

# CHAPTER TWO
## 1869–1902

# Her mother's daughter: The Lyceum's apprentice

For an authoritative account of Edith Craig's early years, readers may expect to turn to her mother's autobiography, *The Story of My Life* (1908). There Edith Craig is depicted as an unusual and forthright child, unhindered by convention. It did not seem out of place for a young Edith to report (in the third person) an occurrence during a church visit that 'Miss Edy has seen the angels!' (Terry 1908: 82).[1] When her younger brother showed fear of the dark, Edith admonished him firmly with a wooden spoon about the head, instructing him 'to be a woman' (Terry 1908: 80). These two anecdotes remain in the revised *Ellen Terry's Memoirs* (1933) co-edited by Edith Craig and Christopher St John, the 'literary hench-man' who had assisted Terry in the 1908 publication.[2] The anecdote about femininity, reported by Craig herself at a women's suffrage commemorative event in the 1930s, reveals the significance for the adult woman of the little girl's response to a family environment where performance and imagination held sway under the protector-ate of a fearless mother. Still technically married to the artist G. F. Watts (1817–1904), Ellen Terry had embarked on an unmarried life with Edward Godwin, the brilliant and charismatic architect and designer.[3] Rather than taking the 'six year vacation' euphemis-tically mentioned in her autobiography, they seem to have set up home with the expectation of its continuation. In Hertfordshire they were relatively safe from metropolitan prying eyes with their two children, Edith Craig and Edward Gordon Craig. *The Story of My Life* (1908) runs through Edith Craig's early years diplomatically in a fairy-tale spin. The narrative takes its episodic journey led by Ellen Terry, with the ghost-writing assistance of Christopher St John, as she alights on significant events that are suitable to recount to a respectable readership while the causal connections fade into the darker corners of the vividly painted scenery.

Edith Craig was born on 9 December 1869 in Hertfordshire. Ellen Terry was apparently attended by Elizabeth Rumball, the wife of a local doctor; from that time onwards Elizabeth Rumball, later known as 'Boo', had a firm place in Terry's family as friend, companion and carer for the children. In 1872 the relationship with Godwin seems to have taken a decisive turn with the birth of a second child, Edward, and the expansion of the Godwin-Terry family. The children, described by Terry as 'the chicks' or 'pretty buds', became accustomed to their mother's self-sufficiency and their father appearing on visits. The repercussions of Godwin's tendency to let any income slip through his fingers were severe. However, the early memories of childhood, the sights and smells, the colours and tastes, would have been delightfully attuned to the development of the children's aesthetic tastes. The Arts and Crafts ideals of beauty and utility were the guiding lights of their early years. Two photographic portraits show mother and daughter in Japanese dress. Edith Craig appears somewhat uncomfortable, in a kimono gift from the artist, Whistler. Ellen Terry, by contrast, faced the camera smiling, with hands on hips, exuding delight and confidence. This image is used by the actor Johnston Forbes Robertson (1853–1937) to illustrate his first meeting with Terry at Taviton Street:

Presently the door opened, and in floated a vision of loveliness! In a blue kimono and with that wonderful golden hair, she seemed to melt into the surroundings and appeared almost intangible. This was my first sight of Miss Terry. I was undergoing a sort of inspection, but her manner was so gracious that it soon cleared away my embarrassment. I was afterward shown Master Gordon Craig in his cradle, and Miss Craig, a lively little girl, black-haired, with great inquiring eyes. (Forbes Robertson 1925: 66)

Photography was to dominate cultural life as the medium for documentation of everyday experiences as well as the public record. Craig's mother had been photographed by the world pioneer in the new medium, namely Julia Margaret Cameron (1815–79),[4] as well as Charles Dodgson (1832–98), whose photographs of children continue to provoke controversy today. Terry bought shares in Kodak and inadvertently invested in the archival legacy, having made sure her children were well-equipped with cameras. This particular theatrical family embraced new technology and were very much exemplars of the new photographic generation.

The children's educational development and cultural influences were carefully considered by their mother. They were given hand-crafted toys to cultivate their impressionable minds towards a life in art and encouraged to read and engage with different cultures and experiences. Terry brought novelties such as a hammock and a canoe back from her travels. Cycling became a family passion and featured frequently in Terry's correspondence: Gordon Craig had to be reminded to take care of his tricycle and Edith Craig went on formidably long cycle rides. Their household always included animals which regularly featured in official photographic portraits as if they were members of the family.

In 1875, when Edith Craig was in her sixth year, Terry and Godwin separated and, although Terry and the children moved house several times, Terry usually found a way of fending off insecurity by story-telling. In 1880 Terry was living at Rose Cottage, Hampton Court Road, in what she fancifully described as 'just a labourers [sic] cottage' ([24 May 1880]; *CLET* 1: 45). Stephen Coleridge described it as a haven with an unexpectedly expansive view:

> The little cottage at Hampton Court was in the row between the gate into Bushey Park and the corner where the road turns down to the bridge. Its windows at the back looked out into Bushey Park though there was no access to it. The deer would sometimes come under the windows to be fed. It was a very quiet restful little place then before the advent of the motor car and its horn. ([24 May 1880]; *CLET* 1: 45)

A similar bolt-hole was found at an inn called the Audrey Arms, Uxbridge. In October 1886 Terry offered it to her visiting American friends Elizabeth and William Winter (1836–1917), the influential drama critic:

> I wish, *wish* you could both just tide-over the winter & come together here in the spring. – You stop – & he come over I mean – I have 'all-but', taken a cottage at Uxbridge – such a *bit* of a cottage = You might live in it part of the time!! (October 1886; *CLET* 1: 20)

To her friends Stephen and Gill Coleridge her letter suggests that she is posing as 'Audrey', The Innkeeper, extending an invitation to visit and make a contribution to its decor: 'Do come & see my "Pub." – I think you'll like it – I want you to give me one of your photographs for it – & a wee book of some sort' ([29 November 1886]; *CLET* 1: 149). Edith Craig's mother would often refer to their properties in a self-deprecating or mock-grandiose way. When the dramatist Henry Arthur Jones (1851–1929) made a present to her of a tea-pot she was delighted but wrote that 'it is much too grand for "The Audrey Arms – Uxbridge" –, & so I shall keep it up here at my town mansion!!' (15 November 1886; *CLET* 1: 146). In a society in which fine distinctions would be used to calibrate social class and respectability, Edith Craig must have been regularly made aware that the family's standing was an unfinished business. In October, the attention-seeking behaviour of her mother was more acute than ever, if not manic, for a tragic reason: Terry was mourning the death of Edward Godwin. She admitted the impact it had on her and the part her daughter played in returning her to good health:

> [...] I didn't know how terribly it would alter me – I went on at my work for a time but broke down at last & sent for Edith to be with me. Selfish & wrong but I couldn't help it – I think I shd have lost my wits from misery = I'm all right now – Edith did that. (23 December 1886; *CLET* 1: 151)

This episode brought mother and daughter together in a way which was restorative and seems to have bound them together psychologically, reflected in lifetime mutual dependence.

From 1878, when Terry joined Henry Irving's Lyceum Theatre company, the family fortunes rose. By 1888 this enabled them to move to 22 Barkston Gardens, a towering red-brick terraced house in a square overlooking a formal, enclosed residents' garden.[5] The kind of education, as well as housing, Edith Craig experienced as a child was determined by the changing circumstances of her mother. At first, arrangements were somewhat erratic and later regularized when Craig attended Mrs Cole's school, where she met fellow pupils with a distinguished future ahead of them: Walter Raleigh (1861–1922), later the first Professor of English literature at Oxford University; and the artist Walter Sickert (1860–1942) (Rachlin 2011: 26–7). Ellen Terry had a great respect for education and was an avid reader. She enjoyed the works of Robert Louis Stevenson and Charles Dickens but had some strong opinions about Thomas Hardy's novels, especially *Jude the Obscure* (1894).[6] Always reading and studying for her next role on the stage, Terry urged her children to apply themselves to their work. She encouraged Edward Gordon Craig to consider the commercial application of his artwork. However his bookplates appealed to the individual bibliophile. He produced a book for children, entitled *Gordon Craig's Book of Penny Toys* (1899) which was promoted in the United States for the burgeoning Christmas market by Ellen Terry while on the Lyceum's sixth tour.

Edith Craig's artistic skills in the field of drawing and painting were limited. According to her memoirs, Edith Craig remembered her own favourite as Harriet Beecher Stowe's *Uncle Tom's Cabin* (1852).[7] On their first American tour, Ellen Terry and Henry Irving had forged a strong friendship with the author's brother, the Rev. Henry Ward Beecher, a preacher of the fire and brimstone style who supported the women's suffrage, temperance and abolition of slavery movements. He had also dealt with public scandal.[8] Terry's friendship and support of the Beechers in the 1880s is particularly significant, providing an opportunity for her daughter to become aware of the furore surrounding the debates about hypocrisy, free love and women's rights: the depth of feeling these issues provoked and the feasibility of taking an unorthodox stance on them.

Ellen Terry chose wisely in the educational influences for her daughter when she sent her to stay with the Mallesons, at Dixton Manor in Gloucestershire. In September 1884 Terry wrote to her daughter there, urging her to behave well. Although I have discovered no records of a school there, there is ample evidence that the Mallesons were involved in teaching in different ways locally and in pedagogical research. Elizabeth Malleson's professional expertise was demonstrated by her own published monograph *Notes on the Early Training of Children* (1854) and association with Dorothea Beale (1831–1906), the second principal of Cheltenham Ladies' College and founder of St Hilda's College, Oxford. Malleson was particularly known for her promotion of district nurses and the positive benefits this brought to rural communities; she also campaigned for women's enfranchisement and other social reforms. Edith Craig was put into the care of Malleson's daughter, Mabel, a history graduate from Cambridge University, who became her companion during her education in Germany.

In the summer of 1886 Edith Craig apparently went on holiday to New York with her mother and Henry Irving (Rachlin 2011: 59–60), and accompanied them, with Joe and Alice Comyns Carr, to Nuremberg where they used their holiday to prepare for the forthcoming Lyceum production of *Faust*. Joe Comyns Carr recalled that

> Our holiday had a practical purpose. Irving and I made an exhaustive study of the gardens of the old German city in order to find suitable material for the scenery of the play, the greater part of which was to be painted by Mr Hawes Craven. We even carried our researches as far as Rothenberg on the Tauber, a most beautiful example of a medieval fortified town; and at the last Irving deemed it wise to summon Craven from London in order that he might make a few preparatory studies on the spot. (Comyns Carr 1907: 243)

Germany became a significant part of Edith Craig's upbringing. Numerous letters from Ellen Terry urged her daughter to improve her spoken German and emphasized the importance of learning the 'language conversationally' (11 February 1887; THM 384/1/2/3). Craig seems to have had international cultural interests, characterized by Terry's designation of her as the 'German-Japanese-English girl in Heidelberg' (4 March 1887; THM 384/1/2/5). Terry reported to her son that she had great ambitions for her daughter's education at Cambridge University:

> Do you know that Edie is at work to pass for Girton? It's 'a <u>coiker</u>' to pass & I shd say her spelling – like yours – wd have to improve first – however Mrs Malleson says 'she can pass

easily' – & <as> all Mrs Mallesons [*sic*] girls are Girton girls, she
<u>ought</u> to know. ([9 April]; *CLET* 1: 272)

Perhaps she hoped that Edith would become an Honorary Malleson
and some of the other achievements of the exemplary sorority would
rub off. It may have been somewhat tactless but this comment may
also have served to make Edward raise his own game at school.
Formal education, particularly that of the public school variety, did
not capture his imagination and he baulked at the rules and regulations. At school he may well have been bullied by other boys who
would scorn the son of an actress let alone one whose parents were
unmarried. The issue of illegitimacy is a significant feature in the
children's development, their social status and identity. Although
in theatrical circles the tolerance of the unorthodox was considerably more flexible and the adoption of stage names familiarized the
idea of multiple personae and identities, the force of the patronymic
was considerable. Their peers in the Lyceum Theatre did not always
share this tolerant attitude.

# The children of Ellen Terry, 'the scarlet woman of the Lyceum'

In *The Successors* (1967), Henry Irving's grandson, Laurence
Irving, wrote a group biography of his father and uncle, the 'successors' of Henry Irving depicted as if an emperor. He positions
Ellen Terry as 'the scarlet woman of the Lyceum', a morally dubi-
ous influence causing a rift in the Irving family, and 'the obstacle to any understanding with their father' (Irving 1967: 161).
Henry Irving's sons, Laurence and H. B., were only a few years
older than Gordon Craig. The Irving boys were both educated at
Marlborough College and began brief careers in diplomacy and
the law respectively before taking to the stage. Laurence went to
College Rollin in Paris and then began a career in Russia with
the Foreign Office. H. B. Irving went up to New College, Oxford
and began a career in law. When Henry Irving proposed that his
sons join the Lyceum Theatre company, Laurence wrote to their
mother, Florence, referring to Ellen Terry in morally judgemen-
tal terms as 'the wench' and 'the serpent at the Lyceum' (Irving

1967: 161–2). There is evidence that Ellen Terry was fond of Henry Irving's 'successors' and especially Laurence, whom she designated 'my Irving boy' (*CLET* 4: 1021).[9] However, at this point in a private letter to his mother and perhaps crafted in a way that would be well-received, Laurence Irving revealed the Irving boys' resentment and repudiation of her. Terry's wench/serpent designation contrasts with Oscar Wilde's defiant reversal when he rehabilitated her as 'our lady of the Lyceum' (Robertson 1931: 149). Terry's children, the heavenly offspring, were not only close to hand, they also shared Henry Irving's affection and respect. It has been noted that Irving gave the same gold watch to Gordon Craig as to his own son Laurence (Irving 1967: 174), perhaps designed to avert potential jealousy. Henry Irving's actions seem to suggest he was insensitive or oblivious to the customary expectations for different gifts reflecting the fact that Edward Gordon Craig was not his son.

Both Terry's children benefited from the invented patronymic, masking their illegitimacy and providing them with a sense of autonomy and uniqueness. The circumstances of Edith Craig's upbringing were irregular and erratic; uncertainties about parentage and status may have been exacerbated by the peripatetic father figures in the generally unpredictable life of the child of a touring actor. Following the separation from Godwin, Terry returned to work on the stage, apparently inspired to do so by the author Charles Reade (1814–84) (Terry 1908: 82). However, she urgently needed to support her two children. Godwin managed to get himself into shape and turned his attentions to Beatrice Philip, whom he married on 4 January 1874. In 1877 G. F. Watts divorced Terry, naming Godwin in the proceedings. This released both Watts and Terry to marry again but it brought into the public domain her adultery with Godwin.[10]

Terry immediately married Charles Wardell and the entire family took his surname. Wardell had had a career in the army, with service in the Crimean war as a boy soldier. Wardell acted under name Kelly, and he had performed with Terry in various productions. In 1878 Edith Craig joined her mother for a brief visit at Charles Wardell's father's rectory in County Durham. Meanwhile six-year old Edward Gordon Craig, presumably under the supervision of Elizabeth Rumball, kept in touch by letter. In 1879 Ellen Terry remarked in a letter to Tom Taylor and his wife that Edith Craig had travelled by train from London 'quite alone!' (September

[1879]; *CLET* 1: 39), to join her in Liverpool and on to Newcastle where she was touring in Tom Taylor's *New Men and Old Acres*.[11] This report is quite unusual since Terry tended to put the children in the care of women whom she had employed for the purpose, such as Elizabeth Rumball or Nannie Held (c. 1887–9). The exclamation mark may imply some sense of the risks involved in that kind of journey for a child who was not quite ten years old. It would have taken several hours. Some form of supervision may have been afforded by travelling with a more expensive ticket. In 1880 Edith Craig, at age eleven, joined her mother and stepfather on tour. By 1881 Ellen Terry was seeking advice from her trusted legal adviser Stephen Coleridge on the best way to keep her new husband at a safe distance. On 4 October 1881 Terry wrote asking Coleridge to look at some letters regarding 'the legal separation', to which Coleridge appended the note, citing the notorious *R. v Jackson* (1891) legal case which tested the husband's rights to ownership of his wife's body having abducted her, a case which became a legal landmark in women's rights:

> The allusion at the end of this letter to my part in arranging her legal separation from her drunken husband Wardell. We had to buy him off with £100 a month, afterwards reduced to £60. This was before the Jackson case, when a husband could claim legal possession of his wife's body. So it had to be done. With her money so paid him monthly by for years, he kept a mistress! (4 October 1881; *CLET* 1: 65)

Four years later Wardell was dead. Nevertheless, Ellen Terry was not quite released. Wardell's relatives continued as her dependants. It is not clear whether Terry's children witnessed any drunkenness or brutality or were aware of the situation at the time.

Ellen Terry seems to have welcomed the idea that her children would take to the stage whereas Henry Irving actively discouraged his two sons, Laurence and H. B, who were of similar age to Terry's. However Terry had a kindergarten teaching career in mind for Edith Craig, inspired by Nannie Held who was the 'first lady to teach kindergarten in America'; Terry wrote to her daughter, 'I've often thought you might some day do that for Mrs Cole – at Mrs Cole's – Meanwhile tho' you've lots to learn my darling' (6 May 1887; THM 384/1/2/9). Terry was determined that her children would have the best training in theatre work by which she meant practice in regular and varied performance.

The year 1887 seems to have been a decisive one for Terry's arrangements for her family. She sorted out her finances before she left for the American tour and the children underwent another transformation by christening on 11 January 1887 at Exeter Cathedral by the bishop, Dr Bickersteth.[12] The invented name 'Craig', apparently inspired by Ailsa Craig, gave them autonomy from patrilineage. Both children were sent to study abroad so their theatrical apprenticeship was not to be relied upon solely for a future livelihood.

## Heidelberg days and nights

Fully equipped as a christened personage, Edith Craig set off for Germany with Mabel Malleson as her companion. Edith Craig trained with Alexis Hollaender as his private pupil for £20 a month, a figure that Terry justified as he provided the best quality of musical tuition. She was delighted to report that Edith was practising piano five hours a day and had sung in public in a choir in Berlin (22 November 1888; *CLET* 1: 242). Ellen Terry expected her correspondence with both children to be strictly regular: her son must write on a Sunday and her daughter on a Monday. Terry gave various pieces of advice and guidance as well as the general items of news. In sending her daughter a dress and wig for a Bal Masqué she advised:

> Remember you must (of course) be more reserved with a pack of folk you don't know *well* (& one changes one's first opinions of some people –) than with old friends & people who know you – & you know I used (long ago) to have to tell you to keep a little steadier in shops & places where strangers were about. (4 January 1887; THM 384/1/2/1)

Terry had some worries about her daughter's lack of awareness about the consequences of an unguarded or uninhibited manner, signing off one letter: 'Be a good girl, & a lady (you & I know exactly what I mean by that term a lady –)' (4 March 1887; THM 384/1/2/5). Three months later she is more specific and emphatic, after finding that her daughter had written to a German actor with whom she was not acquainted: 'be careful for I wd be vexed if some fool or other thought you vulgar' (3 June 1887; THM 384/1/2/11). Another cause of concern was her daughter's poor eating habits and also the discovery that she was grinding her teeth in the night: 'You know it is connected with "The Interior" trouble, & that lies in your own hands to cure by habit. I beg you to pay attention to that most regularly = '(18 October 1888; THM 384/1/3/5). Whether Terry's euphemistic expression refers to psychological or gastro-intestinal causes is not clear but she was more explicit in another letter: 'You must get your <u>own</u> Diapers my dear out of yr allowance' (3 November 1888; THM 384/1/3/7). This is a rare insight into the management of menstruation and advice from a mother to a nineteen-year old daughter in difficulties while travelling abroad.[13]

## 'The wild west fever'

On Edith Craig's return from Germany, there were great things afoot at the Lyceum and some painful family matters to settle. Ellen Terry had an energetic son to deal with who had become much inspired by the dramatic appeal of cowboy culture. She confided in Edith Craig about the effects of her brother's encounter with Buffalo Bill,[14] mimicking the reverential designations used in publicity materials:

> Mr, the Hon William Cody, has set his poor little brain & heart on fire & he thinks & dreams of nothing but 'Bill' – Mr Cody offered to teach Ted to '<u>real</u> ride' if I'd let him join the camp for <u>two</u> months on a visit – but Bradfield is best for him so he goes back this afternoon. (Friday, 29, 1887; THM 384/1/2/12)

The whole family had joined what the press described as 'the wild west fever' (*Columbus Journal*, 1 June 1887). The furore over the cowboy phenomenon was confirmed by Queen Victoria's endorsement of the American Exhibition when it took place at Earls Court. In June 1887 Buck Taylor, known as the King of the Cowboys, was badly injured at the American Exhibition during what sounds impossible: a horseback dance of the Virginia Reel. He fell and broke his leg badly, as Terry reported to her daughter: he had been 'dreadfully hurt' (3 June 1887; THM 384/1/2/11; *Reynolds Newspaper*, 5

June 1887). Edith Craig, who refrained from correspondence, was a frequent reference point in Gordon Craig's letters to his mother.

In the summer of 1887 Edith Craig accompanied her mother and Henry Irving to Queen Victoria's Jubilee thanksgiving at St Paul's (Terry 1908: 370). Craig was enlisted to accompany her mother to visit the grave of her father, Edward Godwin. Once this had been dealt with, Henry Irving, Ellen Terry and Edith Craig enjoyed a holiday in Germany before a very busy and somewhat fraught autumn. Mother and her nearly-eighteen-year-old daughter set off with the third Lyceum tour of North America.[15] The following year, in August 1888, Ellen Terry visited Venice with Henry Irving, reporting to both children in a playful mock character-acting voice: 'Venice is 'ot–& Venice is mosquito-y!' (14 August [1888]; THM 384/1/3/2). Letters were a vital means of keeping in touch and providing some parental guidance at a distance.

However, a few months later Ellen Terry discovered that there was trouble at Heidelberg College. In October 1888 sixteen-year-old Edward Gordon Craig had apparently absconded at night on a cycling jaunt which led to his expulsion. The details remained obscure for some time as Terry struggled to ascertain what exactly had occurred and enlisted her trusty legal adviser Stephen Coleridge to act as her representative. Terry was particularly frank in her letter to her daughter about this incident. In revealing her opinions about the situation, about her son and also about the reaction of Coleridge, she treats her daughter very much as an adult and an equal as well as a confidante:

> I was horrified for I knew in a moment how <such> a think [*sic*] handicaps a lad in the future – I telegraphed for details at once – Meanwhile I got a letter from Ted himself & from the earnest & at last grave tone of the letter I was convinced it was <u>entirely</u> true – & that's all I <u>really</u> care for that he sd [should] have understanding enough to know me for his <u>friend</u> who would fight for him, if trusted with all the truth = It was as I imagined at once – The foolish boy had capped many acts of insubordination by what Laurence described as 'breaking out of the house with 2 other lads at 11.30 at night & going for a tricycle ride until 3–4 in the morning!!' […] Stephen is furious & thinks the worst of Ted –.(28 October [1888]; THM 384/1/3/6)

Terry was mortified, going through a period of disbelief and then concern for the family's reputation. In the absence of Buffalo Bill's mustangs, Gordon Craig had taken off on his tricycle. Oblivious to the precarious position he had in terms of social status, he also seemed unaware that any improper conduct would bring disgrace upon the rest of his family. Stephen Coleridge was unable to rectify the situation and the boy was brought back to England, and placed temporarily in the care of his grandfather and then Mr Wilkinson.[16]

Meanwhile Ellen Terry's next major production was *Macbeth*. The play took up all of her energy from January to June 1889 during which time she performed as Lady Macbeth 150 times, and in May 1889 Terry's portrait in the role of Lady Macbeth by John Singer Sargent was exhibited at the New Gallery, London. Royal approval was granted when the Lyceum Theatre company gave a Royal Command performance at Sandringham in April 1888.

# Musical training and the Bach inheritance

On her return from Germany in spring of 1890, Edith Craig found her musical education had been entrusted to Sir Alexander Mackenzie (1847–1935) of the Royal Academy of Music and in March she duly passed her piano exam. At this time, her mother's standing as a performer was such that she expected to secure only the best for her daughter's education. Edith had just reached twenty-one years and time was running out to make plans for her future. There seems to have been no question about whether she would be directed towards a field of employment. Music was the first choice and it was based on her very real talents. Ellen Terry could be relied upon to be enthusiastic about her children's abilities, but in later life Ethel Smyth, the world-leading composer, included Edith Craig in the short list of her most musical friends, an illustrious catalogue of names.[17]

An awareness of Craig's genuine musical talents as judged by a world-class composer such as Ethel Smyth and an insightful anecdote from Ellen Terry help the reader to make more sense of Gordon Craig's essay, 'Edy Playing', which was his contribution to *Edy: Recollections of Edith Craig* (1949). In 1902 Ellen Terry wrote to her son about Bach, recalling her passion for the fugues and determination to learn the treble part, committing two hours every evening to practise so that she could improve when playing it with Edward Godwin. The anecdote demonstrates Terry's perseverance and her appreciation of music. Significantly, it reveals the shared understanding of Bach that triangulated Godwin, Terry and Edith Craig but excluded Gordon Craig:

> Edy understands Bach better than any kind of music– Do you know that? & we too understood it, but at first it seemed impossible to get through with it at all – but practice practice [*sic*] we did every evening from about 9 to 11 [...] but [the organist of the village] did not feel it half as understandingly as your Father – who somehow got thunderous climax – but learning it on the organ was fine for me I tell you – The wonder to me about Purcell is that he was before Bach!! (19 January 1902; *CLET* 4: 1214)

Gordon Craig's letters to his mother occasionally referred to his own musical appreciation including a performance of Bach (THM 384/5/2), as if to provide evidence to change his mother's mind. The memory of the Bach inheritance and his own dispossession seems to have haunted Gordon Craig's 'recollection of Edith Craig'. An appreciation of music was something which, for their mother, differentiated the two children. As Terry noted tactlessly in the same letter to her son: 'You were extraordinarily bored by music when you were little!! – odd – wasn't it?' (19 January 1902; *CLET* 4: 1214). Terry's emphasis on the Bach inheritance casts new light on Gordon Craig's choice of topic, focusing on his sister's musical talents in 'Edy Playing'.[18]

Craig shared musical interests with her friend Vera Holme, who had been in the Gilbert and Sullivan chorus and with Christopher St John, who was a music critic. At the Lyceum Theatre, Craig was familiar with the integration of music into the production, exemplified by Sir Arthur Sullivan's incidental music composed for the Lyceum production of *Macbeth*.[19] Kenneth DeLong has established how, in the Lyceum Theatre, the music 'contributed to the total dramatic effect' achieved by the large orchestra of forty-six players (DeLong 2008: 149). Edith Craig's productions were to benefit from her own musical training and she was particularly interested in early music.[20] Edward Gordon Craig's experiments in productions with the Purcell Operatic Society included the opera *Dido and Aeneas*, *Acis and Galatea* and the *Masque of Love* in 1901. In 1902 when Ellen Terry wrote to her son, comparing Purcell and Bach, she remarked that 'Edy understands Bach better than any kind of music' (19 January 1902; *CLET* 4: 1214). In this she implies that her daughter may have inherited the intensity of experience that she had had, of playing fugues on the village organ with Edward Godwin. The inference that this was an exclusive inheritance may have been one of the contributory factors to Edward Gordon Craig's possessiveness in later life with his own unique recollections of his mother.

## Dressing for revolution

In her memoirs, Edith Craig connects her interest in the French Revolution with childhood visits to Madame Tussaud's (Rachlin 2011: 16). Craig became something of an expert in the staging of plays about the French Revolution, catching the fashionable wave of the centenary. In 1899, as Joy Melville noted, Edith Craig's career took a different turn (Melville 1987: 171), when she was given the responsible task of producing all of the costumes for Henry Irving's production of *Robespierre* as well as appearing in a small part, as Madame de Lavigne.[21] Ellen Terry reported the scale of the project to Graham Robertson: 'Did I tell you Edy had under-taken all the women's dresses, & many of the mens [*sic*]? She engaged women in the Wardrobe of the Lyceum, & has been for about six weeks almost living in the Theatre' (15 April 1899; *CLET* 4: 989). Audiences were fascinated by the costumes in the Lyceum productions. Terry gives some insight into the use of costume to convey the subtleties of a character's demeanour, in her description of Irving's presentation in the title role:

> H-I – will be splendid! Almost grotesque in the first acts, in the end, with his curled wig uncurled & his bluebell-coloured coat & white shirt ruffled up, he looks most beautiful – & so young! Nelson's grandson sort of look – in form. (15 April 1899; *CLET* 4: 989)

Terry praised her son's sketches of *Robespierre* that were published in the *Daily Mail* and concluded: 'It's not a play after my own heart = Henry was <u>frightfully old</u> in first act Exquisitely beautiful <u>(& youthful)</u> in the last act – when he was all rumpled up [...] Edy's work was a real success – & that has delighted me' ([April 1899]; *CLET* 4: 993).

By June, the impact of Edith Craig's artistic work with the costumes was being realized, as Terry informed her niece, brother Charles's daughter, Minnie Terry (1882–1964): 'Edy is full of business – do you know she did all the dresses for Robespierre & has orders for other Plays since' (10 June 1899; *CLET* 4: 1000).

These lavish Lyceum Theatre productions contributed to the Terry's family income and gave the children a general confidence, if not often a complacency, about their place in the world. In July 1899 Ellen Terry bought another property: Vine Cottage in Kingston Vale, which became a bolt-hole for her and was made available by her to other women of the theatre. At that time Edith Craig was living at 15 Barton St Westminster, where she was joined by her American friend Satty Fairchild ([12 July 1899]; *CLET* 4: 1005). Ellen Terry was concerned about her daughter's grasp on her own finances, writing to Stephen Coleridge: 'She is going on capitally with this new work of hers – but I do wish she cd have her accounts Audited =!! she is constantly <u>careful</u>, but doesn't know how she stands' (17 July 1899; *CLET* 4: 1006).[22] Coleridge reflected on Terry's attitude to her daughter, annotating the letter: 'Endless struggles to believe in Edie – constantly disappointed' (30 July 1899; *CLET* 4: 1009). Terry's maternal concern extended also to Craig's rented accommodation. The owner, the Hon. Maude Stanley (1833–1915), was a philanthropist and social reformer, but under suspicion in this instance, signalled by Terry's punctuation:

The Hon'be (?) Maude Stanley has taken the <u>House</u>, cleaned it out as to Drains (?) & put in Electric light – but she charges Edy £<u>2-10-0</u> for 4 rooms & ~~I believe~~ I <u>would</u> like to know what she (Miss Stanley) pays for the house = I <u>believe</u> it wd be far better for me to let the house, & live in the above parts (Edy in the <u>lower</u> rooms) & get rid <u>if I can</u>, of this Barkston <u>Gds</u> – [...] If you cd find out the Rent Miss Stanley pays for that house, & <u>if you wd look over it first</u>, I shd be much gratified = I'd like all this <u>done quietly</u> at first before we speak to Maude Stanley – Oh,

\*<u>doesn't</u>\* she like to make a pretty penny!' (17 July 1899; *CLET* 4: 1006)

A month later, Terry was more forthright in her opinion; she gave instruction to Coleridge to sort out the accommodation for Craig and alluded to Maude Stanley's work in setting up girls' clubs: '(& Miss S. poses as a helper towards young women!!) She is very well known as a "regular screw", & you cd tackle her splendidly' (24 August 1899; *CLET* 4: 1018). Given these extensive protective interventions, it is perhaps surprising to note that at this time Edith Craig was approaching her thirtieth birthday. So independent in many ways, Craig and her brother both found it difficult to separate themselves from their mother's supervision. It created a sense of dependence as well as complacency that was to have a long-lasting impact on the ever-extending family.

From July 1899 Craig's theatre practice focused on costume design and her costumier business was financially supported and promoted by her mother.[23] Stephen Coleridge reflected that 'Edie's "business" was conducted with hopeless irregularity & ended in an awful crash with thousands to pay out!' (31 July 1899; *CLET* 4: 1010). After so much hard work, described by Terry as 'slaving away like a house a fire!' ([1899]; 1053; *CLET* 4: 1053), Craig went to Bath for a rest and allowed her brother to stay at Barton Street, much against her mother's advice (7 August [1899]; *CLET* 4: 1013). At this time he was in a relationship with the actor Jess Dorynne and looking for somewhere to stay.[24] Although his marriage to May Gibson had come to an end, 'M & the Babes' were still in evidence in his mother's life and staying at Vine Cottage, Kingston. So Terry offered her son and Jess Dorynne temporary accommodation in principle at the end of September at the newly acquired Elizabethan Farm at Tenterden with the proviso, 'but surely an undrained house wd make you both ill' (22 August 1889; *CLET* 4: 1017). Terry took her daughter with her to visit The Farm.

Terry relied on her opinion of Shaw's latest plays, *The Devil's Disciple* and *Captain Brassbound's Conversion*. Craig was sceptical about the character of Lady Cicely Waynflete, as Terry candidly reported to the author:

it seemed to her you \*<u>thought</u>\* yr Lady C. one sort of woman, & have <u>written</u> her another = conveyed another idea = She don't think Lady C. is shown to be either very clever or humourous = or vital & certainly not "of great humanity" = I shd have to get you to let me know more about Lady C's <u>inside</u> before I – <u>did</u> her! (Did for her =). (11 October 1899; *CLET* 4: 1037)

Both Shaw and Terry respected Edith Craig's opinion and Terry relied on her daughter in many ways, especially theatrical matters.[25] When at the beginning of the sixth American tour, Terry wrote to her friend Elizabeth Winter, she mentioned only one of her children: 'Edy is not with me, & I miss her all the time' ([October 1899]; *CLET* 4: 1045). Terry's correspondence reveals her endless patience with her children, even giving extensive advice to her son on how to deal with the mother of the young woman with whom he was living. The priority for her was always their happiness. Gordon Craig seems to have shown some sibling concern, to which Terry replied with similar equanimity: 'Don't you trouble about Edy – You <u>don't</u> suppose <u>she</u> is not going to have her bad & absurd times, & make mistakes, & all the rest of it? <u>Of course she will</u>. All one must do is to help = '(1899; *CLET* 4: 1058).

Edith Craig had had several years to get used to a variety of roles: being a sister-in-law and then aunt to her brother's four children and then his separation from them, generated a new family structure. Terry supported her son throughout this transition and typically invented a new phrase to make the unorthodox seem familiar. She wrote to him in December 1900, a month after the birth of his child to Jess Dorynne: 'we will be, you & I, & Edy & Jess, a "<u>mutual-admiration Society</u>"' (11 December 1900; *CLET* 4: 1122). In emphasizing the support from this close family circle, she was probably recalling her own experiences of exile when she had her children outside marriage. And endeavouring to provide her son with more support than she had enjoyed from her own family. In 1900 Terry and her daughter travelled to St Albans to see Gordon Craig's youngest four children, whose mother he had divorced. In August 1902 Edith Craig was at The Farm looking after these children (30 August [1901?]; *CLET* 4: 1173). In April 1902 Craig accompanied her mother to Stratford for a production of *Henry VIII* and Terry found time for relaxation 'with Edy & a crowd of young people on the River' (24 April 1902; *CLET* 4: 1232).

In January 1900 Terry wrote to Stephen Coleridge for reports on her daughter's health and on her business, relieved that 'Chris Marshall, & Alix Egerton have been magnificent friends to her in my absence' (8 January 1900; *CLET* 4: 1066). In August 1900 Terry visited Aix-les-Bains for a 'rheumatism cure' with her friend Edie Lane (20 August [1900]; *CLET* 4: 1096), mentioning her daughter's need for recuperation.[26] The following August, Edith Craig accompanied them on another visit, benefiting from car rides in the mountains and the experience of the latest fashions: 'The dresses here are a sight to be seen – Good for Edy to see = They are <u>outrageous</u>' (7 August 1901; *CLET* 4: 1167).

# The secret of costume: 'a question of omission'

Edith Craig wrote articles on costume for the *Kensington* and *Fortnightly Review* and was acknowledged by the Stage Society, the organization leading experiments in stage production, in its annual reports as 'Mistress of the Robes' (*SSAR* 1900–1: 8). She thought that costumes should be designed and made by the same person and that costumes for a historical period should reflect that age rather than look shiny and new (EC-G180). The influences on Edith Craig as a costumier were varied. They certainly developed from practical experience in watching Mrs Nettleship and Alice Comyns Carr make and design costumes for numerous lavish productions. Typically Ellen Terry was on hand to provide relevant stimuli for her children. In 1887 she gave her daughter a well-chosen book.[27] Terry described her daughter as 'a born archaeologist' (Terry 1908: 215) probably alluding to Craig's father, Edward Godwin, who wrote extensively on historical costume design.

Literary adaptations and productions designed for children were ones for which Craig designed costumes, such as *The Snowman* in 1899, and for which she was praised for the detailed representation of the artwork: 'no pains have been spared to secure absolute fidelity' in their interpretation of Walter Crane's designs (E.V.6.4). When she produced the costumes for *Shock Headed Peter* at the Criterion Theatre on 31 December 1900, Ellen Terry was disappointed that she was unable to see the production and the costumes. She asked for press cuttings so she could get some impression of her daughter's creations: 'That's the proper kind of entertainment for Children – or at least it <u>should</u> be!' (10 December 1900; *CLET* 4: 1121). Terry's interest in her children's theatrical work never faded.

Christopher St John wrote to Ellen Terry to report on Edith Craig's costume designs for Laurence Irving's *Bonnie Dundee* (13 March 1900; ET-1,411). Edith Craig had been the designer of costumes rather than Tom Heslewood. Craig had chosen to use all sorts of reds and types of material because otherwise it 'promised to be a monotonous show of red'.[28] In her costume design Craig always demonstrated an awareness of the effect of different textures in stage lighting.

Inevitably Craig gained experience by designing for her mother and other willing family members. In 1900 her costume designs for her aunt, Marion Terry, as Rosalind at the Stratford Festival were reviewed in *The Lady*, highlighting the leather tabard having been inspired by the Renaissance artist Pietro Perugino (*Lady*, 3 May 1900). In 1901 Craig designed costumes for Lillie Langtry's production of *Mademoiselle Mars* and *The Sacrament of Judas*, a play by Louis N. Parker (1852–1944) who became nationally known for his work as a producer of historical pageants. In 1902 Craig provided the historically accurate costumes for the procession of thirty characters including Milton's daughters, Katharine Parr, Elizabeth I and Queen Victoria in the Kendal celebrations to mark the coronation of Edward VII on 9 August 1902 (E.V.6.4 5/5). Ellen Terry was obliged to make arrangements for her own costumes when she toured independently while with the Lyceum. In these circumstances her daughter made dresses for her for *Madame Sans-Gene* (3 June 1901; *CLET* 4: 1161). In July 1902, when Terry played Mistress Page in *The Merry Wives of Windsor* at His Majesty's Theatre under Beerbohm Tree's management, it was in a costume made by Edith Craig. It is not clear exactly how it was designed but Terry wrote to her son thanking him for sending a design but explaining that she had to wear the costume 'provided for me' (30 May 1902; *CLET* 4: 1239). In her autobiography, Ellen Terry recalls the fire in her theatre dressing room prompting Edith Craig's courageous commitment to make a replacement dress before the evening performance: 'My daughter says to know what not to do is the secret of making stage dresses, it is not a question of time or of money, but of omission' (Terry 1908: 352). This illuminating description of Craig's method points to a domain of suggestion, impression and minimalism rather than the elaborate and lavish features typical of the commercial theatre.

In 1901 Edith Craig designed costumes for an unusual play by Russell Vaun entitled *Nicandra*, with Cora Brown Potter in the lead role, and topical allusions to the fashion for mysticism and magic. Special effects created the necessary magical atmosphere for the transformation of the Egyptian snake woman Nicandra, but her costume was of central importance and Edith Craig was involved in its creation. A review suggests that the glittery fabrication of the dress may have borne some resemblance to Terry's Lady Macbeth costume:

> [The] gown is so cleverly designed and made as to carry out the serpentine idea to perfection for every curve of her supple figure is followed by a sheath-like robe of emerald-green tissue, shot with gleams of vivid violet, and now and again with a shimmer of silver. Over this comes a transparent and trailing drapery of black net wrought with a scale-like device in jet paillettes, while scarves of violet and green chiffon are draped at the décolleté, and caught together here and there on the white arms by jewelled clasps. Two great square-cut emeralds fall low down on her forehead from strings of pearls wound in her ruddy hair. Altogether, Nicandra is a veritable enchantress. (*Modern Society*, 20 April 1901, p. 757)

The dress was ingenious in its exploitation of the reflective and transparent properties of the fabric and jewels. The fit of the garment implied the sinuous profile enhanced by an intriguing 'scale-like device'. The *Illustrated Sporting & Dramatic News* satirized Brown-Potter, drawing attention to the revealing aspects of the costume: 'She is seen in but one dress or what would be one dress were it cut more liberally where the sleeves should be' (20 April 1901, p. 289).

## Acting unusual parts

Edith Craig learnt a great deal from Cora Brown Potter, Sarah Bernhardt and Lillie Langtry.[29] She had walk-on parts as extras in Bernhardt's plays from which she learnt the importance of correct

presentation of supers.[30] Edith Craig made her New York debut in
*Barbara* by Jerome K. Jerome, in which the orphaned Barbara dis-
covers that she has a fortune, enabling her friend Lillie to marry the
impoverished author, Cecil, who is revealed to be Barbara's brother.
In 1890 she appeared as Polly Flamborough in *Olivia* under
the name 'Miss Hallet' at the Grand Theatre Islington (Rachlin
2011: 80).

Craig worked for the Lyceum Theatre company as a performer
from 1887 to 1899. In July 1895 for the Lyceum's production of
*Macbeth*, Henry Irving cast Edith Craig as Donalbain (Cockin
1998a: 41; ET-D715). Irving also cast male performers in the role
of the witches; Mr Valentine, Mr Hague and Mr Archer played
first, second and third witches respectively. William Poel's cross-
gender casting of Rosencrantz and Guildenstern attracted critical attention but Irving had already experimented in this way. In
1891–93 Edward Gordon Craig was a regular performer with the
Lyceum Theatre company in *Becket*, *King Lear* and *The Merchant
of Venice*. Edith Craig tended to perform Ursula in *Much Ado
About Nothing* (ET-D712), Jessica in *The Merchant of Venice* (ET-
D714) and Clarissant in *King Arthur* (ET-D713).[31] In 1895 Edith
Craig appeared in the 100th performance of *King Arthur*. As a
character actress, she was able to portray older women and convey
distinctive personalities as Alice Comyns Carr recalled, when Ellen
Terry and Edith Craig transformed on stage from youth to old age
at a fund-raiser for the Winchelsea lace-making industry (Adam
1926: 114). Craig occasionally appeared as Terry's understudy,
including in *Journey's End in Lover's Meeting*.[32] Pearl Craigie
met Edith Craig at Daly's, presumably when Craig was working
for Sarah Bernhardt. According to Edith Craig's memoirs, Craig
had been employed as an extra (Rachlin 2011: 100). Edith Craig's
experience in productions included the tour of *A Doll's House* and
*Candida* with the Achurch-Charrington company in 1897, placing
her at the centre of developments in performing the New Ibsenite
Woman.

Craig's financial situation probably led to her return to acting.
Her costumier business had not flourished and she had got herself into significant debt to her mother. Terry wrote to Stephen
Coleridge asking him to arrange for her daughter to repay her on a
monthly basis from her reduced allowance (12 March 1901; *CLET*

4: 1143).[33] Craig's role in Frederick Fenn's *A Married Woman* may have been an attempt to earn some money although she was apparently nervous about her return to acting, as Christopher St John informed Ellen Terry: 'Three years absence from it – no wonder she was a bit frightened' (25 November 1902; EC-1,420). She may have also been concerned about her mother's reaction to an all too-familiar plot. The play featured the difficulties of a woman married to an alcoholic husband and there were other aspects which made it controversial. As Lady Muriel, Craig performed the supporting role of the unattractive spinster who gains revenge on the misogynists by altering her appearance so much that they fall in love with her. More attention is given to the leading character, Cicely Kent, who is married to an alcoholic husband and, in order to escape him, cross-dresses as a 'Mr Holroyd'. In this disguise, she enters into the masculine world, discovering that Richard Strake, a young man, is attracted to Cicely Kent.

Although the plot seems to offer scope to explore the desires of women who are unmarried or unhappily married, most reviewers regarded this aspect of the play with suspicion. The concept of an unhappy marriage was unintelligible to the reviewer in the *News of the World*: 'the woman in question, is one of the modern neurotic type, who is by no means satisfied to take married life for better or worse, but sighs for liberty and ideals' (30 November 1902; EC-G1651). Max Beerbohm (1876–1956) seemed alone in understanding the threatening potential of the play.[34] In his contribution to the *Saturday Review*, he highlighted the cross-dressing in the play, using it as an opportunity to explain the success of male impersonators such as Vesta Tilley,[35] and to demonize as 'irrelevant monsters' those women who cross-dress off the stage:

[Although there have been] in modern history several well-known instances of a woman palming herself off as a man for many years [...] these deceivers have been, invariably, women of a peculiar kind – women whose nature was more masculine than feminine, and who chose a masculine life, not by caprice, but because a feminine life dissatisfied them. But Mrs Kent is quite an ordinary woman, and she falls duly in love with the baronet who harbours her. Being an ordinary woman, she is bound to look more than ever womanly in masculine attire, and could not for a moment impose on anyone except on a blind man; [...] She could not possibly (unless she were one of the irrelevant monsters whom I have mentioned) look like anyone but Miss Tilley. (*Saturday Review*, 29 November 1902; EC-G1648)

The strength of Beerbohm's response reflects the climate of homophobia generated after the trial of his friend Oscar Wilde in 1895. Beerbohm had Ellen Terry in mind in writing his brief verdict on her daughter's performance: 'Miss Edith Craig, in a lesser part, grafted the Terry charm on a brusque and un-Terryish realism, all her own' (*Saturday Review*, 29 November 1902; EC-G1648). In using a horticultural term for creating new breeds, Beerbohm identified a difference about Craig which cannot quite be articulated but fundamentally separated her from the Terry family.[36]

## Transatlantic adventures and family foundations

Edith Craig first visited North America on holiday in August 1886, before she arrived there for work on tour with the Lyceum Theatre company in the autumn of 1887. She recalled meeting Horace Furness in 1888 (Rachlin 2011: 74). In 1897, during the transatlantic sea voyage, she was a captive audience for Bram Stoker when he tested passages from *Dracula* on her; he read with relish the details of Renfield's consumption of insects (Rachlin 2011: 97). By contrast, Edith Craig often refused to eat and her lack of appetite disturbed her American hosts (Rachlin 2011: 73).

Edith Craig acquired another sibling of sorts when in 1899 her mother informally adopted the adult Pamela Colman Smith,[37] and brought her into the Lyceum Theatre company. Colman Smith was known for her story-telling performances; as 'Galukiezanger' she would tell Jamaican folk stories. The programme for a New York event described it as 'an absolute novelty: folk stories from Jamaica' and quoted endorsements from several illustrious celebrities: Ellen Terry confirmed, 'Since hearing your stories I have told no others'; W. B. Yeats implied that Colman Smith was operating in another dimension: 'Our father "time" and our mother "space" have said to her – as they say to none but excellent artists "you are as good a child that we need not trouble about you" ' (ET-D2094). A sense of the performance is given by Arthur Symons who describes the sound of her voice: 'I am proud to add a word of mine to those who have already praised you. What you do seems to me exquisitely right, like an instinct; out your croon comes into silence like a bird's chuckle among the leaves outside the window' (ET-D2094). Colman Smith's unusual blend of artistic skills as a visual artist, performer and author and her serious interest in the occult brought her into the circles of Jack B. Yeats, W. B. Yeats, Arthur Ransome and Lady Gregory. She became a regular visitor at Terry's Kent home.

The Terry family became accustomed to having several properties. They were bought outright or on lease: a fortunate situation directly related to the success of Terry's acting career. In July 1892 Ellen Terry's purchase of Tower Cottage, Winchelsea from Joe Comyns Carr was made possible by the success of her tours of *Nance Oldfield*.[38] The extent of the family resources in the 1890s meant that Terry could buy six cottages in Brancaster.[39] These effectively represented Terry's pension fund for Elizabeth Rumball. Brancaster became something of a family bolt-hole but the details of Terry's financial involvement was probably concealed from her children.

Although Terry owned several properties, she was frequently on tour and tenants were arranged. Increasingly, driven by financial exigencies, the family was involved in a high degree of mobility.[40] While on tour in America Terry wrote to Mrs Rumball about her plans to arrange tenants for her daughter's No.7 Smith Square flat during the coronation period ([28 October 1901]; *CLET* 4: 1185). Its prime central London location next to Westminster Abbey made it an ideal temporary residence during such a historic occasion.

## Her Master's voice and Ellen Terry's 'literary henchman'

Christopher St John and Edith Craig met in 1899, backstage at the Grand Theatre Fulham. St John had arrived by bicycle and was dressed in the military costume of a Chelsea veteran, with her red coat and tricorne hat (Rachlin 2011: 118). The two women shared interests in theatre, literature and the arts generally. They formed a relationship and lived together for over 40 years at various addresses: 7 Smith Square, Adelphi Terrace, 31 Bedford Street, Covent Garden and when in Kent, at Priest's House, the cottage neighbouring Ellen Terry's Farm. St John had studied history at Somerville College, Oxford and worked as secretary to Lady Randolph Churchill. As a writer, she worked on a freelance basis for various publications, notably for *Time & Tide* and the *Lady*, often reviewing musical and theatrical productions. In 1902 St John's letter to Ellen Terry provides an insight into the intensity of St John's feeling for both mother and daughter:

> You have given me the best, the most superb gift of my life in Edy. So my worship of you as the most wonderful of all women is steadied & deepened by the gratitude of a saved soul to its redeemer. For you, if it were asked of me, I think I could have strength to render up the gift. Do you know that not a day passes when I take it as a matter of course that you should smile at her living with me. I realize more & more poignantly with time what depth of love there is in that smile.
>
> Christopher (your ghost) (27 June 1902; ET-1,413)

The signature, promising a haunting and persistent presence, also looks forward to St John's role as Terry's ghost-writer in her autobiography (1908), Shakespeare lectures (1910) and *The Russian Ballet* (1913).

The influence of Henry Irving was imperceptible and comprehensive in Edith Craig's approach to theatre work as an all-consuming enterprise. It explains her statement that 'the stage is too much a part of my life to theorise about it' (EC-G174). After Irving's death in 1905, Craig's memento of Irving was kept close at hand; imperceptible because repurposed in a way that would only occur to Craig. When Gordon Craig spotted that her bed covering was Irving's Romeo cloak, he immediately commandeered it.[41] Ellen Terry's children grew up with the theatre in their bones and souls; it was their daily breath. For Edith Craig, a physical reminder of Irving's performance enveloped her when she woke and retired to bed. With her own body heat, she willed the costume to come back to life. Henry Irving was the people's knight and his death devastated Ellen Terry who noted 'I think the whole world mourned for him = he is buried in the people's hearts' (ET-Z2,174). His funeral on 20 October at Westminster Abbey was effectively a state occasion.[42]

Irving's henchman Bram Stoker was on hand to support Irving's theatrical enterprise. He took on other duties, helping Terry at times of difficulty and even attempting to provide a guiding hand to her son. Edith Craig seems to have assisted in the copyright reading of his dramatization of *Dracula* at the Lyceum Theatre (Cockin 1998a: 49). She also provided a reliable audience for his reading of the novel as it developed (Rachlin 2011: 97). Edith Craig was attentive to Her Master's voice; like Renfield for Dracula, she did Henry Irving's bidding to ensure that the Lyceum costumes were just right. Eventually the time came to break away from the gothic family of the Lyceum and find her own path.[43]

# After Rubens: Edith Craig & Co., *The Green Sheaf* and other magical workings

Edith Craig is described in a striking and memorable way in an article on her costume work in a column aimed at female readers of the *Free Lance* in 1901:

> She looked like some stately lady of rich old Holland, who had stepped out of the shadows of Rubens to look out at our vulgarities with grave, grey eyes, and who would bye-and-bye go back again to her grander world of bygones. (5 October 1901)

Craig's knowledge and expertise in historically authentic costumes is here attributed to her time-travelling as if she has magically walked out of a seventeenth-century oil painting by Rubens. The specific artist and period suggests a world of patronage in which artists engaged with the wealthy. By contrast, Craig's treatment of her workers was rather more egalitarian.

With Edith Craig & Co., her business run from Henrietta Street, Covent Garden, Craig was directing her time towards her expertise in costume design instead of acting. The business was financially supported by Ellen Terry and ultimately could not sustain a competitive place in the market. It was given prominent and regular advertisement, taking one third of a page, in Pamela Colman Smith's short-lived little magazine *The Green Sheaf* (1903–4).[44] The extension of theatrical costume into social events is noteworthy and will be examined in Chapter three. It indicates the prevalence of fancy dress as well as public pageantry, in which Edith Craig had a significant role.

The promotion of Edith Craig & Co. to the readers of *The Green Sheaf* was a significant marketing strategy. It promised access to an influential circle of authors and artists, including W. B. Yeats in the period before the Abbey Theatre was founded in Dublin. Christopher St John, who made four signed contributions to it, reported to Ellen Terry the advent of this new magazine in a way which provides not only an insight into the circumstances of its development and the artistic leadership of *The Green Sheaf* but also the significance of Yeats's support:

> Pixie is starting another paper – an affected, dilettante sort of affair, but as her Irish god 'Mr Willie' has blessed it, she thinks it will be the most original journal ever produced.[45]

Ellen Terry had been sceptical about Yeats's poetry, writing to her son in 1900: 'after Tennyson the <u>wee-est</u> bit of old Swinburne for <u>me</u> before bucketsful of Yeats – I've tried for a whole year to "<u>acquire the taste</u>" for Yeats, & can't = <Yeats> – Phillips – Watson all <u>good</u>, but not <u>good enough</u> I feel' (20 August 1900; *CLET* 4: 1095). If Yeats was Pixie Smith's 'Irish god', he was sparing in his contributions although what little he did provide was highly symbolic. Yeats's signed input was restricted to one short story and a reproduction of his pastel sketch of the lake at Coole. His choice of subject matter for the sketch is revealing; in his essay 'Magic' (1901) Yeats meditates on the banks of the lake at Coole as the site of spiritual enlightenment.[46] St John and others were more in evidence than Yeats was as contributors. It has been assumed that W. B. Yeats was responsible for the inspiration and founding of the magazine, attributing the principal creative features not only to Yeats but also his brother Jack,[47] who had edited a similar magazine with Colman Smith:

> No magazine called the *Hour-Glass* appeared, but the young American artist Yeats wrote about, Pamela Colman Smith, did

come out with a slight and lovely periodical about which hovers the spirit of make-believe Yeats alluded to. Instead of a preface by Yeats, there is one by Smith – a versified editorial statement accompanied by a colored drawing, both of which appear on the cover of each issue of the *Green Sheaf*. (Sullivan 1984: 155)

The appearance of *The Green Sheaf* after the *Hour-Glass* and the similarity of its interests, could be over-interpreted. *The Green Sheaf* was not the *Hour-Glass*. If what is taken as a substitute for a preface can be accurately described as a 'versified editorial statement', it is certainly unconventional and it is unsigned, like several contributions in each issue. *The Green Sheaf* does not present itself to its readers with a clear manifesto and the 'versified editorial statement' requires some interpretation. Until issue No. 4 it appeared on the back cover:

My *Sheaf* is small…but it is green.
I will gather into my *Sheaf* all the young fresh things I can –
  *pictures, verses, ballads*, of *love* and *war*; tales of *pirates* and the
  sea.
You will find ballads of the *old world* in my *Sheaf*. Are they not
  green for ever…
Ripe ears are *good* for *bread*, but green ears are good for *pleasure*.
  [emphases in original]

As an enigmatic lyric, it plays with the word 'sheaf', a bundle of corn or of papers with 'young and fresh' items, caught at an early stage with potential for development. As a pastoral image of cultivation, it is distanced from the industrialized process of printing and consistent with the Arts and Crafts aesthetic of other *fin de siècle* little magazines. It has escaped critical attention in recent years. The magazine itself resembles the little sheaf of papers, tied with green ribbon. Produced in the laborious and intimate process of hand-made paper and hand colouring, *The Green Sheaf* also promoted, through its advertisements, traditional crafts such as weaving and lace-making.

There is therefore evidence that Edith Craig was one of the influential circle of theatre practitioners who promoted *The Green Sheaf*. Colman Smith's relationship with the Lyceum Theatre, where Ellen Terry worked with Henry Irving until 1902, has been identified as a significant feature of *The Green Sheaf*. In issue No. 5 one of the contributions is an anonymously authored short story entitled 'The Lament of a Lyceum Rat'. Under the imprint of 'The Green Sheaf' but after the magazine had ended, she published Christopher St John's elegiac pamphlet, entitled *Henry Irving* (1905). It depicts a sketch of an extinguishing lantern on the front cover, symbolizing the expiring flame and spirit of Irving. *The Green Sheaf* magazine No. 3 carried an advert for *A Masque of the Harvest Home*, organized by Edward Gordon Craig and the musician Martin Shaw, offered with a forty-five minute running time and with music by Purcell as well as unfamiliar folk music. This was apparently never produced.

Although Ellen Terry did not relish 'bucketsful of Yeats', Yeats himself greatly appreciated the work of her children. It was after Edith Craig showed him backstage at Gordon Craig's production of Laurence Housman's play *Bethlehem* in 1902 that Yeats wrote to Lady Gregory, 'I have learned a great deal about the staging of plays from "the Nativity"' (Kelly and Schuchard 1994: 285). In the years before the Abbey Theatre was opened in Dublin on 27 December 1904, Yeats was writing plays and becoming drawn to the theatre. Edith Craig was one of those theatre practitioners who enabled him to see how words could be transformed in performance on stage. In 1903 Yeats, Pamela Colman Smith and Edith Craig were all involved in an intriguing, ambitious and ultimately thwarted theatre society called The Masquers.

# CHAPTER THREE
## 1903–7

# The New Woman experiments and the genealogy of the 'Scala masque'

In the early twentieth century there was, as Roger Savage (2014) has noted, something of an English revival of interest in the masque. Three hundred years earlier, this spectacular dramatic form incorporating dance and music would introduce an evening of entertainment and feasting to delight the early Stuart court. Ben Jonson's court masques were lavish productions served for the benefit and reassurance of the aristocratic elite. The ceremonial processions, music and dancing signified structure and order, hierarchy and power whereas the anti-masque engaged with the anxieties and conflicts of the period; disruptive elements were given vent but subsequently controlled and restrained with the entrance of the members of the court in the masque. The staging of these performances, centrally at court or in country houses that might serve as a rest stop along the royal route, indicates the importance of the sense of occasion and place to the masque and its knowable audience. The significance of the performance was therefore time- and site-specific.

The end of Queen Victoria's reign was a prime time to revive the masque and three or four productions in the period have been identified.[1] In July 1903 Philip Comyns Carr (b. 1874) produced Ben Jonson's *Hue and Cry after Cupid* in Regent's Park in which Ellen Terry's sister Marion appeared as Ceres and Ellen Terry contributed a recital,[2] and in 1908 Lena Ashwell (1872–1957) organized *The Vision of Delight* at the Kingsway Theatre and repeated it on 27 June 1911 for the royal gala performance in order to provide a vehicle for female performers to take part in the coronation of George V at His Majesty's Theatre (Leask 2012: 77, 96). These productions shaped the expectations that early twentieth-century audiences had for masques or pageants and, as Roger Savage argues, Philip Comyns Carr and Lena Ashwell had all endeavoured 'to free the masque from the absolutist court ethos of the Stuarts and make it safe for constitutional monarchists, even for democrats' (Savage 2014: 65). Savage notes the wide appeal of the hybrid and multi-media form of the masque, with its poetry, song, dance and visual arts:

> It is apt, then, that our small renaissance of Jonsonian masquing should begin with Philip Carr giving his *Hue and Cry* its public premiere in Regent's Park in July 1903, within a week of the first formal meeting of the Masquers Society: that high-Aesthetic venture which would have been called 'the Theatre of Beauty' if Yeats had had his way and which hoped to stage, another sort of non-naturalist drama (ancient Greek, modern *symboliste* and so on), a revival of Gordon Craig's *Masque of Love* and a 'masque of beauty' that Yeats himself had in hand. (He would never finish it, though his detailed synopsis of a related 'Opening Ceremony for the Masquers' is extant). (Savage 2014: 65–6)

The Masquers society was thwarted for various reasons but, as will be discussed later in this chapter, its prime mover was Edith Craig.

Edith Craig's involvement in the Edwardian masque and related networks informed her nationwide productions of one of the most effective and influential British women's suffrage plays. This was *A Pageant of Great Women* by Cicely Hamilton, who dedicated the play 'To Edith Craig, whose ideas these lines were written to illustrate' (Hamilton 1910: 9). This play has been associated with the tradition of *tableaux vivants* and pageants, but in this chapter

I will be arguing that it was influenced by the revival of the masque. Instead of making these new masques, as Savage suggests, '*safe* for constitutional monarchists, even for democrats' (Savage 2014: 65; my emphasis), Hamilton and Craig redeployed its promise of danger, packing the stage with women portraying historical precedents as evidence for the merits of women's enfranchisement, and reactivating the tense political reverberations and the site-specific significance of the audience and participants gathered for the event.

Prompted by the discovery of Ellen Terry's designation in private correspondence of *A Pageant of Great Women* as the 'Scala masque' (11 November [1909]; *CLET* 5: 1570), this chapter will both establish the genealogy of this extraordinary play (extending three hundred years back to Ben Jonson) and restore Edith Craig to the historiography of the twentieth-century vogue for masques (Savage 2014: 35). Edith Craig's work as a director was influenced by her knowledge and understanding of theatre history, dramatic forms and her commitment to authenticity of costume and staging. As a contemporary of figures such as William Poel (1852–1934) who founded the Elizabethan Stage Society (1893–1905), Craig followed a similar path but her work as a director was eclectic. Instead of regarding her career as entering a different discrete phase with her women's suffrage productions, I suggest that she simply applied the same knowledge and expertise as a theatre practitioner to the political project. If Craig's direction of *A Pageant of Great Women* is situated in a tradition of Jonsonian masque, its production for knowing audiences in designated venues on the route of the national campaign tours may be considered as appropriating the masque form for the great and the good of women's suffrage activism and their invaluable groundling activists in a spectacle to inspire and transform them. In resituating some missing fragments in the history of the Edwardian masque tradition, this account of Edith Craig's productions of *A Pageant of Great Women* demonstrates how they mounted a highly effective political intervention and a well-timed deployment of theatrical formal experiment. By tuning in to the topical interest in civic spectacle in the consolidation of national identity at the heart of the British empire, the play appropriated for women's suffrage activists a central place at their imagined court in their new regime. Cicely Hamilton, author of *A Pageant of Great Women*, created with Ethel Smyth the famous women's suffrage anthem entitled 'The March of the Women'.

All that remained was their establishment of a new feminist world order. The extent to which this feminist cultural work was being felt as a radical force is suggested by Beerbohm Tree's marshalling of beautiful female bodies in 1911, as a rather feeble anti-suffrage epistle to the radical force that Edith Craig's direction of Cicely Hamilton's *A Pageant of Great Women* had become.

# *King Arthur* (1895) and *Comus* (1903)

Edith Craig had acquired a great deal of first-hand experience of staging visually stunning productions at the Lyceum Theatre where her mother's performance style was particularly defined as 'pictorial', with an emphasis on her artistically innovative costumes. In 1895 Edith Craig had appeared as Clarissant in Joseph Comyns Carr's play *King Arthur* at the Lyceum Theatre with Henry Irving and Ellen Terry performing as respectively King Arthur and Guinevere. *King Arthur* exploited the fascination in this period with medievalism, envisaging chivalric knights in combat and quests for prized ladies. Meanwhile in the Lyceum Theatre and the wider empire a precariously balanced power structure was being nibbled away from the margins by raucous beasts and sarcastic jesters.

The story of King Arthur, so popular in the nineteenth century, is described by Jeffrey Richards as 'the ultimate Victorian chivalric myth' (Richards 2005: 24). Cultural references to innocent ladies at risk and protective knights battling magical spells were ubiquitous in poetry, drama and the visual arts. The King Arthur story offered particular attractions to Henry Irving, still sensitive about his own social mobility. Richards interprets Irving's desire to play King Arthur because the role was 'linked by a powerful commitment to the chivalric vision but also one that is doomed to end in failure. As a self-made gentleman, Irving was always conscious of the fragility of gentlemanliness' (Richards 2005: 30). However, in his portrayal of King Arthur, a character linked elsewhere to Prince Albert, Irving was asserting himself as King of his Lyceum Theatre domain with his Queen, Ellen/Guinevere. Rather than a sign of insecurity, it was a performance of power and influence supported by established social networks of drama critics, theatre managers, artists, investors and freemasons. In 1877, a year before he took up the management of the Lyceum Theatre, Irving had become a freemason; by the time he appeared as King Arthur he had already proceeded to the level of master mason and been involved in founding the new Savage Club Lodge No. 2190, of which Albert, Prince of Wales, was an honorary member (Prescott 2003: 15). Any anxieties Irving may have had about his social status were mitigated by his confidence in the approval of the Brotherhood and other influential circles that welcomed him internationally. As members of the younger branches of the inner circle at the Lyceum, Edith Craig and her brother would have benefited indirectly in some ways by association.

Irving commissioned *King Arthur* from Joseph Comyns Carr (1849–1916), who was at the centre of cultural innovation. A barrister, drama critic, theatrical entrepreneur and patron of the arts, Comyns Carr had also been one of the first directors of the Grosvenor Gallery when it opened in 1877 and, with Charles Hallé (1819–95), was co-founder of the New Gallery in 1888. These were the centres of the latest in contemporary art. Sir Edward Burne-Jones (1833–98), one of the Pre-Raphaelite artists promoted by Comyns Carr and who had exhibited at both of these galleries, was commissioned by Henry Irving to design costumes for his lavish production of *King Arthur*. This winning combination, with Sir Arthur Sullivan (1842–1900) providing the music, guaranteed a wide network for publicity and consequently a prospect of large audiences interested in the visual arts as well as theatre. The Comyns Carr family was part of the Irving-Terry intimate inner circle. Alice Comyns Carr designed some of Ellen Terry's most famous costumes, notably the Lady Macbeth 'beetle-wing' dress and the crinkled dress of Ellaline in *The Amber Heart*. The production of these costumes was the result of a creative understanding between actor and costumier. Joseph Comyns Carr was the vendor when Ellen Terry bought Tower Cottage, Winchelsea in 1896, her rather grand country residence, in contrast to Rose Cottage about which she had felt obliged to create an apologetically mock heroic narrative.

Philip Comyns Carr, one of the sons of Joseph and Alice, was well-placed to secure the implementation of his ideas for theatrical innovation in the development of the masque. In 1903 he founded the Mermaid Society, with five productions offered for five guineas.[3] *Comus* was staged in the Royal Botanical Society grounds in Regent's Park, apparently making good use of the lake and intriguingly included a 'Miss Wardell' as one of the three graces (*Athenaeum*, 11 July 1903, p. 71).[4] In 1897 when Philip Comyns Carr was secretary of the Oxford University Dramatic Society (OUDS, founded in 1885), he wrote to invite Edith Craig to take part as Katharine in *The Taming of the Shrew*; he apologized for the short notice as it would mean taking part from 27 February to 2 March. He also briefly mentioned John Milton's *Comus (A Masque Presented at Ludlow Castle 1634)* in this letter (EC-Z3, 127). As Humphrey Carpenter noted in his history of OUDS, the Vice Chancellor of Oxford University forbade the production of *Comus* and it was replaced by *The Taming of the Shrew* (Carpenter 1985: 59). Six years later when Comyns Carr produced *Comus* for the Mermaid Society, Edith Craig attended it and, evidenced by her annotated playscript, was at least an attentive observer if not also with some input into its production (EC-H192). Edith Craig had a continuing interest in the play. When it was performed in 1934 at Ludlow Castle along with the *Shropshire Pageant*, Craig seems to have attended (EC-D260).

# *The Masque of Love* (1901) and *The Vikings* (1903)

In the Terry family, masques were firmly associated with Edward Gordon Craig. Gordon Craig's first three influential productions which used simple staging, curtains, gauzes and lights were *Dido and Aeneas* (1900), *The Masque of Love* (1901) and *Acis and Galatea* (1902). In 1901 Edward Gordon Craig had collaborated with Martin Shaw on *The Masque of Love* for the Purcell Operatic Society. As Christopher Innes describes, in *Edward Gordon Craig: A Vision of Theatre* (1998), Gordon Craig's work at the Hampstead Conservatoire involved improvisation within an unpromising space but he developed a process that he was to use elsewhere: by lowering the proscenium to create an impression of extra width and 'he also found...stepped platforms made three-dimensional groupings and movement possible, and promoted as well a symbolic ranking of characters' (Innes 1998: 38). Unfortunately, the second production of *The Masque of Love* at the Coronet Theatre, as Innes notes, 'attracted numbers of the regular and less artistically inclined patrons of Notting Hill Gate because of the presence of Ellen Terry in a crowd-drawing curtain raiser, there was raucous laughter from the gallery and heckling at some points' (Innes 1998: 44). This observation highlights the specialist audience that had been expected for this production and the apparently contrasting audience drawn by Terry: Gordon Craig and Ellen Terry seemed to occupy different aesthetic positions. Ellen Terry's correspondence reveals the practical reasons for Terry's performance as a strategically designed element of the production to ensure some financial security for these very costly productions which she was underwriting for the sake of her children's careers. She continued this support by leasing the Imperial Theatre. Having left the Lyceum Theatre, which was being run as a syndicate, Ellen Terry became an independent actor-manager of her own productions with the help of a business manager and her children.

The staging at the Imperial Theatre in April 1903 of Ibsen's *The Vikings at Helgeland*, with Terry as Hiordis, seemed to be an odd decision for Terry although the topic had the potential to attract an audience. As Andrew Wawn (2000) has established, the history and culture of the Vikings were popular in the nineteenth century, and were deployed in complex and conflicting ways, drawing enthusiastic support from linguists, historians and artists. In some ways 'the Vikings' became a passionate obsession and politically resonant, engaging with the global perspective of cultural tourists and imperialists alike. Although Wawn makes no mention of Ibsen's *The Vikings* or Terry's production of it, these competing tensions are at work in its London production by the former leading actress at the Lyceum Theatre where transatlantic tours were part of a cultural ambassadorial project. In *Ibsen's Women* (1997), Joan Templeton shows that Ibsen's play foregrounds the tragic conflict between male allegiances and the self-determination of a powerful and passionate woman. As a play about the anguish caused by marrying the wrong person, albeit driven by ideas of loyalty, duty and honour rather than love, *The Vikings* provided a rich source of material to spark familiar emotional memories from which Terry's performance might draw in what otherwise seemed to be a play that was drastically out of character for Terry. The role of Hiordis posed a challenge to the costumier, requiring as it did historically plausible Viking apparel and features that would accentuate her power. In her portrait,

Pamela Colman Smith depicted Terry as Hiordis, emphasizing her upright stance by means of the vertical lines of her costume and the background. With her spear tilted towards the ground and breaching the border of the picture, Ellen Terry as Hiordis appears to be indisputably ready for action.

Terry would probably have known of Sigurd from William Morris's epic poem, 'The Story of Sigurd the Volsung and the Fall of the Niblungs' (1876). Some critics have noted the unsuitability of Terry in the role of Hiordis and emphasized the folly of entering into such a large speculative project. There is however evidence that she scrutinized the accounts, demonstrating sound business sense. A large proportion of the costs went on the costumes, scene designs and lighting but unfortunately the venture was based on unrealistic expectations of audience numbers. Terry's loyal followers expected from her another appearance in the familiar Womanly Woman role, as a carefree handmaiden or wittily bantering comic foil to her leading man. In this case, Hiordis, with bristling headdress and formidable armour, would have been unpalatable to them. The appearance of Terry as this Viking warrior was too reminiscent of the demonic New Woman. However, the very name of Ibsen was enough to keep some people at a great distance from the theatre's box office. In a letter of 9 December 1902 to Lady Gregory, W. B. Yeats referred to Ibsen as 'the accursed Norwegian cloud' (Kelly and Schuchard 1994: 271). Ibsen had come to symbolize campaigns for social reform and political challenge. Edith Craig had been in the thick of a renowned tour of Ibsen (*A Doll's House* as Mrs Linden and Shaw's *Candida* as Prossy) with Janet Achurch (1864–1916) and Charles Charrington (1854–1926) in the Independent Theatre. According to her mother's opinion, confided in a letter to Shaw, the tour risked leaving an indelible mark on her daughter's very appearance and blighting her future:

A clever friend of mine said to me

Yesterday – 'If Edy stays long with the Independent Company she will get dull –

Heavy – conceited – frowsy – [illeg.] & dirty!! – in fact will look moth-eaten!! & no one will see her again because nobody goes to their Theatre' –.(Tuesday [14 September 1897]; *CLET* 4: 851)

Edith Craig's role in *The Vikings* was in the production of the costumes. In her memoirs, she recalled several unforgettable details of the tasks she tackled for the production: her brother's insistence on the use of a specific shade for the cloth, requiring it to be sent to Germany to be dyed at great expense; his impossible designs for a cloak; and the extraordinary porcupine quill headdress that Oscar Asche (1871–1936)[5] had refused to wear (Rachlin 2011: 146) but Ellen Terry wore with a good grace if not also a great deal of forbearance. Terry had invested heavily in the production to give her children opportunities to demonstrate their talents but they failed to work within a budget. This had severe consequences for them all for some time to come, although Terry maintained a stoical silence as she planned and manoeuvred behind the scenes to restore the family's fortunes.

## Edith Craig, The Masquers (1903) and the lost minstrels

Edith Craig's involvement with the production of masques and pageants could be ascertained from details given in the advertisement for her Edith Craig & Co. costumiers. The business also catered for the general interest in historical performances of various kinds: not only historical plays in the professional theatre but also for individuals taking part in costume balls with historical themes. The advertisement provides a helpful note about the availability of historical costumes:

Edith Craig & Co, 13 Henrietta Street, Covent Garden, WC
COSTUMES, THEATRICAL AND PRIVATE
Telephone no. 3345 Gerrard Office hours 11–5 Saturdays 11–2

Beg to draw your kind attention to the HIRING DEPARTMENT they have opened at the above premises, where a large selection of artistic and valuable costumes is now available for hiring for balls, Theatricals, etc. They can also supply at reasonable charges all requisite properties and costumes of correct period for costume plays or tableaux. These can be sent any distance, with full instructions for use, or, if desired, a competent person can be sent to arrange them. – This is strongly advised for Tableaux. (*The Green Sheaf*, No. 4; BL)

This demonstrates the flexibility of arrangements whereby a package of necessary costumes and other accessories could be made available. However, the emphasis on the need for an expert to arrange tableaux specifically reflects Craig's experience of the complexities involved in setting up the stage for the best effects. Historical performances also featured in public events such as galas, festivals, fetes and pageants, traces of which are hard to find. The vast collection of printed ephemera preserved by John Johnson (1882–1956), who recognized their value, now provides a rich resource at the Bodleian Library Oxford for insights into these events.

Edith Craig shared John Johnson's appreciation of ephemera, recalled by her contemporaries, and exemplified by the National Trust's Edith Craig archive. There is ample evidence of Craig's intense interest in historical pageants and a small collection of documents – a prospectus, letters and a sample of headed notepaper – provide further evidence of Edith Craig's involvement in The Masquers, a short-lived theatre society which developed at a pivotal moment for all of those involved. W. B. Yeats left for a lecture tour in United States which lasted from November 1903 to March 1904, and the Abbey Theatre was founded in December 1904. Craig was an active committee member of the Stage Society, with sufficient power in that organization to arrange for plays (such as Yeats's *Where There Is Nothing*) to be produced in 1904. The Masquers has been discussed in some detail in the context of W. B. Yeats (Schuchard 1978, 2008; Chapman 1989).[6] In *Edith Craig: Dramatic Lives* (1998) I reassessed Edith Craig's role in The Masquers in a reading of the further correspondence in the Gilbert Murray and W. B. Yeats collections and with reference to the newly identified evidence in her own archive (Cockin 1998a: 73–5). I established that Edith Craig was the prime mover of The Masquers, evidenced by W. B. Yeats's letter to Edith Craig. Other correspondence also established that the tensions arising in the managing committee centred on the ideas and plans of some of the female theatre practitioners and male authors and artists. Ronald Schuchard's *The Last Minstrels* (2008) therefore prompts my further analysis in this chapter.

The Masquers had progressed beyond a few informal discussions in which conflict would be likely to arise and be resolved before any formal organization was instigated. A managing committee had been formed, a prospectus drawn up with a list of proposed plays and even official headed notepaper was printed in anticipation of the business correspondence needed to run a theatre society. Edward Gordon Craig was not a member of the committee but Edith Craig was and even described by Gilbert Murray as 'our one vital capable member' and to whom the artist Walter Crane (1845–1915) wrote, suggesting either F. R. Benson (1853–1939) or William Poel as stage manager (21 July 1903; EC-3,170). It is therefore likely that stage manager was not her role in the society; it seems instead to have been a more senior role as artistic director. The first meeting of the committee was held on 28 March 1903 at 13 Henrietta Street, Covent Garden, where Craig ran her costumiers. The official address of The Masquers was 7 Smith Square, Craig's home. Extant correspondence shows that individuals such as Lady Gregory, patron of W. B. Yeats, Walter Crane and Jane Ellen Harrison (1850–1928), the classical scholar, had signed up for membership. Craig and Harrison shared an acquaintance in Mabel Malleson.[7] Harrison's experience as a performer in *Alcestis* for OUDS in 1887 would have been useful to this new society which had ambitions to produce ancient Greek drama.

The archival records show that there were particular concerns about control over the staging and style of performance of the plays and different degrees of enthusiasm and commitment to the project. This reflects to some extent the kind of squabbles that characterize any enterprise of this kind but in the case of The Masquers it reveals that Edith Craig was both at the centre of the conflict and the creative drive for it to succeed. Others had doubts that increased and developed into antipathy.

Gilbert Murray had held a chair at the University of Glasgow for a decade (1889–99) before returning to Oxford where his academic career as a classicist continued to flourish. In 1908 he was appointed as Regius Professor of Greek. It is relevant therefore that at the time of The Masquers' interest in enlisting him on their managing committee, Murray was an internationally renowned expert in Greek translation. His recently published translation of Euripides' *Hippolytus* was one of the plays The Masquers planned to produce. Murray had been invited officially to join The Masquers by W. B.

Yeats on 17 March 1903 but only seven months later, in October 1903, Murray used a typed memorandum to the management committee to convey his significant doubts about The Masquers and Mrs Patrick Campbell in particular:

> At one time, I remember, she said that she saw her way to the performance if she might chalk herself over and pretend to be a statue! At another she proposed to act it in the Chinese style. [She was interested in what I was able to tell her about Miss Farr's performance on the psaltery,[8] as a means of dealing with the choruses, and has, I believe, bought a psaltery. But I think that is the only practical outcome of the interview]. Even if she were willing to do it now, I should rather hesitate about asking her. I had formerly imagined to myself how good she might be in the part of Phaedra; but during this interview I began to imagine how bad she might also be...fidgety and unclassical. (27 October 1903; EC-Z3,598; parentheses in original.)

Murray mentioned the undesirable inference of nepotism if his translation of *Hippolytus* were to be included as one of the productions. He was concerned, if not also alarmed and repelled, by Stella Campbell's ideas for performing it in an orientalist mode and lacked confidence in her attitude. These two issues appear to relate to his quite reasonable concerns about his own reputation and how this theatrical venture, with some potentially bizarre performance strategies, might reflect upon him. He was not averse generally to experimentation or unorthodox ideas and expressed opinions on various political issues, including Irish Home Rule. He was also supportive of theatrical productions and was to become involved in this context with George Bernard Shaw, W. B. Yeats and Harley Granville-Barker (1877–1946).[9] It may well have been the rather unpredictable and irrepressible behaviour of Stella Campbell and the determined attitude of Edith Craig that made him pause for thought. Those involved in The Masquers had different investments in its success. Gilbert Murray expressed his opinion in emotive terms, saying that for The Masquers, its 'suicide' was preferable and he consequently set about entreating the organizers to wind it up (EC-Z3,598). However, the correspondence of the committee members of The Masquers, especially that between W. B. Yeats and Edith Craig, reveals what kind of role she had in the organization.

This was a substantial role and appears to have been directorial rather than costumier.

Gilbert Murray was also concerned about the involvement of acting members, Edith Craig, and those who may have been influencing her, specifically an unnamed collaborator. He wrote with some relief to William Archer after The Masquers had collapsed, 'I felt that I should have no control when once Miss Craig's poodle had got the bit between his teeth, and I did not know what might happen' (20 January 1904, quoted in Schuchard 2008: 440). 'Miss Craig's poodle' has subsequently been assumed to be the musician Martin Shaw (Schuchard 1978: 440; Chapman 1989), with whom Edward Gordon Craig had collaborated on the Purcell Opera Society productions. However, other female candidates such as Pamela Colman Smith and Christopher St John are equally likely. Craig had been living with St John for four years by this time and St John was using The Masquers' headed notepaper. However, it was Colman Smith with whom Craig had collaborated on costume and scene design and who wrote to Yeats referring to their shared opinion of the demise of The Masquers.

Four months after Yeats had invited Murray to join the committee, and by which time considerable progress had been made in discussing the work of the society, Arthur Symons wrote, in confidence, to Gilbert Murray about the direction events were taking and the potential inference of dishonourable behaviour towards their female colleague (18 July 1903). Symons revealed not only that it was Edith Craig in particular who was leading The Masquers, confirming the impression given by W. B. Yeats himself, but also that Gilbert Murray and others were planning a coup:

> I am desperately afraid I agree with everything you say. I don't quite know what we should do. Miss Craig evidently will not give up: What Yeats feels now I don't know. Can we, in any case, desert in a body if she insists on going on? That scarcely seems fair. (Gilbert Murray papers, fol. 70–71)

A later letter to Murray from Yeats confirms his own support of Stella Campbell's ideas and, presumably those of Edith Craig, and his amusement about the comments made by the poet Thomas Sturge Moore (1870–1944). Furthermore, Katherine Bradley (1846–1914) and her niece Edith Cooper (1862–13), who wrote poetry and plays together under the single pseudonym 'Michael Field', apparently judged that on the managing committee of The Masquers there was 'much stubble to be burnt' (Schuchard 2008: 151). The rift was therefore taking a particularly decisive and destructive turn, with some members planning a mutiny in The Masquers and others contemplating a sinister immolation couched in the familiar terminology of the natural process of harvesting the remains of the old crop giving way to the new green shoots. Yeats confided in Edith Craig his opinion about the débacle:

> I have heard from Miss Smith and others about the collapse of the Masquers. I was doubtful somewhere about midsummer when I thought we were not going to get subscribers, but I don't think that the Society should have been dropped, once that it got so much into the public eye and got so much money. Such things should be left undone or done altogether. Personally it rids me of some inconvenience, as my time will be so much taken up with the theatrical movement in Dublin. I am sorry, however, that an idea of yours should have gone astray. (6 December 1903; EC-3,788; Kelly and Schuchard 1994: 478)

Edith Craig had responded decisively, proposing formally an amendment to the proposal made by Acton Bond that The Masquers be suspended. Craig proposed that activities cease altogether and, as Gilbert Murray reported to Yeats, she would then turn her attentions to 'improving the Stage Society' (12 November 1903; Finneran et al. 1977).

Thoughts of The Masquers seem to have lingered for Michael Field and their close friends, the artists Charles Ricketts (1866–1931) and his partner Charles Shannon (1863–1937). In 1904 Ricketts sent a scenario of a cross-dressing mock tragedy entitled *Giuliano or Never, Never Let Us Part*, suggesting they might act it in masks privately with Ricketts as Diana in a mask of silver lace, Katherine Bradley as the Old King François in pink satin, Edith Cooper as Catherine de Medici in black velvet and Shannon as the 'shut door'; Ricketts directed that in the masque they should exclude all 'inferior married people from the cast and exclude the audience too since "art is self sufficient"' (Donoghue 1998: 117). As an elite form, the masque had been taken to extremes in Ricketts's scenario, removing the audience, restricting the eligibility of performers and rendering it solipsistic.

The end of The Masquers did not bring about the end of the association of W. B. Yeats, Edith Craig and Colman Smith. Craig and Colman Smith had collaborated on the designs for Yeats's *Where There Is Nothing* (designed in 1902; produced in 1904) and went on to design for Synge's *The Well of the Saints* at the Abbey (1905). However, the relationships between writers and actors were problematic in both The Masquers and the Abbey Theatre. In his essay 'The Irish Dramatic Movement', Yeats recalled the frustrations felt by the writers during the pre-production process at the Abbey Theatre:

> [And] our theatrical organization was preposterous, players and authors all sitting together and settling by vote what play should be performed and who should play it. It took a series of disturbances, weeks of argument during which no performance could be given, before Lady Gregory and John Synge and I were put in control. (Yeats 1964: 199)

The sometimes unpleasant clashes of personality, mistrust or prejudice experienced in the organization of performance had a particularly threatening effect on the aesthetic position of this group of individuals since it brought (instead of Beauty) the much despised Reality unwelcomely to the fore. Gordon Craig regarded the actor as a creative force, once freed from the limitations of self-awareness and becoming a vehicle for the art of the theatre. In theatrical cultural practices which materialized only through social interaction, the realization of the mask, the dream and play through performance problematized the distinction between the real and the mystical which obtained in symbolism. It tended to produce anxieties about the process: of the need to get it right and to retain control. Such matters can perhaps remain dormant or repressed in the ideal text in literary criticism but in theatre practice a final performance is achieved, however fleeting it might be.

Roy Foster has assumed that, for Yeats, the attraction of the Irish theatre was ultimately stronger than anything happening in London and that the loss of Gordon Craig was a fatal blow to The Masquers (Foster 1997: 291), but it was his sister, Edith Craig, who was in Yeats's confidence, receiving private letters evaluating the other committee members. Anxieties and tremors were set in motion by the collision of actors and writers, authors and artists, symbolists and careerists. For Yeats, the intensity of drama meant that it was the ultimate art form. He declared, 'What attracts me to drama is that it is, in the most obvious way, what all the arts are upon a last analysis' ('First Principles'; Yeats 1964: 140).

## Aftermath: On tour, the death of Irving and the jubilee

The intense disappointment when The Masquers was wound up must have been difficult for Edith Craig to bear. The experience would have reinforced the need to be careful about selecting congenial collaborators. It familiarized her with the kinds of behaviour that can arise when conflicts, centred on powerfully driven egos, are left to fester. Edith Craig resolved that it was in the field of theatrical direction that her talents should be applied, and it was on her mother's British and American tours that she gained considerable experience with relatively little interference.

Edward Gordon Craig referred to his mother's regional tour of 1903 in disparaging terms. In later life he failed to acknowledge the financial motive that drove the tour, after the significant financial losses incurred by him in the Imperial Theatre and implicitly dismissed his sister as a competent manager for Terry to have chosen for her tour: '[Terry] never found any first class manager to organize her affairs for her, and her theatrical course, during and after "The Vikings" was zigzag, for she was rudderless' (Gordon Craig 1931: 140). Oddly he was named as producer for many of these productions. Edith Craig was named as stage manager for this recuperative tour with The Good Hope by Herman Heijermans, translated from Dutch to English by Christopher St John providing many sound parts for female performers. In its naturalist exposure of social inequality, The Good Hope was as challenging as any Ibsen play. Ellen Terry's involvement in the productions of this play with her daughter provides a new perspective on Terry's supposed rejection of Ibsen on grounds of dramatic form or political critique.

The death of Irving on 13 October 1905 at the Midland Hotel, Bradford while on tour was devastating for everyone. Edith Craig wrote to her mother straight away, offering to be by her side. Effectively given a state funeral at Westminster Abbey, Irving was honoured by interment in Poets' Corner and acknowledged as an international figure by representatives of the Comédie Française. Although Terry and her children had already found their separate paths in the theatre by this time, the loss of Irving, was profound. Neither Edith Craig nor her brother regarded Henry Irving as part of a theatrical past to be rejected in favour of a distinctly new modernist aesthetic. They both drew on aspects of Irving's example and methodology in their visions of the art of the theatre. Edward Gordon Craig was to publish his own full-length study, *Henry Irving* (1930). Characteristically refraining from publication, Edith Craig instead continued to draw on the lessons she had learnt from Irving at the Lyceum Theatre. Terry's children, who were both over thirty years old but still relied on their mother's resources, needed to be mindful of their own transition into adulthood however reluctant they were to accept this. Irving had been planning to retire from the stage. A year after his death Ellen Terry was having similar thoughts and this had consequences for her reluctant dependants.

In the tradition of both celebrating the long career of a performer and securing a pension fund for her, a stage jubilee event was organized for Ellen Terry in 1906. It was marked by a lavish production at the Drury Lane Theatre promoted by the *Tribune* newspaper. The jubilee production involved various performances by distinguished actors, a production of *Trial by Jury* directed by W. S. Gilbert (1836–1911) and tableaux with Ellen Terry and her two sisters, Marion and Kate. Acton Bond and the dramatist A. W. Pinero (1855–1934) were the principal organizers of the production.

Most of the extant correspondence (forty or so letters) is addressed to Bond or Pinero, with the exception of three letters to Edith Craig,[10] suggesting that Craig had a minor role as an assistant. Ellen Terry's consternation about the absence of female performers from the production is widely known. She wrote to express her concerns to Pinero, threatening not to appear herself unless she shared the stage with other women ([11 May 1906] *CLET* 5: 1449; Thursday, 24 May [1906] *CLET* 5: 1452). In *Ellen Terry, Player in Her Time* (1987), Nina Auerbach foregrounded this intervention by Terry in the staging of her jubilee, describing a series of tableaux which were added to the programme and attributing the overall direction of these tableaux to Edith Craig (Auerbach 1987: 10). Ellen Dolgin has recently described Craig's 'visually and intellectually stunning pageant for her mother, Ellen Terry's Jubilee in 1906. It featured twelve tableaux vivant about historically important women from Cleopatra to Joan of Arc to the Madonna' (Dolgin 2015: 123). However, in the programme for the event, the arrangement of these tableaux is attributed to various other named individuals. The extent of Edith Craig's involvement in Terry's stage jubilee is somewhat unclear.[11] The debacle of Terry's jubilee was mentioned eight years later by Edith Craig when she advised her mother to get up a programme of events and to employ female managers such as Lena Ashwell, Gertrude Kingston, Lillah McCarthy and Eva Moore. Craig reminded her mother: 'There are a good few now & they are always left out of the usual committees – like they were at your jubilee = Lena, & Gertrude, & Lillah, & Eva Moore etc.' (30 August [1914]; THM 384/4/4). She provides no further details, and makes no mention of having organized the tableaux.

Other complexities included the financial consequences created by an accumulation of responsibilities from the period of Craig's costumier business and Gordon Craig's lavish expenses on the staging at the Imperial Theatre. Edith Craig was probably not aware of the details of this financial situation since Terry kept such matters confidentially. The jubilee marked the rehabilitation of Ellen Terry, the fallen woman, with the symbolic gift from the Royal household of a diamond brooch.[12] Terry cautiously but persistently sought confirmation that the source of the gift could be disclosed. This public display of recognition clearly signified a rite of passage for Terry as a formal acceptance by royalty. For her children, both of whom had surnames that evaded the patronymic, it would have been a highly significant change in the family's social standing.

## Edith Craig, stage director and strategies for producing a play (1907)

Edith Craig's role in her mother's American tour in 1907 prompted an article entitled 'Producing a Play'. The placing of the article in *Munsey's Magazine*, which catered for a mass market readership, guaranteed that it would reach over half a million readers. Craig's approach as a producer is described in detail and, inevitably perhaps, in comparison with Henry Irving and Edward Gordon Craig. She is described in terms of a landmark trailblazer, as the first female stage manager and a new profession for women. The claim is somewhat over-stated, given the female predecessors who had operated as actor-managers in commercial theatres and in the experimental theatres. However, Craig was committed to achieving a coherent aesthetic. She was influenced by Irving's autocratic control over the details of staging and his openness to the involvement of all practitioners. She rejected Edward Gordon Craig's control over the performers and the over-reliance on technology, arguing that 'everyone ought to contribute a little bit of life to the performance'. She had specific strategies for lighting, to accentuate mood and atmosphere, 'as a means of helping the acting' and she had strong views about 'the mania for lighting a scene like a saloon bar'. She gave an example of her lighting of a scene in Herman Heijermans's *The Good Hope*, an interior with women talking, which she chose to light in a sombre way to accentuate the gloomy atmosphere and to give a natural impression of lamplight. She prioritized a combination of 'pictorial effect' and 'dramatic situation'.[13] She argued that every play has scenes that need to be accentuated and these feature as 'certain pictorial moments' to be enhanced. This example demonstrates how Craig was concerned with the visual interpretation of the play to ensure that all aspects of the staging presented a coherent whole to the audience. With a detailed understanding of colour and space, she observed mistakes with the shade of costumes and the number of actors used in crowd scenes. She had learnt a great deal from Irving's designs for the Lyceum Theatre productions.[14]

The article demonstrates the shifting theories of staging in this period which were reflected in the fluid terminology for the roles of stage manager, producer and stage director. In the same article it is claimed that Edith Craig is 'the first woman stage-manager on record' but she describes her work on her mother's American tour as 'stage-director' and refers to control of the staging. Her method seems to have been to conceptualize staging as a series of visually significant tableaux, which anticipated the later development of film direction. In this approach, she shared the views of Max Reinhardt (1873–1943) who directed *The Miracle* at Olympia, London in 1911 and productions at the Volksbühne (1915–18), and who was also co-founder of the Salzburg Festival in 1920 before moving to the United States for a career in teaching and film.

Edith Craig observed a cultural difference in America where her experience was that her ideas as a director were politely implemented whereas in England they would be resented. Given the focus on gender in the article and Edith Craig's pioneering role as stage director, it is surprising that the campaign for women's suffrage is not mentioned. The article predated Craig's own foray into the direction of women's suffrage drama but the campaign itself was highly topical on both sides of the Atlantic. A different impression is given in an article in a Brooklyn (United States) newspaper which reported on Craig's approach in managing the actors on tour, including her mother, in a profoundly autocratic and mercenary fashion, notably by fining actors for forgetting their lines.[15] In 1907 Edith Craig was named as 'stage director' for *Captain Brassbound's Conversation* at the Empire Theatre (ET-D754). She was effectively actor-director, performing as Saart, the widow of a fisherman, in *The Good Hope*, alongside James Carew as Geert and Ellen Terry as Kniertje at the Empire Theatre (ET-D755). In this period Edith Craig was willing to adopt a subsidiary role and on occasions acted as understudy for her mother,[16] Craig also continued to design her mother's costumes.[17] The tour of Ellen Terry with James Carew apparently had a mixed reception for reasons related to the audience's interest in the actors' lives off-stage. In Stephen Coleridge's opinion: 'He was as young as her son, and the public & her best friends were grieved at such an act' (3 November 1907; *CLET* 5: 1506). At a time when Edith Craig was just becoming familiar with the role of director, circumstances prevailed to distract the audience from the quality of the performances and the overall staging and to put obstacles in the way of her continued presence as her mother's stage director. The principal obstacle presented himself in the figure of James Carew.

## Publishing debacles

Another difficulty which came between mother and daughter before the marriage to Carew was Terry's decision to publish her autobiography, probably prompted by the success of her jubilee and encouraged by the reinforcement of her reputation, signalled by the royal acknowledgement. In 1906 Christopher St John sent 18,000 words

to Ellen Terry similar to the earlier series of autobiographical article entitled 'Stray Memories', explicitly drawing attention to their
similarity. She advised Terry about the arrangement with the publisher, Heinemann, minimizing the difficulties and planning what
was a high-risk strategy of getting publishers to negotiate through
A. P. Watt for the manuscript.[18] In a later letter Terry's annotation
seems to imply that she acknowledged the earlier arrangement with
Heinemann as a problem but did not understand or acknowledge
any attempt to pass off as original what was effectively already
published material.

Edith Craig became drawn into these difficulties and they were
probably heightened because of the rift created by Terry's marriage to Carew. In the summer of 1907, several months after the
controversial marriage, St John and Edith Craig were called for
what must have appeared to be a very daunting meeting about
the publication problems at the office of Terry's solicitor, the formidable Sir George Lewis (1833–1911). Although for Craig, he
was a longstanding family friend and had sorted out the difficulties surrounding her brother's divorce, Sir George Lewis had a
reputation for his expertise in cross-examination in criminal cases.
The issue he took up on behalf of Ellen Terry was an allegation
of self-plagiarism but it also related to the appropriate payment
of Christopher St John as Ellen Terry's ghostwriter.[19] In 1907 the
autobiographical manuscript that was sent to *McClure's* magazine had previously appeared in the *New Review* in 1891 under
the editorship of Archibald Grove, meaning that McClure's series
had to be suspended. Terry had already made an arrangement
with Heinemann to publish her autobiography for which she
had been given an advance payment (ET-SC22-A1). Heinemann
too was therefore unhappy about this publication. Terry subsequently published *The Story of My Life* with Hutchinson in 1908
for £1700 advance, having had an offer of £1500 from Methuen
(ET-D2269). It is not clear what, if any, advice she had taken before-
hand. From Edith Craig's perspective, this increasingly fraught
situation was additionally *politically* compromising. The rights of
the author, especially female authors, were to become a matter
of political debate, for instance, to the Women Writers' Suffrage
League (WWSL) formed in 1908. A few years after this incident,
both Edith Craig and Christopher St John appear with Cicely
Hamilton in a street procession holding the WWSL banner and

were officially photographed by Christina Broom.[20] Christopher St John's involvement in Ellen Terry's publishing matters, the copyright infringement and ethical issues were therefore potential points of acute embarrassment for Edith Craig.[21]

Ellen Terry's financial situation always had a significant impact on her daughter and it made these publishing difficulties even more complex. A firm of accountants drew up Ellen Terry's balance sheet on 2 January 1907, providing a useful snapshot of her financial situation at a time which happened to be only a few months before she married James Carew.[22] In the autumn of 1908 she had to explain to Boo that she could not fund Boo's niece's husband in a new venture and confided that she was in financial difficulty (19 November [1908]; *CLET* 5: 1544). In August 1907 she had rented out The Farm to Gabrielle Enthoven and Edith Craig made herself scarce (18 August [1907]; *CLET* 5: 1495). Ellen Terry and her new husband spent Christmas 1907 in Boulogne. Edith Craig had moved into her flat in Adelphi Terrace in October 1907.

Throughout 1907 and 1908 Ellen Terry and Christopher St John were in conflict and Edith Craig was caught in the middle. It raises some questions perhaps as to why Craig chose to dictate her own memoirs to Vera Holme and not to St John. In a letter in 1908, Terry wrote to her daughter frankly about the conflict and referred to the circumstances of St John's publication of her biography, *Ellen Terry* (1907) published by J. T. Grein in the 'Stars of the Stage' series, suggesting that it deliberately stole Terry's thunder:

> Please tell C. I will not write to her. As to the money when I get it I'll send to her – As to the Story I think she did her work wonderfully – but I am not in the vein to express myself at all to her since whenever she writes to me her words are full of abuse, & threat, of all things in the world!! From her – to me!! – Your mother, & always, for years her friend. Does she really think it wd have made the least bit of difference to me if she had written my 'biography by C St J' or C.M. or what she likes? I had my own opinion of the exceedingly clever little book she published just before mine came out – I mean I had my opinion about the straight-ness (?) of her doing it =. (THM 384/1/31/31)

Edith Craig found herself in the position of not being credited for her work when she made the costumes for a ground-breaking charity production in 1908 of Ben Jonson's *The Vision of Delight*. She was omitted from the credits but the costume designs were attributed to Charles Ricketts (Savage 2014: 42). According to Savage, this production emphasized women's independence,[23] contrasted with that of Beerbohm Tree, which exploited the display of beautiful women. Although Savage does not elaborate on the circumstances in which Craig worked with Charles Ricketts, this episode reflects the subsidiary role assigned to women in the theatre, especially in the field of costume. This was a state of affairs which women, like Edith Craig, actively involved in the women's suffrage movement were keen to challenge ideologically and in practice, by taking control of their own productions with good reason. Unlike Ashwell's *Vision of Delight*, Beerbohm Tree's production in 1911 for the coronation celebrations seemed to appropriate and subvert the autonomy of the female performers who were described by reviewers, as Savage notes, in objectifying terms (Savage 2014: 60). As the director of Edith Craig & Co. costumiers, Craig was in the service industry to the theatre arts, where those involved in the field of theatrical costume have not always been officially acknowledged. A complication seems to arise since one aspect of Edith Craig's modus operandi was to focus on the end results of the production which sometimes led to circumstances where she was not always acknowledged.

## *A Pageant of Great Women* as the 'Scala masque'

Edith Craig was centrally involved in the creation of a pageant for the new world for women using women's history at its centre. Between the time of her mother's stage jubilee in 1906 and the staging of *A Pageant of Great Women* with Ellen Terry featuring at the Scala Theatre debut as herself, Edith Craig, Christopher St John and Terry had come through an extended period of litigious feuding; and Edith Craig had gained a stepfather. At the time of the new family arrangement, Craig was nearly thirty-eight years old and her new stepfather, the American actor James Carew, was thirty-one years old. Her mother's clandestine marriage rocked Craig's foundations. However, Carew was not a stranger. Edith Craig had been on tour with them both having had secured the position as stage manager. Ellen Terry continued to tour with Carew but without her daughter. Communications between mother and daughter became fraught. Precisely what the marriage may have represented to her daughter has perhaps not yet been established. For Terry's family and the wider world, the marriage raised some other issues: the significant age difference between the two; the antipathy towards Americans and a concern that Shakespeare's heroine had become American; and that Irving's 'Beatrice' had married an actor who could come nowhere near the Lyceum Theatre quality of performance. In the context of Edith Craig's women's suffrage politics, Ellen Terry's decision to marry at all was a cause for concern. In August 1907 Terry confided in George Bernard Shaw that her daughter disliked Terry's new husband (13 August [1907]; *CLET* 5: 1493). For suffrage activists, Terry had become an icon, as the archetypal 'free-woman'. Consequently when Terry returned with her new husband from America, there may have been something of a sense of betrayal or embarrassment for Craig and more widely in that the mother of the 'Proteus of suffragists' felt the need for a husband.

Cicely Hamilton's *A Pageant of Great Women* (1909–12) involved both professional and amateur actors, and it made use of the generosity of theatre practitioners who were committed to the political cause of women's suffrage. Extant documents in the archives – programmes, photographs and press cuttings – have revealed some significant aspects of this production, notably its mobility, flexibility and consciousness-raising use of women's history.[24] When Ellen Terry referred to *A Pageant of Great Women*, on the occasion of its debut, as 'the Scala masque' (1909) there is evidence that Terry's conceptualization of the play as a 'masque' makes sense in the context of her own family history. The use of the masque and the pageant in service to a political movement predicated on claims for equality is ideologically conflicted. In theatrical production and in literature, the posing of women for an audience's gaze has been subject to critique.[25] Silence and disguise, ceremony and procession, 'great women' drawn from the exceptional and the elite, all provide contradictory elements in Craig's production of Hamilton's play which nevertheless succeeded in pleasing its audiences and riling its critics.

Ellen Terry's reference to *A Pageant of Great Women* as a 'masque' uses unexpected terminology that raises some questions about whether this was her own attribution or picked up from her daughter. The term would have had particular resonances in the Terry household. In the context of theatre history, I want to consider to what extent 'masque' is an accurate or relevant term for Ellen Terry to have used for *A Pageant of Great Women*. The play was staged in the context of the wide-ranging strategies for addressing the class conflicts at the heart of the political debates. The 'women' who would be enfranchised on the same basis as men were wealthy and not the working-class women.[26] With these associations in mind, *A Pageant of Great Women* features a great number of actors on stage (similar to the numbers Gordon Craig had envisaged for one of his unperformed masques); they were arranged in groups; and steps were used to enhance the arrangement. There are even points of similarity in the costumes of Justice and Woman in 1909 and those in Gordon Craig's 1901 *Acis and Galatea* and the 1912 Moscow *Hamlet*.

In addition to the associations for Terry with the 'masque' form in Edward Gordon Craig's experiments, the term highlights some aspects of *A Pageant of Great Women* that have been overlooked. These include the ceremonial dimension, the multi-media aspects, the combination of song, dance, movement, stasis, silence and the staging of the spectacle in a specific setting and occasion. Ben Jonson's court masques were characterized by such features and also included an anti-masque section explaining the inclusion of Cicely Hamilton's 'Anti-suffrage waxworks' in a production of *A Pageant of Great Women* (Cockin 2005: 532). Although little trace has been found of this curtain-raiser, it seems to have involved the recreation of various anti-suffrage representations of women with a critical commentary provided by Hamilton as 'The Showman' (EC-D180). The following play would therefore have served to undercut these anti-suffrage arguments, in the manner of a masque. This dramatic form, of course, also attributed to the women's suffrage audience members a great deal of power. They were assembling in their own court (like the Woman's Parliament formed in February 1907 which sent a deputation to Westminster); it was a setting in which one could write a masque for today.

# Theatrical alchemy: Masques of the future and past as 'The Woman's Century' dawns

Although the literary history of the masque form draws on the work of Ben Jonson, with the ceremonial use of movement, costume, gesture and symbolism, it also has a place in the history of occult practices and elite cultural formations. Edith Craig's close friend and collaborator Pamela Colman Smith was a member of the Order of the Golden Dawn, a Rosicrucian organization that admitted women and men to membership on equal terms. Women such as Constance Wilde (1859–98) and the Hon. Gabrielle Borthwick were members.[27] The actor and author Florence Farr and theatrical patron Annie Horniman (1860–1937) both held higher office than W. B. Yeats. In *The Magicians of the Golden Dawn* (1985), Ellic Howe notes, 'In some respects the ritual ceremonies were like complicated theatrical performances' (Howe 1985: 57). Mary K. Greer's *Women of the Golden Dawn* (1995) provides an insight into the complex cultural and social networks involved in this organization and helps to establish the significant role played by financially powerful women such as Horniman, who had sponsored Florence Farr's theatrical productions. Edith Craig's brother Edward Gordon Craig had published plays co-authored by Florence Farr and Olivia Shakespear, *The Beloved of Hathor and The Shrine of the Golden Hawk* (c. 1895). Craig and Colman Smith were apparently unhappy when Florence Farr's organization, The Dancers, appeared in 1903 after The Masquers had ground to a halt. The prospectus for The Dancers described its interests in ceremonies and pageants. Colman Smith wrote to Yeats, emphasizing her conspiratorial collaboration with Craig and their shared attitude towards Farr's new enterprise. She depicts The Dancers as humourless and lacking insight:

> The Masquers is dead – at least for the present – The Dancers – came out with a flourish of news paper notices – and thinks its self very grand – Most people I know, won't join – Edy Craig & I think of getting up a grand mock dance & offer to do it for them! (16 December 1903; Finneran 1977: 132)

Colman Smith's allusion to a proposed 'grand mock dance' had something of the anti-masque about it as well as the kind of dialectical, ironical positioning that Yeats favoured. Nevertheless his allegiance to Farr was strong and he would be unlikely to relish the idea of her public humiliation.[28] The posturing in Colman Smith's letter is in tune with the performative style of the period, defined by cultural feuds and manufactured conflicts. In the context of occult factionalism, this vying for the spotlight was all too familiar to Yeats, Colman Smith and Farr who had been through the ruptures of the Order of the Golden Dawn resulting in Farr's appointment as the new national leader. Her opponents had fearsome reputations.[29] The debacle had been mocked in *Nicandra*, the play for which Colman Smith and Craig had been involved in costume design in 1901, discussed in the previous chapter. It was originally produced in 1898 at the time of the scandals surrounding fraud in the Order and concerned Nicandra, an 'Egyptian priestess famous for her wickedness – she worshipped serpents' (p. 20). In the play Nicandra arrives and departs to the sound of the musical chanting of her name, reminiscent of Florence Farr's expertise in chanting to the psaltery. Nicandra appears in different forms: dressed in Egyptian costume; cross-dressed as the male secretary of Professor Townsend who brought her back from his expeditions in Egypt and, crucially, she also appears in serpentine guise. Colman Smith's letter to Yeats positions Craig and herself as allies, keeping their powder dry along with their sense of superiority, in the battle over cultural innovation.

Florence Farr was in the ascendant as superwoman: a fellow warrior enjoying temporary success. In 1906 Farr published an article entitled 'Music in Words', referring to words in religion – words of power – mantras and also to spells such as those in *Macbeth*.[30] In 1905 Farr published *The Mystery of Time: A Masque* with the Theosophical Publishing Society. It was produced at the Albert Hall Theatre on 17 January 1905.[31] The conflict between The Past and The Future is resolved at the end of the masque with The Present asserting that peace, eternity and a life free from fear are all to be found within the present. The introduction to the masque describes experiments reminiscent of meditation and mindfulness. Farr believed the future was female. In the preface to her later radical book *Modern Woman: Her Intentions* (1910) she begins: 'There is a great difficulty in writing of the women of the first ten years of the twentieth century. This is to be the Woman's Century. In it she is to awake from her long sleep and come into her kingdom' (p. 7). However, Farr identifies contradictions. In her first chapter, 'The Vote', she notes the difficult circumstances women experience and how the women's suffrage movement 'has raised up a powerful body of feeling on both sides, that will end in one of the greatest social revolutions of the time' (p. 16). Published in the year when Edith Craig's productions of *A Pageant of Great Women* were regularly highlighted in the women's suffrage newspapers, Farr's book discouraged her readers from dwelling on the past: 'For I want the women who read this book not to dwell upon the past, but to look forward to the great century that is waiting for their alchemy, to transmute its life by giving it a more intent purpose' (Farr 1910: 92). Instead she urged women to action. In tune with the slogan of the militant WSPU ('deeds not words'), Farr emphasized a political turning point. In 1912 she settled in Ceylon (now Sri Lanka), committed to the education of girls. Edith Craig turned to theatrical alchemy.

# CHAPTER FOUR
## 1907-14

# The art of women's suffrage theatre and the 'fire of Prometheus'

In the manner of stars of the women's suffrage campaign, Edith Craig, Ellen Terry, Christopher St John and the author and performer Cicely Hamilton all featured in photographic portraits by Lena Connell (1875–1949), which were exhibited at the Royal Photographic Society, London in 1910 and 1911.[1] These portraits showed the women in their stage costumes in Edith Craig's productions of Cicely Hamilton's *A Pageant of Great Women*, a play which achieved a central position in the cultural representations of the women's suffrage movement. The play even featured in the highly visible and popular merchandise on which the women's suffrage political organizations came to rely as an income stream to fund their activities. Print publications and photography were significant media for exploitation. As a result, traces have survived to provide an insight into the visual impact of the theatrical production. In 1910 Lena Connell was interviewed in the Women's Freedom League (WFL) newspaper the *Vote*, where she described her photographic studio staffed by women. Sheila Neale has noted that Connell, a member of the Hampstead branch of the Women's Social and Political Union (WSPU), became known for her specialism in portraits of suffrage activists whom she depicted as 'dignified and calm, quietly dedicated to their cause' (Neale 2001: 62), contrasted with the orthodox representation of 'the suffragette' as deranged. Connell's numerous portraits of performers in their stage costumes for *A Pageant of Great Women*, including Edith Craig, Cicely Hamilton, Christopher St John and Ellen Terry, were reproduced in the edition of *A Pageant of Great Women* published in 1910 and the later edition published in 1948 by the Marion Richardson Fellowship. Visitors would have been struck by Connells's serious treatment given to these portraits of suffrage activists in contrast to the newspaper coverage. Connell's photographs were probably displayed and sold in sets,[2] at the International Suffrage Shop run by Sime Seruya,[3] which operated until February 1911 from Edith Craig's Bedford Street flat in Covent Garden. The International Suffrage Shop and the marketing of women's suffrage merchandise were therefore associated with Edith Craig and the Pioneer Players from the outset. In 1912 the Pioneer Players even staged a fund-raising production for the International Suffrage Shop with *The Coronation* by Christopher St John and Charles Thursby[4] and *The Man of Destiny* by George Bernard Shaw.

Women's suffrage organizations were alert to the effects that the press could have on their campaigns. In December 1908, when Emmeline Pankhurst and her daughter Christabel were to be given a reception on their release from Holloway prison, a directive on the appropriate dress code was issued to those supporters who intended to appear:

> We heartily urge all those who can do so to make a special effort to wear uniform. It will consist of a short skirt of purple or green, a white golf jersey and a simple hat of purple or green. The regalia [sash] will be worn over the right shoulder and will be fastened under the left arm. (quoted in Atkinson n.d.: 23)

The visibility of suffrage activists in this period was a sign of the challenge they posed and their organization of the paraphernalia of identification suggests that they were using the surveillance mechanisms to their own advantage. Specifically they adopted a military masculinity in defining their costume as 'uniform' and 'regalia' and this performative aspect provided a visual sign of the strategic organization, scale and extent of their militant activities which would be troubling to the forces of law and order. It presaged a highly organized military body of others prepared to follow, taking up their positions to provide a continuous onslaught in what became an extremely destructive period of civil warfare. Costume, public performance and the ability to organize innovative events were all vital skills for this political campaign.

Edith Craig's skills in set design were called upon in a most unusual manner. When Sime Seruya was imprisoned in Holloway she managed to have smuggled out a clandestine letter written on lavatory paper. This letter was addressed to Craig, containing detailed instructions for creating a demonstration prison cell as an exhibit at the forthcoming WFL's women's suffrage fair. This attraction was used to raise funds by charging an entrance fee to view the interior of the cell and to obtain an impression of the experience of imprisonment.[5] A photograph by Christina Broom shows that attendees at the fair would pay 6d admission to observe a suffragette inmate in the cell (Atkinson n.d.: 21). *Votes for Women* described what amounted to a re-enactment of imprisonment: 'Three times a day viz at 3.30, at 5 and at 8 – the prisoner represented by an actual ex-prisoner will be seen in the cell performing the ordinary daily duties allotted to her. She will scrub the floor – scour her pans – make her bed, and then sit down to make mail bags, sew shirts, and knit stockings' (quoted in Atkinson n.d.: 21). In making visible and commercializing the women's suffrage prison experience, the women's suffrage activists combated in the most undermining way the power of the state to repress them. The customary seclusion of imprisonment and site of torture was turned inside out; spectacularized and domesticated, it became a powerless fairground attraction rather than a deterrent.

The pursuit of the spending power of women in this period was evident in newspaper advertisements for products aimed at the female market for the preservation of the home and family. The women's suffrage organizations harnessed the purses of their supporters for revolutionary purposes. The production and consumption of women's suffrage merchandise was a material form of political support by means of the donation but the use of the objects themselves *performed* as a visible sign of affiliation and allegiance. The products were imaginative and diverse, comprehensively covering aspects of daily life, ranging from postcards and board games to jewellery and clothing but they also included re-enactment experiences and theatrical performances. Edith Craig was at the centre of this cultural production.

Supporters of the campaign had the opportunity to publicize their support, enlisting others by using women's suffrage postcards in correspondence and choosing to wear women's suffrage insignia at social functions; they also chose to conceal their activities and allegiances when necessary. In *Holloway Jingles* (1912), a collection of sixteen poems published originally by the Glasgow WSPU, a poem entitled 'A Strange Sort of College' by E. A. Wingrove represents 'Holloway Gaol' as a college from which a fellowship (the FHG or Fellowship of Holloway Gaol) might be awarded, reconfiguring prison as an educational rather than corrective institution:

> There we take our F.H.G.,
> A very high degree,
> And the hand-grip of true friendship that's the prize. (Norquay 1995: 174)

The poem alludes to clandestine signs of association by means of a handshake, providing an additional context for understanding an observation about the cultural practices of the women's suffrage movement: 'There was a new Freemasonry amongst women since the movement had begun. For one woman Suffragist to know that another woman held the same views was to trust that other' (*Vote*, 12 March 1910, p. 232). Furthermore, the wearing of specific colours as insignia became institutionalized and familiar to the general public. Purple, white and green symbolized the values of the WSPU, formed in Manchester in 1903. By means of its colours, the WSPU was not only explicitly associated with the military and the warrior but also with the elite, as Emmeline Pethick Lawrence explained: 'purple stands for the royal blood that flows in the veins of every suffragette' (quoted in Atkinson 1992: 15). The chorus of the purple, white and green march reinforced the symbolism of the three militant colours:

> Purple stands for the loyal heart,
> Loyal to cause and King;
> White for purity, Green for hope,
> Bright hopes of spring. (quoted in Atkinson 1992: 17)

The WSPU activists, known popularly as 'suffragettes', were there-fore associated with a militant vanguard, pioneering the move-ment with deeds and actions that promised to bring about political change but claimed at the same time to be patriotic and royalist.

Edith Craig became a highly valued figure in the women's suf-frage movement – as a director, performer, leader – and she lent her skills and time to a wide range of activities and organizations. In addition to directing plays, Craig sold suffrage newspapers on the street, attended political meetings, organized street processions and promoted the publication and international performance of wom-en's suffrage plays. This chapter will explore the central role played by Craig in the women's suffrage movement's cultural campaign in which the flow of work, life and politics characterized this first wave of feminist activism. A selection of new discoveries, some cor-respondence from George Bernard Shaw and Ethel Smyth, and new readings of two lesser known women's suffrage plays directed by Craig – a play about vegetarianism entitled *A Modern Crusader* by Florence Edgar Hobson and a play about the persecution of Polish nuns namely *Macrena* by Christopher St John – will demonstrate how diverse in form and treatment was women's suffrage literature and how it emerged within a holistic approach to political argu-ment and social reform. The kind of women's suffrage politics Edith Craig was interested in was international in outlook, committed not just to securing the vote for women but also to changing a whole way of life.

Craig's theatrical work for the women's suffrage movement had an inter- and transnational perspective, bringing the drama of American authors, such as Charlotte Perkins Gilman and Susan Glaspell to a London stage and acting as agent for performances of women's suffrage plays abroad. In America, as Leslie Goddard has noted, the allegiance between the theatre and women's suf-frage was both a matter of public debate and taken for granted; in 1897 in America the *New York Dramatic Mirror* claimed that the theatre provided equality for women and in 6 November 1909, the *Billboard Magazine* headlined an article 'Women of the Stage all desire to vote' (Goddard 2002: 138). In Britain, performers were highly visible and versatile in the political campaigns. Craig was involved in the Women's Freedom League (WFL) which had a particularly international perspective. Craig's transatlantic and European travels had already provided her with this outlook.

A well-travelled woman, she was educated in Germany, had worked in North America and Canada on theatrical tours and holidayed in Europe. The travel and communication systems in this period enabled women to be in dialogue across the world, travelling to speak in public and take part in events. They wrote articles with a potentially international readership in mind. Muriel Matters, Australian activist for the WFL, was photographed with Edith Craig in the *Daily Express*, the caption revealing that militant activity was not confined to 'suffragettes': 'Suffragists marching Towards Martyrdom' (THM 384/33/1). Matters was notorious for engaging in memorable publicity stunts involving chaining herself to the grille in the Strangers' Gallery of the House of Commons and distributing leaflets from a hot air balloon. This reminded the opposition that the threat would come from all directions and the least expected quarters, the air as well as the river. It pre-empted the threat of aerial bombardment when it came during the First World War. For pacifists, when that war broke out, the International League for Peace and Freedom was a logical step because suffragists had already established international networks. This innovative thinking was in contrast to the anglo-centric patriarchal party politics and macho posturing that drove much of the war strategy and its implementation. Edith Craig's work in theatre predisposed her to this transnational perspective.

Women's suffrage drama was highly popular and effective in disseminating the arguments, publicizing the campaign and training participants in public performance as well as recruiting new members. Edith Craig was one of the most famous directors of women's suffrage drama, working independently and as a freelance for the Actresses' Franchise League (AFL) and as Honorary Managing Director of the Pioneer Players theatre society. Ellen Terry wrote to her daughter appreciative of Elizabeth Baker's play: 'Have you seen *Chains*? Ain't it 'ot?' (THM 384/1/40/4). Some women were not convinced about the use of drama for political purposes. Rebecca West (1892–1983) reviewed *A Modern Crusader*, to be discussed later in this chapter, one of the Pioneer Players' fund-raising women's suffrage plays in 1912 in the most dismissive manner, rejecting it on aesthetic grounds and revealing her failure to understand or appreciate either the staging of the play or the political argument. At that time, Rebecca West was working as a journalist, writing articles and somewhat controversial reviews, one of which, in

September 1912, prompted an invitation from H. G. Wells that was to lead to their long-term relationship. It is one particular drama review by West earlier that year, in May 1912, in *The Freewoman* that inadvertently raises questions about what was at stake (then and now) in a lack of understanding and awareness of women's suffrage drama. West's principal concern appears to have been the lack of artistic merit in the play, condemning both the play and those who were involved in producing such politically driven plays: 'the Actresses' Franchise League and the Pioneer Players, whom nothing but the fire of Prometheus could make into artists' (*The Freewoman*, 1912, p. 8). West was particularly incensed by the outrage constituted by women's suffrage drama. *Votes for Women*, the earliest suffrage play, written by the American actor and promoter of Ibsen's drama Elizabeth Robins (1862–1952) had been produced successfully in April 1907 at the Royal Court theatre.[6] In many respects it conformed to the conventions of naturalism in its domestic setting and dialogue tense with contemporary debate but several features unsettled the audience. A scene in Trafalgar Square reconstructed political speeches and a heckling crowd, transporting the comfortably sedentary audience to the centre of political conflict. It is easy to categorize as a 'women's suffrage play': the title is explicit; the characterization and plot directly cite political debates about enfranchisement and the persuasion of others to support the campaign.

Other suffrage plays were sometimes less easy to identify from any textual cues in terms of the title, form or content and instead were recognizable by means of the context of performance. In January 1914 Edith Craig directed *Paphnutius* by Hrotsvit, the tenth-century nun said to be the first female dramatist.[7] The context of this production, alluding to the imprisoned suffrage activists prepared to sacrifice themselves, appropriated it for the women's suffrage movement. On some occasions in order to reach wider audiences who would be willing to watch a play but not attend a political event, plays addressed broader social reforms, embedding women's independence within them. Many plays tended to be relatively short, focusing on incidents that highlighted sexual inequality or emphasized women's worthiness and strength and used comedy to expose the redundant arguments of the anti-suffrage lobby.

Women's suffrage drama has been identified, collected and analysed, but it tends to be discussed in the context of women's writing,

gender studies and history rather than literary studies within which
it still has an uncertain place.[8] One factor relates to the aesthetic
criteria used to evaluate literary texts and the extent to which the
wider socio-political issues addressed by women's suffrage literature are so little understood. As a consequence, the tone is often
misread; an ironic slant is treated as a serious statement; and the
domestic sphere is seen as an inevitably containing space rather than
one which is staged and constructed in order to be dismantled. For
women's suffrage audiences, the principal crime depicted in Ibsen's
*A Doll's House*, a play in which Edith Craig had toured regularly
as Mrs Linden, was that of Norah's deliberately limited education
rather than her act of forgery. The liberating act of her departure is
simultaneously tragic because she is obliged to sacrifice her children
who are left at home with her husband Torvald.

In 1908 the AFL was formed at a meeting attended by 400
performers and speakers included Cicely Hamilton (Holledge
1981: 49). It aimed to co-ordinate and apply the skills of theatre
practitioners for the best effect in the campaign. Edith Craig was
involved in the AFL but also operated independently.[9] The Women
Writers' Suffrage League (WWSL) was led by Elizabeth Robins, a
specialist suffrage organization which similarly welcomed authors
who would write material to promote the movement. Craig held
the performance rights to at least three plays by WWSL authors
and supported the WWSL in a street procession.[10] Printing presses
were used to disseminate their writings and the major organizations had their own newspapers and periodicals.[11] In the tradition
of effective political movements, suffragists took control of the
means of production, but they innovated and excelled in the diver-
sification of cultural practices and the appropriation of otherwise
apolitical forms, organizations and spaces. Plays were performed
in supporters' houses, in public halls and in skating rinks. This
active engagement and broadening of their audiences was a deliberate strategy. The women's suffrage movement exploited the new
marketing deployed by journalism at a time when women were
being identified and exploited as a new market. This symbiotic
relationship led to some high visibility and mutually beneficial
engagements.

In Britain the political campaigns to enfranchise women took
the form of lobbying, letters and petitions from the middle of the
nineteenth century, but from 1905 a more militant strategy was

emerging that involved deliberate law-breaking, civil disobedience and destruction of property. Many suffragists, including Edith Craig, did not work on the basis of single-issue politics; the vote for women promised to change society. So their cultural activities were diverse and demonstrate a range of allegiances and interests that sometimes appear difficult to understand one hundred years later. All kinds of cultural interventions were used in order to reach the widest audiences. The use of performance – scripted, site-specific, partially improvised, rewritings and parodies – by activists in the women's suffrage movement was highly effective in persuading audiences that enfranchisement should be extended to women.[12] A great deal more was involved in this process than simply the use of drama as a vehicle for the political ideas of 'the suffragettes'.

To some extent there was an awareness of the implications of the relationship between performer, space and place but accounts of the productions often provided an insight into the tensions and conflicts of various kinds that fundamentally defined the political movement. Some plays made use of stratifications of social class (female servants and employers, aristocrats with inherited wealth and middle class with new money) but offered no realistic solution beyond an optimistic gesture towards enfranchisement. Since legislative change was proposed on the same basis that men had the vote at the time, it meant enfranchising the wealthier class of women. Craig was in an ambivalent position. The daughter of a famous and wealthy mother, she had also experienced intermittent hardships and the lifelong stigma of illegitimacy concealed in plain view by her invented surname.

## 'A very Proteus of suffragists'

Edith Craig, like other leading activists, was featured as a role model or pioneer in the women's suffrage newspapers, and in an article an observation is made about her low profile:

> The enthusiastic master of our pageants, the kindly daughter of our good friend delightful Ellen Terry, the most genial of workers – and the easiest to work with – the most painstaking of picture-makers, the quickest to grasp a telling incident, and the most understanding of teachers, choose which description

you will, and you instantly conjure up the figure of Miss Edith Craig. A very Proteus of Suffragists, she comes continually to our assistance, [...] The work which Miss Edith Craig has done for us on various occasions [...] has not always received its due notice, owing to her habit of laughing self-effacement. ('Miss Edith Craig', *Vote*, 12 March 1910, p. 232)

The interview drew attention to the way in which Edith Craig prioritized activity but avoided self-promotion: by her deeds was she known and to some extent it seems that by her own 'laughing self-effacement', as well as the institutionalized prejudices and exclusions, has she become hidden from history.

There are numerous literary examples of the valuable effects of performance, especially costume as disguise, for the women's suffrage activist. Edith Craig's fervent belief in the political efficacy of drama was quoted in the suffrage press: 'One play is worth a hundred speeches!' (*Stage*, May 1911). Craig was so committed to this that she had plays printed and obtained performance rights.[13] In her collection is a play by J. L Austin, *How One Woman Did It*, which features cross-class dressing, exemplifying the preoccupation in women's suffrage literature with the facility with role play and disguise as enabling suffragettes to gain access to prohibited spaces and intimate contact with individuals in order to extend the lobbying.

In H. Johnston's novel *Mrs Warren's Daughter* (1920), Vivie has an alternative life as a lawyer, going by the name of Mr Michaelis: 'But she was Protean. Much of her work, the lawless part of it was organized in the shape and dress of Mr Michaelis' (Norquay 1995: 264). The details provided about her expertise in transformation reveal the close affiliation of political activism and theatrical costume:

> Thus disguised she elicited considerable information sometimes, though she might really be on her way to organize the break-up of the statesman's public meeting, the enquiry into discreditable circumstances which might compel his withdrawal from public life or merely the burning down of his shooting box. (p. 265)

Protean transformations describe Vivie's shape-shifting as Mr Michaelis, Edith Craig's work as 'a very Proteus of suffragists'

(*Vote*, 12 March 1910) and characters in several women's suffrage texts who disguise themselves as servants.[14] The implication of rendering social class roles as performative and a matter of costume was fundamentally destabilizing.

Hats became highly politicized, as symbolic markers of social class and gender conformity. In Gertrude Colmore's short story 'Oh Richard!', the suffragette character notes that 'the working man's cap covered more helpfulness than the tall hat or the policeman's helmet' (p. 367). This evocatively recreates the perspective from within the crowd such that people are identifiable only from the features that are visible: in this case, their hats. The encounters in public demonstrated that there were alliances between the women's suffrage activists and the working man but this is revealed at moments of violent conflict. In the East End of London the People's Army, seen parading on the streets with their rifles, could be relied upon to protect Sylvia Pankhurst and suffragists committed to social justice.[15]

Violence was an integral part of the anti-suffrage response and simmered just beneath the surface of polite domestic encounters. In Gertrude Colmore's short story 'The Introduction' (1912), the male perpetrator of physical violence against a suffragette is brought to account in a middle-class social setting. Having been asked for a formal 'introduction' to a young lady at a party, the male protagonist finds that she presents herself with a broken arm and then learns, to his horror, that he was responsible for the injury at a recent political meeting where he had acted as steward. This narrative operates on the basis of an ironic reversal with the revelation at the end, drawing much of its powerful effect from the contrast between violence and politeness. It leaves the suffragette in a position of strength and the male anti-suffrage character exposed, undermined and with a great deal to reflect upon. The narrative perspective provides an insight into the consciousness of the anti-suffrage character. The open-endedness of the short story emphasizes the process of reconsideration required as a basis for adopting a political position. The authoritarian directives of propaganda that instruct the reader or audience to take up a specific position are seldom used in women's suffrage literature. Instead the reader is engaged in a thoughtful reflection and the invitation to share an ironic joke and in so doing the process of affiliation would exploit those shared values further along the route towards political conversion.

## *How the Vote Was Won*: With defiant laughter

An effective means of combating the ideologies which promoted violence was the undermining, deflating power of comedy. In 1908, only a year after her mother had married so controversially, Edith Craig had performed in the role of Mrs Bridgnorth in George Bernard Shaw's comedy *Getting Married*. The timing of the play and Shaw's casting of Terry's daughter sheds another light on the continuing involvement of Shaw and the Terry family. The play challenged the dominance of marriage and the need for more flexible divorce arrangements, especially for women such as Reginald Bridgnorth's wife whose circumstances bore some resemblance to those of Mrs Ellen Wardell. In a letter to Shaw, Ellen Terry tauntingly referred to his play as a 'low comedy' but added her own comic suggestion that she and her new husband perform in it (13 April [1908]; *CLET 5*: 1528).

Edith Craig directed and appeared in *How the Vote Was Won* (1909), co-written by Christopher St John and Cicely Hamilton. This was one of the British women's suffrage movement's most popular comedies. Susan Carlson has explored the political effects of comedy in women's suffrage drama (2000). *How the Vote Was Won* incisively exposed the hypocrisies at the heart of the anti-suffrage position and the compromises required from the suffragists. It featured in a long programme of entertainments at the 'Green White and Gold Fair', the political festival organized by the WFL alongside a variety of other performances, including Cicely Hamilton's satirical 'Anti-suffrage Waxworks', a demonstration of jiu-jitsu and tableaux of 'Famous Women of History' (15–17 April 1909 at the Caxton Hall, Westminster; EC-D435) and presumably the reconstructed prison cells designed by Craig and Seruya. Women's suffrage drama focused on issues relating to the political debates (inequalities in marriage and work; the phenomenon of prostitution; the separate spheres; the worthinesss of women as citizens). Monologues relied on the strength of a single character to gain attention and achieve credibility on the basis of reported speech of others and descriptions of past events. In this way 'Jim's Leg' and 'A Chat with Mrs Chicky' gave a voice to the overlooked wife and servant and made domestic labour visible as work.[16] Other plays such as *How the Vote Was Won* re-enacted the community of women on stage, brought together with a common purpose in spite of their different social class positions. The play's comedy focuses on the dilemma for capitalism and patriarchy when women are mobilized collectively to use their power and take action. The exploitation of women, including the exploitation of women by other women, was the subject of women's suffrage literature and visual art. For this reason, the literary, dramatic and cultural *forms* adopted as well as the cultural *processes* needed to address the problems of inequality rather than reproduce them. *How the Vote Was Won* uses the small domestic space and large number of women to make a striking political point by enacting a strike of women. The female relatives of Horace Cole descend on him as their patriarchal provider and occupy what little space he has to offer in the parlour.

As Ann Ardis argues in *Modernism and Cultural Conflict* (2008), the ascendency of particular aesthetic concerns that came to characterize modernism was achieved at the expense of others. In Britain, women's suffrage literature was associated with various projects that were anathema to the leading modernists populating the literary canon today. However, it has been established that 'realism' does not account for the range of narrative uncertainties, episodic structures and eclectic range of myth and imagery found in women's suffrage fiction and poetry. In drama, Sheila Stowell has argued persuasively in 'Rehabilitating Realism' (1992b) that this mode had 'the effect of making visible traditionally invisible processes of capitalist production' and 'is capable of presenting a range of ideological positions' (Stowell 1992b: 85; 87).[17] The range of scripted women's suffrage performances was broad and included short plays and monologues as well as the self-referential and interrogatory, the comic, the pageant, the masque and processional, the use of dance and the staged female body. These forms invited completion by the audience of committed activists, sharing with them a sense of alienation from the current state of the world, sufficiently defamiliarized for the critique to be dramatized and requiring their action to change it. If some women's suffrage performance seems to have anticipated modernist performance methods, the invitation is to consider how they relate to what we currently understand as modernist and whether their inclusion prompts a reconfiguration, especially given the positioning of drama and performance as parallel, semi-autonomous operations in relation to modernist literature. Naturalist modes were used to exploit the claustrophobic aspects of the domestic space, to defamiliarize the patriarchal family and the expected position of women in it and to familiarize the prospect of women extending their reach outside in the wider political, public sphere. In women's suffrage performance spaces, the fourth wall rarely existed; audience and performers were ideologically unified and the practice of using activists as performers generated a closer relationship between audience and performers.[18]

## The four musketeers

In the deployment of drama, literature, art and music to campaign for women's enfranchisement in Britain, many activists came together in new collaborative ventures. Such collaborations were exemplified by Edith Craig's most famous women's suffrage productions namely *A Pageant of Great Women* and *How the Vote Was Won*; these received requests for repeat performances at highly publicized political events. Edith Craig performed in both plays as well as directing them. Craig, Ethel Smyth, Cicely Hamilton and Christopher St John brought musical and theatrical talents as well as generosity and exuberance to the many cultural events which they organized. The wider discourse of militancy and violence appears to have shaped personal relationships and artistic creativity as well as political strategy in the British women's suffrage movement.[19] Unpublished letters of Ethel Smyth to Edith Craig explored here for the first time provide a new perspective on the cultural references made by suffrage activists to cross-dressing female soldiers and sailors of the past, such as Christian Davis and Hannah Snell; they illuminate their own military and outlaw self-presentation and interest in romantic tales of smugglers and shipwrecks and the complex range of anti-feminine dress in anti-suffrage iconography.

Smyth's correspondence with Craig principally concerns their artistic collaborations. At that time Craig continued to be highly active as a theatre director with regular coverage in the national press but Smyth received official recognition of her work as a composer and her contributions to music in the honours list when, in 1922, she was awarded the title of Dame. By 1911, when Smyth composed 'The March of the Women', the rousing anthem especially for the women's suffrage movement, she had already established herself in the music world, with her *Mass in D* (1891) and an opera, *The Wreckers* (1906; produced 1909), about smugglers deliberately wrecking ships on the Cornish coast. Craig brought to her friendship and collaborations with Smyth more than an amateur musical knowledge and extensive knowledge of the theatre, from costume and performance to lighting and directing. *A Pageant of Great Women*, within which groups of characters portrayed the great women of the past, was directed by Edith Craig who appeared as Rosa Bonheur, the artist in each production. Ellen Terry wrote on 12 November: 'A few days rest will do you good & then – my eye!! You'll have to go it again for the Pageant. Bless you my bonny boots! You did look "spiffer" as Rosa!' (THM 384/1/40/39).[20] George Bernard Shaw wrote to Edith Craig on 17 June 1910 declining any potential invitation to process as a great woman: 'No use. I am not a woman; and I will not be led in triumph' (THM 384/9/ 2). This play was first performed for the AFL and the WWSL at the Scala Theatre in London on 12 November 1909, and its realization depended on the writing skills of another talented woman with a national profile in women's suffrage campaigns: Cicely Hamilton.

## 'Very violent in a deadly underground way'

An actor as well as an author, Hamilton was responsible for rousing a multitude of women to march for women's suffrage. She wrote the words to 'The March of the Women' as well as the script for *A Pageant of Great Women*. A hitherto unpublished letter from Ethel Smyth to Edith Craig encapsulates something of the particularly dynamic interactions between these women. Thus, Smyth confided in a letter to Craig about the effect Hamilton had on her and where it might lead:

Miss Hamilton's ways (handwriting, verses & words & sentiments, & general fierce fling) makes me feel we ought to do something big together – If we didn't kill each other (*both being very violent in a deadly underground way*) over it, we shd produce something worth doing! (n.d.; EC-3, 638; my emphases)

Smyth's turn of phrase in this private correspondence reveals her exhilaration in finding a kindred spirit, marked by vitality and virility; it is a matter of kindling with a view to a pleasurably incendiary outcome. It also points to something more significant about the dynamics of art and politics in the transformation of female subjectivities in a world beginning to imagine women as free to think and act as they wished. Smyth's letter provides the kind of detailed (but unfortunately fleeting) articulation of a sense of self that raises useful questions about how those involved understood, perceived or had an awareness of their opposition and how this was effected. In *Disturbing Practices* (2013), Laura Doan proposes

> [...] a new practice, a queer critical history that seeks to understand the multiple, contradictory, and overlapping configurations of the sexual that are unmappable within the epistemological apparatus of modern sexuality. The payoff lies not in its potential to satisfy queer yearnings for collective belonging but in its alertness to other *structures of knowing*, including residual knowledges now vanished. (Doan 2013: 198; emphasis in original)

My reading of Smyth's encounters with Craig and Hamilton suggests that in the period of militant women's suffrage from 1905 to 1914 and the interwar years, militancy, violence and military-style uniform – especially that of the seafarer and any associations with the pirate, the outlaw, the highwayman and the (French) revolutionary – warrant reassessment.

In considering the available 'structures of knowing' for Smyth and these other women involved so closely in women's suffrage stage performances, it is relevant to note that the 'cultural topsy-turvydom' and 'utter confusion over gender' that Laura Doan has identified (Doan 2013: 133), also had a literal, *theatrical* provenance. The phrase 'topsy-turvydom' was notoriously associated with W. S. Gilbert's libretti for the comic operas at the Savoy Theatre which had succumbed in the 1890s to the formulaic, in improbable plots and startling reversals of convention.[21] Craig's friend Jacko (Vera Holme) had worked at the Savoy Theatre in the chorus of these comic operas. As Laura Doan argues there is no 'secure link between the masculine woman and the modern lesbian' (Doan 2013: 106), but there is evidence of a wide variety of cultural representations of gender inversion, especially in clothing and demeanour, apparent in the context of British women's suffrage militancy that were connectable to the strategy of marriage resistance performed by women, including women who were celibate or living a woman-centred life of various kinds including cohabitation. This is demonstrated by the performance of a female military masculinity and a theatricalized self-presentation which are most apparent in Edith Craig's circle and during the militant women's suffrage period of productions of *A Pageant of Great Women*; however they extend well beyond this period too. It is likely that this rich cultural provenance of the cloak and tricorne hat informed the self-fashioning of Una Troubridge and Radclyffe Hall and explains why they may indeed have shopped for unusual everyday clothing at the theatrical costumiers Nathan's in the early 1920s (Doan 2001: 116). Successful theatrical productions inspired fashions. Ellen Terry's character as the outspoken laundress who marries above her social class in *Madame Sans-Gene* had inspired a fashion in white caps. The tricorne hat had been highly fashionable,[22] but it also acquired a specific range of reference after *A Pageant of Great Women* when various military hats were worn by Cicely Hamilton as Christian Davies, Lina Rathbone as Mary Ann Talbot and Christopher St John as Hannah Snell (photographs by Miss Leon reproduced in Hamilton 1910: 41, 43).

The misogynistic depiction of the suffragette in anti-suffrage postcards typically used a variety of features that signified the 'spinster' stereotype but it is worth reconsidering how the suffragette-spinster iconography served to reinforce the institution of marriage and mark as deviant certain females outside it, notably those who were disruptive or making claims for themselves instead of serving silently in socially acceptable occupations such as teaching or charitable works. The behaviour and demeanour of the women who publicly committed themselves to women's suffrage have been explored by historians and cultural critics in great detail. Women, and indeed men such as Laurence Housman, were exploring new ways of living, working and collaborating; they were exploring the potential for commercialization in different forms of cultural intervention. Women's suffrage militancy often drew on Christian religious precedent, notably such rebellious antecedents as Joan of Arc. The hitherto unpublished correspondence of Ethel Smyth with Edith Craig reveals the seamless and determining way in which unfeminine and sometimes perceived unseemly behaviours inspired women to action and cultural production in the period of women's suffrage which was perpetrated, as Smyth indicates, 'in a deadly underground way'. Letters from famous suffrage activists Annie Kenney and Emmeline Pethick Lawrence to Edith Craig have survived and confirm the esteem with which she was held as well as the breadth of her influence. A discourse of militancy, virility and violence (imagined, planned, realized, failed, postponed, remembered) shaped their interactions, informed political strategies and inspired new cultural practices, manifesting itself in metaphor and the expression of desire as well as in literal statements of intention to commit illegal acts. A consideration of the interweaving of expressions of violence or dissidence in the common daily correspondence of a leading militant activist like Ethel Smyth demonstrates both the familiarization with violence and militancy which took place in this context and the possible eroticization of these cultural values for these women. While cross-dressing has been widely analysed as a sign of potential lesbian identification in this period, the lesbian significance of violent expression in specific relation to the cultural arguments of women's suffrage invites some scrutiny. This nexus of military masculinity emerges in the correspondence quoted above between Ethel Smyth and Edith Craig, revealing the prestige associated with the potential violence to be perpetrated by the activist warrior (familiarly symbolized by heroic martyr figures, such as Joan of Arc) and the sorority arising from collective action for those prepared to fight for the vote.

## Hearing 'The March of the Women'

It is widely known that, as the women's suffrage campaign progressed, the need for increasingly confrontational and spectacular events was identified and promoted by the more militant groups, notably the WSPU. Less famous, but equally spectacular, were the tactics of the WFL, of which Edith Craig and Cicely Hamilton were active members. The WFL formed when leading members of the WSPU, including Teresa Billington-Grieg, Emmeline Pethick

Lawrence and Charlotte Despard, became disaffected with the strategic direction of the suffragettes. It may be the aftermath of this phase to which Ethel Smyth refers to in the careful qualification she makes in the letter to Edith Craig, taking up the invitation to help in a suffrage fund-raising event. Smyth was committed to the WSPU and Mrs Pankhurst in particular. She promised to help, on the understanding that 'Theresa' [Billington-Grieg] was not involved: 'She I believe is trying to hurt my friends – so of course wd not cooperate with her' (April 1911; EC-3, 644).[23] Although the women's suffrage movement did not escape the banal betrayals and breakdowns in relationships often arising from political activism, it was also characterized by those many acts of generosity, collaboration and leaps of faith which are generated by the political direction of energy towards social change. One such is evident in the creation of the inspirational song 'The March of the Women', originally dedicated to the WSPU. One of its strengths is its memorable lyrics. Many phrases from the song – 'shoulder to shoulder' and 'laugh a defiance' – have had afterlives as titles of women's suffrage autobiographies and documentaries. It became an audible reminder of suffrage militancy and solidarity when on 6 March 1930 it was performed by the Metropolitan Police Band at the unveiling of the statue of Emmeline Pankhurst at the Houses of Parliament (Smyth 1933: 272).[24] The significance of this particular song for women's suffrage veterans in attendance, including Kitty Marion (1871–1944), music hall performer and suffragette, may have undermined the attempts, outlined by Laura E. Nym Mayhall, to rewrite women's suffrage activism through Emmeline Pankhurst in terms of a sacrifice that could be domesticated, contained and rendered compatible with the status quo (Mayhall 1999: 6).

Although 'The March of the Women' had a significant part in the 1930 commemoration of the WSPU leader, Cicely Hamilton's lyrics have subsequently been described by Hamilton's biographer, Lis Whitelaw, in different terms:

Cicely admired Ethel Smyth's energy and wholeheartedness and was elated to be her collaborator – even though she had not been Ethel Smyth's first choice and had a justifiably poor opinion of the verses she eventually wrote: they are fervent but otherwise undistinguished. (Whitelaw 1990: 123)

Ethel Smyth was of a different opinion. She noted, '[...] the March does seem to excite people I play it to – & seems easy to pick up' (EC-3,641). Although she created the music first and then Cicely Hamilton wrote the verse, Smyth felt that the two were ideally suited: explicitly referring to the works of art but implicitly, perhaps, revealing her perception of their creators' natural affinity. Aesthetically, she argued, the chronological sequence could easily have been reversed: 'This poem of hers might have made the tune instead of vice versa!' (EC-3,637) Smyth was keen to develop the song and was moved to write to Edith Craig with suggestions for its adaptation for the trumpet. In *Female Pipings in Eden* (1933), she recalled thus:

> In those early days of my association with the WSPU occurred an event which, in her pride, the writer must recount 'ere the pace becomes such that a personal reference would be unthinkable; namely the formal introduction to the Suffragettes of 'The March of the Women', to which Cicely Hamilton fitted words after the tune had been written – not an easy undertaking. A Suffragette choir had been sternly drilled, and I remember Edith Craig plaintively commenting on the difficulty of hitting a certain E flat. But it was maintained that the interval is a peculiarly English one (which is true) and must be coped with. We had the organ, and I think a cornet to blast forth the tune (a system much to be recommended on such occasions), and it was wonderful processing up the centre aisle of the Albert Hall in Mus. Doc. robes at Mrs Pankhurst's side, and being presented with a beautiful *bâton*, encircled by a golden collar with the date, 23rd March 1911. (Smythe 1933: 201)

Generously, Smyth sent Edith Craig a score for the trumpet which she had transcribed herself.

She could rely on Craig understanding the musical significance and referred to its political efficacy, in the stirring effects its rousing tones promised:

> If ever you want to do the March with trumpets etc...there is a 3 part edit (2nd I think) for female voices – let two trumpets & one baritone (a bass instrument!) play the 3 parts. Each wd write out the part in his own way on a bit of music paper for 3d I shd say – or rather I'll write out score for you (enclosed) – All you

have to do if you want it is to copy each part on a little bit of music paper. I shd say the many you employ – or one of them wd write it out for you for 6d.

Keep the score I send & return some day – no sort of hurry – & no sort of necessity to do it...but there it is as it may come in useful in yr shows. I'm never going to take part in any Suff. again – except deputation on March 4th or whenever it is...as I think that essential for all to have done once. The Govt literally mind nothing else.

Yrs E. (n.d.; EC-3,634)

Craig never did return the score. Whether she put it to use in a production is not yet known. The aesthetic significance of the trumpet in delivering the song is worth further consideration. As an instrument the trumpet is ubiquitous in women's suffrage iconography

**FIGURE 1** *Score for trumpet in 'The March of the Women' composed by Dame Ethel Smyth, n.d. (reproduced with permission of Higham Associates); EC-3,634.*

and it features in *A Pageant of Great Women*.[25] The female bugler and warriors in *A Pageant of Great Women* and the Renaissance masque form provided a powerful combination, drawing on the literary prestige and historical associations of Edmund Spenser's *The Faerie Queene* (1596). Britomart provided a female Arthurian model that added to the cultural layers at work in these historical allusions. Susan Clayton has argued that 'female chivalry' was promoted in this period by literary and visual depictions such as Joan of Arc and the bugler but also the literary depiction of the female knight specifically in various editions of Spenser including that by Walter Crane (1900) and Mary MacLeod's edition *Stories from the Faerie Queene* (1897) in which Britomart successfully passes for a knight (Clayton 2010: 329). Chivalry is depicted as both anachronistic and retaining a powerful force in contemporary culture in Evelyn Sharp's women's suffrage short story 'Shaking Hands with the Middle Ages' (1910). Of course, the clarion was a symbol for socialists in this period too, adopted as the name of a newspaper. The appropriation of Christian symbolism by political movements lent authority and familiarity to the otherwise outlandish aspects of the dawning new age (Taylor 1983). With angelic heralds signalling the apocalypse, the new revolution, whether manifested through socialism or feminism, was going to be no apologetic affair: heard as well as seen, it would be welcomed in by the loudest of fanfares. The powerful literary and cultural weapons used in this battle were drawn from carefully chosen but often unexpected historical moments.

## Suffragette nuns and historical drama: Irena Macrena

Two of the more unusual plays produced by the Pioneer Players were Christopher St John's translation from the tenth-century Latin of Hrotsvit's *Paphnutius* (in which a prostitute is walled up for her sins) and Christopher St John's *Macrena* (about a period of persecution of Catholicism by Emperor Nicholas in which the Abbess Macrena and the nuns in her order were abused). Both plays concern abjection and violence: violence against a sexualized body and threatened sexual violence against a sanctified body. The Pioneer Players' production of these plays presents unexpectedly topical resonances: the tenth century and early nineteenth century provided dislocated moments from which a new perspective might be realized on the imprisonment and destruction of the suffragette body. This is exemplified by Emily Wilding Davison, who famously died from injuries sustained after collision with the king's horse at the Derby races, and by Lady Constance Lytton (1869–1923), who exposed the iniquitous treatment of working-class women in prison on hunger strike. The threat of rape against suffragettes was implied and widely propagated in anti-suffrage popular postcards.[26] The Pioneer Players responded in an engagement with the political and the play of ideas which was often indirect, thought-provoking and perplexing.

Christopher St John's Catholic beliefs are likely to have motivated her in writing *Macrena*, a play which exposes the persecution of Catholics in Poland under the control of Russia in the 1840s. She took the name of St John the Baptist and Christopher in place of Christabel Marshall, signifying through this masculine name both her sexuality and her Catholicism, which provided an unexpected niche for the lesbian as abject heroine (Glasgow 1990). The political discourses on both sides exploited the idea of a holy war, although this was most visible on the pro-suffrage side where joining the movement was likened to a nun becoming a bride of Christ.[27] The militant WSPU especially chose Joan of Arc as a warrior figure, who became a ubiquitous icon. Macrena's heroic role is described in the author's note to the play where she is presented as defender of the Catholic Church in Poland and comparable to St Thomas of Canterbury:

The story of the coercive measures employed by the Emperor [sic] Nicholas of Russia from 1830 to 1840, while completing the incorporation of Poland into the Russian Empire, is not well-known in England. So it is necessary to say that Irena Macrena, the chief character in this play, was a real person, and that the incidents of which I have made her the central figure are historically true. Macrena's heroic constancy to the Catholic Church, for which many of her nuns suffered martyrdom [sic] stemmed the tide of apostasy in Poland, but it was not until she escaped from the Russians, and told her story in Paris and Rome, that Catholic Europe was roused to a sense of the barbarity of the methods used to force the Poles to join the Russian Church. It is not too much to say that the liberty of the Catholic Church in Russian Poland was secured by the courage and sagacity of Macrena, who emulated St. Thomas of Canterbury in resistance to tyranny. (typescript; EC-H148)

If *Macrena* now seems to be a prototype of T. S. Eliot's *Murder in the Cathedral* (1935), the theatre-going public at the time would have recalled the popular melodrama, Wilson Barrett's *The Sign of the Cross* (1895) but the women's suffrage supporters would locate Macrena in the esteemed company of women recovered from history to establish various historical precedents in their argument for women's enfranchisement. Cicely Hamilton's *A Pageant of Great Women* was the most famous and well-populated drama of recovered women[28]; in the play St John played one of the women warriors, Hannah Snell (1723–92). Macrena's heroic response to 'tyranny' and willingness to risk her own life for her beliefs made her a suitable candidate for recovery and situates her specifically in the context of women's suffrage militancy. Not only was Macrena a proto-suffragette but the male authority figures in the play typified the attitudes of politicians who were attempting to coerce women to accept their unenfranchized status. The play significantly articulates the otherwise repressed fact of the conflict over women's rights: that the extent of the physical threats deployed by the foot soldiers included sexual violence.

In the opening section of the play, before Macrena appears, she is described as having been made to leave her convent by force but having personally chosen to carry the convent's heavy wooden cross. In the first part of the play, in the dialogue between 'Joseph Siemaszko, the Schismatic Archbishop of Lithuania' and 'Colonel Fedor Vassieliewitch Uszakoff, military governor of Polock', Uszakoff controversially corrects Siemaszko: 'If any one says: "Poland must be forced to change her religion before we can govern her successfully", I understand him. But what I don't understand is all this talk about the Poles being brought back to the fold' (EC-H148, 3). He rejects the hypocritical rewriting of history to conceal the brutal force involved in controlling the religious beliefs of the colonized.

Macrena's refusal to pay allegiance to Siemazcko is dramatized by a violent gesture, as she knocks the jewelled cross and White Eagle honour sent by Prince Nicholas, from Siemazcko's hand with the word 'apostate'. This forceful response highlights her strength. The account of the attempts to force the nuns to accept the Russian church are brutal and sustained. These include strategically separating the women in order to try to break their will. The play therefore draws a parallel between the imprisoned women and the treatment of suffragettes.

The turning point in the play reveals Colonel Uszakoff's devotion to Macrena, implying also overwhelming sexual desire. The stage directions indicate some kind of acknowledgement between them: 'There is silence between them, one of those silences when two souls have the courage to see each other without disgust and without fear' (p. 18). Uszakoff replies, desperately: 'Oh, Irena I asked you to sign just now...to save yourself from the beast in me...I ask you again to sign...to save your nuns from the same beast in other men...' (p. 18). Although Uszakoff is presented as capable of transformation, demonstrating an understanding of political and religious positions and a sympathy and admiration for the nuns, he is also symbolically the uncontrollable 'beast'.

The play ends with Colonel Uszakoff colluding in Macrena's escape and preventing Michael from taking any action. When Michael arrives, revealing that he has changed allegiance: 'Resistance is useless...we must all go the same way' (p. 10), Uszakoff physically prevents Michael from raising the alarm: 'Michael tries to open the window, and begins to shout. Uszakoff claps his hand over his mouth and shakes him.' Uszakoff intends to keep Michael prisoner overnight, to give the women chance to escape. Referring to Macrena, Uszakoff says: 'That's the best woman I've ever known...the dearest, the bravest, and she's going to have as good a chance of escape as I can give her. Now make yourself comfortable, for much as I dislike your company, you're going to spend the night here with me' (p. 22). This scene alludes to the threat of sexual violence towards the nuns mentioned earlier in the play. As these are the last lines of the play before the curtain falls, they leave the audience wondering: does Macrena escape? Was Michael correct when he said earlier 'Resistance is useless' in the face of physical force? Between the military colonel and Macrena and her rebellious nuns, unexpected allegiances emerge.

# 'Patrolling the gutter' and *A Modern Crusader*

Edith Craig's commitment to women's suffrage politics was extensive, in the field of her expertise in theatrical production and costume, but also reached to the somewhat less appealing and more
confrontational activities. She was an enthusiastic street-seller of
women's suffrage newspapers and was quoted in the press describing her experience. Craig provides enthusiastic details about
newspaper selling apparently inconsistent with her 'laughing self-
effacement' in terms of her work as a director, about which she is
oddly silent in this interview:

> I love it. But I'm always getting moved on. You see, I generally
> sell the paper outside the Eustace Miles Restaurant,[29] and I offer
> it verbally to every soul that passes. If they refuse, I say something
> to them. Most of them reply, others come up, and we collect a
> little crowd until I'm told to let the people into the restaurant,
> and move on. Then I begin all over again. (*Votes for Women*, 15
> April 1910, p. 455)

Instead of using the interview to seek glory she offered constructive
advice for prospective newspaper vendors:

> It was seeing *Votes for Women* sold in the street in an apologetic
> manner that made me feel that I wanted to do it quite differently,
> and I began joining societies right away. That was some time
> ago, you know, and our sellers don't apologise for their existence
> now. (*Votes for Women*, 15 April 1910, p. 455)

Although Craig emphasized her impartiality, her activism is especially in evidence for both the WFL and the WSPU. Photographs
show Craig getting out of a car driven by Vera Holme and with
Emmeline Pankhurst, leader of the WSPU, in the passenger seat
(Rachlin 2011: xxx). In another photograph (see Fig. 2), Craig is
poised in a doorway ready to sell the militant WSPU newspaper
*Votes for Women*.

The street selling of newspapers for women's suffrage was
a highly visible and risky symbolic form of political activism.

**FIGURE 2** *Edith Craig selling* Votes for Women *newspaper, n.d. (repro-duced with permission of the V&A Theatre Collection).*

It featured in Evelyn Sharp's short story, 'Patrolling the Gutter' (1910). In this story, women acted as fearless pioneers, put on sandwich boards to advertise the women's suffrage movement and take their places in the gutter, off the pavement and therefore removing themselves from the potential charge of obstructing the highway. One of the women describes her sense of aliena-tion in theatrical terms: 'I feel like a pantomime super myself!' (p. 76). The trained bodies of the new suffrage army were also fundamentally theatricalized bodies. The narrative focalization provides an insight into the various motivations of the women involved, from the earnest and committed to the naive and patronising, emphasizing to the reader the compromising position that selling newspapers in the street posed: 'In time, no doubt, it would be possible to acquire the easy swagger of the real sandwich man' (p. 78). The specific activity of campaigning using this method dramatically situated the suffrage activists in the public sphere – the street – putting themselves in harm's way. Towards the end of the story, a nearby postman dismissively retorts: 'Votes for a few rich women, that's all you're after' (p. 82). This dilemma sums up the central problem facing the women's suffrage campaign.

Selling newspapers seemed to symbolize a declaration of solidarity and it was one which Edith Craig was proud to make. However from the perspective of the political campaign, the street selling of newspapers had an extra significance, casting a new light on Edith Craig's emphases in the interview of this form of activism. Kitty Marion was one of the most experienced newspaper sellers and, as Christine Woodworth has demonstrated, even Marion recalled in her autobiography the difficulties involved in this form of activism:

> What a great lesson in selfdenial, self abnegation, self-discipline. The first time, I took my place on the 'island' in Piccadilly Circus, near the flower sellers. I felt as if every eye that looked at me was a dagger piercing me through, and I wished the ground would open and swallow me. However, that feeling wore off and I developed into quite a champion paperseller. (quoted in Woodworth 2012: 83)

Woodworth notes that Marion's skills brought her notoriety in New York as she sold the *Birth Control Review* in Times Square, until she returned to England in 1930 to attend the unveiling of the statue of Emmeline Pankhurst (Woodworth 2012: 86, 88). Woodworth notes that Margaret Sanger appreciated Marion's suffragette training in newspaper selling:

> [...] selling *The Suffragette* on the streets of London had been part of the initiation which duchesses and countesses and other noble

auxiliaries to the Pankhurst cause had had to undergo. Kitty had stood side by side with them. Since we had so experienced a veteran ready for service we began to offer the [*Birth Control*] *Review* on the sidewalks of New York. (quoted in Woodworth 2012: 86)

Sanger understood that newspaper selling was effectively a suffragette initiation process to test the mettle of new recruits from a privileged background. This insight into the training of new recruits casts a new light on Edith Craig's public revelations about her enthusiasm for newspaper selling therefore signalling her rite of passage. In a sense, she was making a formal, public declaration that she had passed the test. That test was staged outside the notorious Eustace Miles Vegetarian Restaurant.

Women's suffrage activists therefore risked physical assault, humiliation and ridicule from their opponents. Hostile responses sometimes came from unexpected directions including supposed supporters. Rebecca West began her review of Craig's production with the Pioneer Players of Florence Edgar Hobson's play *A Modern Crusader* in the most outspoken way: 'I have not the least idea why a play concerned with the troubles of a vegetarian doctor who is in love with a butcher's daughter should be funny. But it is so.' (*Freewoman*, 1912, p. 8). She claimed that the poor quality of the play provided ammunition for the anti-suffrage lobby: 'I am inclined to agree with the Anti-Suffragists in their opinion that "there are some things which can safely be left to the men"' (*Freewoman*, 1912, p. 8). West also objected to the melodramatic aspects of the play and what she regarded as the ridiculous plot and characterization, largely based on her scornful attitude towards vegetarianism: 'I have never seen anything so mournfully comic as the second act, laid in the butcher's shop, with the refined heroine visibly wilting among the joints' (*Freewoman*, 1912, p. 8). When briefly noting the published edition of the play, the *Athenaeum* reiterated West's interpretation; the play was described as 'more pamphlet than drama, but might perhaps be performed with effect to promote a health campaign in villages. The sophisticated town-dweller would be apt to take the scene in a butcher's shop rather as farce than as drama' (*Athenaeum*, 18 May 1912, p. 575). The didactic potential of the play is taken for granted but the vegetarian critique is dismissed as unsophisticated.

West failed to acknowledge the relevance of vegetarianism *as a political position* and sees the play operating only within the frame of reference of realism or naturalism. The terms on which 'ordinary life' was lived were being questioned. As Laura E. Nym Mayhall has noted in *The Militant Suffrage Movement* (2003):

> Suffragettes did not merely stage their exclusion from the constitution: they also repudiated the authority of the law. Rooting their rejection of the law's authority in the principle that 'government without the consent of the governed is tyranny', they claimed the right to withhold consent until they received representation in Parliament. (Mayhall 2003: 59)

In the very spectacular acts of hunger striking and forcible feeding, the suffragette and the repressive forces of the State came into conflict. Lady Constance Lytton famously wrote about her own experiences in prison, especially as a vegetarian, in *Prisons and Prisoners* (1914). In 1910 on release from Walton Gaol, she and her brother Lord Lytton wrote to the Home Office about her treatment and prison conditions generally. It was the prison staff and doctors who came to be represented as torturers. By 1913 new legislation was introduced (more swiftly than the extension of the franchise) to prevent the martyrdom of death in custody: the Prisoners (Temporary Discharge for Ill-Health) Act, known familiarly as the Cat and Mouse Act and depicted in a famous poster symbolizing the predatory process and its fundamentally carnivorous ideology.[30]

In the year 1912 women's suffrage activists regarded Asquith's failure to support their campaign as highly provocative and it saw a rise in militant suffrage activity, with window smashing and arson. This was the fifth year of very active theatre work (writing and production of plays) to promote women's suffrage and additional plays to raise funds for organizations that they supported. Hobson's play was staged at the King's Hall on 30 April 1912 to raise funds for the National Food Reform Association (NFRA), formed in 1908 with Eustace Miles (the owner of the famous vegetarian restaurant) in the chair for the meeting. The NFRA aimed to educate and lobby for reform of institutional catering in prisons and hospitals and publicize the connections between diet, social reform and economics. This seems to have had a suffrage context given that Lady

Constance Lytton's brother was Chairman of the organization. NFRA Vice Presidents included Beatrice Webb, Charlotte Despard (president of the WFL), and Gilbert Murray. Leah Leneman (1997) has established the extent of the popularity of vegetarianism in the women's suffrage movement and examined the ideological points of connection between vegetarianism and women's suffrage. She interprets the emotional and aesthetic arrangement of the scene in *A Modern Crusader* when the protagonist Josephine is in her father's butcher's shop, revolted by the carcases on display and horrified by the squeal of pigs in the slaughter house off-stage as 'melodramatic' and an 'identification of women as victims with animals as victims' (Leneman 1997: 279).

The play powerfully depicted the oppression of women and animals, drawing its strength in some scenes from a modernist mode of representation and treatment of emotion. It also endorsed the political dimensions of vegetarianism and feminism by staging the *feeling for* animals as well as the violent feelings *about* women which underwrote the anti-suffrage movement and the state's torture of women by forcible feeing in the prewar period. It is the way in which this play appeals to the audience's feelings about others (principally animals) that its political significance lies. Implying perhaps a sensational performance designed to elicit an emotional response, Leah Leneman describes as melodramatic a scene in which Josephine is alone in the shop on a windy night, with the joints and carcasses swaying. According to the stage directions a pig starts to 'sway back and forth in a sort of rhythmic motion':

> As it sways its head comes fairly near to Josephine, who stares at it in horrible fascination, her eyes becoming fixed in terror. At last she can bear it no longer; rises slowly like one in a dream, keeping her eyes fixed on the pig as if under a spell, reaches out mechanically and takes down Freddy's apron, hanging on door, walks with it towards pig, holds it up to cover up the pig, when, just as she has raised her arms, holding the apron, still staring at pig, a horrible squeal is heard from slaughter-house of a dying pig, and with a piercing shriek Josephine falls fainting to the floor. (Hobson 1912: 41)

The description of Josephine's fear and her movements ('like one in a dream' and 'as if under a spell', 'mechanically') in their dehumanizing effects, convey the unconscious at work. This is a difficult matter and associated with great risk in the political context in which women as political agents were disempowered as irrational by anti-suffragists.

The scene in the butcher's shop, mocked by Rebecca West, dramatizes the deeply embedded values driving Josephine. Her vegetarianism is most definitely not a fad; it defines her at a profound level and is connected with her world view. Appropriately subtitled a 'pamphlet', the play is full of political dialogue,[31] notably the speeches of Dr Lawson:

> It's not only a question of food: there are lots of other things besides; it's understanding what it means to lead a healthy life altogether – it's the whole field of hygiene and preventive measures. To being with, we want a Minister of Public Health with wide powers and a seat in the Cabinet. This would impress people with the importance of physical health as the basis of a civilised society. (p. 55)

Although the play appears to be about vegetarianism, beginning with Josephine reading Upton Sinclair's *The Jungle* (1906) to Mrs Barrington, it is about 'food reform' as imagined within a system of social reforms including education, housing and health. It is the holistic perspective presented by Florence Edgar Hobson in the play and in her work more generally that Rebecca West rejected,[32] but which Edith Craig and the Pioneer Players embraced.

# CHAPTER FIVE
## 1911–25

# The Pioneer Players as London's art theatre

Edith Craig founded a theatre society called the Pioneer Players which gave three plays for its first matinee for members on 8 May 1911 at the Kingsway Theatre, London, firmly locating the society in the context of women's suffrage and significantly highlighted the history and expertise of female performers. In Christopher St John's play *The First Actress*, Margaret Hughes is seen struggling to fight prejudices about female performers when she becomes the first actress on the English stage after the Restoration.[1] Hughes is given inspiration and encouragement by a vision of actresses of the future, in a metatheatrical scene in which numerous well-known performers of 1911 (including Ellen Terry as Nell Gwynn) appeared as great actresses from history in Hughes's dream vision. Terry was, as ever, willing to support her daughter's theatrical endeavours and described the production positively although in this private correspondence to her stalwart friend Elizabeth Rumball she revealed a surprising vulnerability about her own performance: 'Edy's affair went off all right for the Pioneers – I had only a dozen lines to say & was nervous' (17 May 1911; *CLET* 5: 1636). This private confession emphasizes the difficulties facing even those who appeared to have secured some position of power. Terry was a valuable role model for readers of *The Freewoman* and the newly formed Pioneer Players, which had ambitions to lead London theatrical innovation and subsequently had an international outlook.

With Ellen Terry as its President and a distinguished group of individuals in its Advisory Committee, the Pioneer Players became London's alternative to the much larger Stage Society which had been founded twelve years earlier. The Stage Society's first production on 26 November 1899 had been George Bernard Shaw's *You Never Can Tell*.[2] Edith Craig was acknowledged in the official records of the Stage Society in her capacity as costumier but the extent of her influence is not clear. The Stage Society was able to pay a maximum of three guineas for the three weeks' work associated with each production, becoming a training ground for professional actors and facilitated by income from subscriptions drawn from membership which increased from 300 in its first year to over 1,000 in its sixth year (Woodfield 1984: 61, 65). By contrast the Pioneer Players remained smaller, with 200–300 members annually, and it supported actors and authors in principle.[3] The Pioneer Players' guide 'To Authors' made it clear that no fees were payable to authors but the author was permitted to suggest casting and attend rehearsals on the understanding that decision-making rested with the casting committee and control of rehearsal was solely with the producer. These regulations also implied the Pioneer Players' expectation of global reach and consequent benefits which they were determined to protect.[4] These ambitions were probably influenced by the success of plays such as *How the Vote Was Won*.

Broadly the Pioneer Players' prewar productions focused on women's suffrage and politically orientated drama, and from 1915 the society produced plays often translated into English, bringing to London the innovative and experimental from overseas. Other productions demonstrated the Pioneer Players' interest in specifically transatlantic dialogues, a context which even frames Ellen Terry's Shakespeare lecture that had been performed in United States in 1910.[5] At that time she had issued a press release to distance her North American lecture tour from the international women's suffrage campaign:

> Although it is true that my name is registered [illeg.] amongst the names [illeg.] of those <actresses> who are in favour of women not being excluded from voting; my forthcoming Lecture tour in the States & in Canada has no connection whatever with the subject or object of Women's Suffrage, & I am anxious to deny

at once myself the statement that it has –.(4 August 1910; *CLET* 5: 1599)

Ellen Terry's correspondence has revealed that her difficult financial circumstances had forced her on this international tour. Given the motivation for that tour, this unusually forthright statement is therefore evidence that Terry was keen to maximize her potential sales and therefore could not afford to alienate either anti-suffrage or politically neutral audience members. Such economic motives did not inform her performance of the lecture for the Pioneer Players and the women's suffrage context of the lecture was most certainly brought to the fore. Apparently on home ground, although Terry was still married to an American, her lecture on Shakespeare's triumphant women at the Garrick Theatre, London was followed by a reception for the membership.

In *Women and Theatre in the Age of Suffrage: The Pioneer Players 1911–25* (2001), I have argued that the Pioneer Players was primarily a play-producing subscription society, did not operate as a theatre company or a women's theatre, differed from political organizations such as the WFL, NUWSS (National Union of Women's Suffrage Societies) or WSPU. It aimed to produce 'the play of ideas' as well as supporting relevant fund-raising causes but from the turning point of 1915 it prioritized international art theatre and the production of plays in translation. Several representative Pioneer Players' productions relating to women's suffrage, the political campaign with which they were closely connected, have already been discussed in Chapter Four and elsewhere. This chapter will therefore examine some new insights into Edith Craig's work with the Pioneer Players in relation to her brother's journal *The Mask* (1908–29) and after the outbreak of the First World War (when the society was rebranding itself as an art theatre). Craig's innovative productions were drawn from Russia but also from Japan, Spain, Italy, France and North America. Dance and costume became significant aspects of the cultural engagement of the Pioneer Players' brand of 'art'. As Edith Craig committed herself to the work of London's art theatre in the Pioneer Players, her brother was actively producing *The Mask*, in which he featured the Russian Ballet but appeared studiously to avoid his sister's work with the Pioneer Players.

Gordon Craig's publication of an article about the Russian Ballet is particularly relevant for an understanding of the cultural impact of the female dancing body as highly controversial, provocative and powerful. The publication by the President of the Pioneer Players of *The Russian Ballet* (1913) seemed to position the society in relation to the latest in innovative performance internationally and the entire Terry family with Russia. In 1918 J. T. Grein's London production of Oscar Wilde's *Salome* became embroiled in the notorious scandal, litigation and wartime fears about national security centring on individuals in a position of power whose behaviour placed them vulnerable to blackmail. Grein's Salome, Maud Allan, became the lightening conductor in this furore when Grein financed the joint action against the libel that threatened her reputation and his production and has become known as the Pemberton Billing case.[6] Although this sensational court case is well known, less familiar is the theatrical fallout of this scandal. This was considerable and it had repercussions for Edith Craig and the Pioneer Players. Thirty years earlier, in 1891, Grein had promoted the Independent Theatre's production of *Ghosts* at the Royalty Theatre, the first production of Ibsen in Britain. In some quarters Grein had probably never been forgiven.

A new perspective has emerged on the demise of the Pioneer Players, hitherto regarded as a matter of regret and dispossession for Craig. If Craig's own career plans had gone smoothly, they would have taken her out of the country and consequently compromised her ability to organize and direct plays for the Pioneer Players at all.[7] These plans were devastatingly affected by the fate of J. T. Grein in the cultural retrial of Wilde through the treatment of those involved in staging his play, *Salome*, in 1918. But this debacle was also followed by an unrelated and highly publicized, tragic drugs scandal, which blighted the end of war celebrations in London, attracted sensational press coverage and also indirectly threatened the reputation of Edith Craig and those involved with the Pioneer Players. The details of the unfortunate events seem to have followed the plot of the play *Ellen Young*, a Pioneer Players' production in 1916 only two years earlier.[8] By this point, Edith Craig (like her mother venturing across the Atlantic with her Shakespeare lectures in 1910) could not afford the potential career damage that an association with scandal might bring.

The figure of the female dancer, whose innovative choreography is complemented, if not even inspired by, experiments with sex and drugs became something of a cliché in this period as well as embodied by specific historical figures. Meggie Albanesi (1899– 1923), whose career had been launched by her performance in 1917 in *The Rising Sun* for the Pioneer Players, died in tragic circumstances in 1923.[9] Isadora Duncan, one of the leaders of experimental dance, was personally involved with Edith Craig's family and in correspondence with Ellen Terry about her grandchild. Edith Craig's brother was the father of Duncan's daughter, Deirdre (1906– 13), who died in a tragic car accident in 1913. Other professional dancers linked more closely to the work of the Pioneer Players by their performances in productions included Ethel Levey (1880– 1955) and Margaret Morris (1891–1980).[10] As Tiziana Morosetti (2016) argues, theatrical performances in Britain in the long nineteenth century constructed a range of bodies as 'exotic' or fascinating in various ways. The dancing woman was a central protagonist and an active participant in the organization of the Pioneer Players' work and an apparently peripheral feature of the society's cultural circle, evidenced in the costume balls they organized and even the advertisements in their play programmes.[11]

## The Pioneer Players and 'The fellow of the Royal Society of Literature'

The Pioneer Players theatre society had a management structure involving an elected Advisory Committee, in 1918–19 renamed as the Council. Subscription fees allowed for patrons and charged lower rates to acting members. This is one of the signs that its institutional structure was embedded in knowledge of theatre practice and acknowledged the conflicts at work in expecting professional actors to work on a voluntary basis, learning their lines and attending rehearsals for what was to be a one-off experimental and controversial production. The motivation was, of course, the chance for actors to demonstrate their acting abilities and inspire the managers and directors in the audience to cast them in a commercial production. The Advisory Committee included Charlotte Shaw (Mrs Bernard Shaw) for the years 1911–13. New insights into the Shaws's involvement in the Pioneer Players – how they came to be invited and their responses – are provided by letters to Edith Craig in the Ellen Terry archive (THM 384) at the V&A. Consequently a new way of understanding the comparison between the Pioneer Players and the Stage Society has emerged. It has been the Stage Society, rather than the Pioneer Players and Edith Craig, that has been associated with the drama of George Bernard Shaw. However, the Pioneer Players promoted Shaw's drama during the period when his political views were creating the most controversy. Craig's support of Shaw's plays was sustained later in her career in the interwar years.

The Pioneer Players' reputation and profile as understood by contemporaries has been established by examination of evidence from newspaper reviews, references in published autobiographies of those involved and in unpublished correspondence and the author's interview with a performer who appeared in the first production in 1911, notably providing an illuminating comparison between the Pioneer Players and the Stage Society. The new archival material that has now emerged provides George Bernard Shaw's interpretation of the Pioneer Players. In February 1911 George Bernard Shaw responded to Edith Craig's invitation to support the Pioneer Players. He was clearly interested but confused about the identity of the organization in relation to the earlier Pioneers society,[12] and reveals his cautious approach to subscriptions by proposing anonymity:

> Who the blinkety jink are The Pioneers? Are they your crowd, or are they the imitation Stage Society that called themselves by that name a year or two ago?
>
> On the whole, I think if you feel bound to go through any solemnities on the subject of the fee, I had rather you did not put it in the form of a donation from me to any of those societies, because each of them will write to me every year for the rest of my life reminding me that I gave them a donation and inviting me to renew it. Also, they will be asking me to lecture. Therefore, if you insist on the donation, put it as coming from the Pioneer Players or from yourself, or from A Constant Subscriber, or anybody else you like except
>
> Yours ever
>
> G. Bernard Shaw.
>
> PS. Judy has explained what The Pioneers are. (8 February 1911 at 2 Adelphi Terrace House; THM 384/9/4)

It is noteworthy that Shaw distinguishes the Pioneer Players from the earlier organization which he characterizes as 'an imitation Stage Society'. In doing so he challenges Craig to explain how the Pioneer Players was to avoid the perception of 'imitation' and establish itself with a unique identity. Shaw's involvement with the Pioneer Players was to extend beyond the use of his prestigious name in their official records and his very welcome and much-needed financial donation. In the event Edith Craig directed three of his plays for the society as well as *The Patience of the Sea*, a play modelled on Shaw, by Norreys Connell (Conal O'Riordan). The correspondence between Craig, the Pioneer Players and Shaw demonstrates the extensive involvement of Shaw in the casting of his plays for production by the Pioneer Players. Notes about casting the Pioneer Player's production of *Mrs Warren's Profession*, a play he advised against performing given the previous problems with the Lord Chamberlain, provide evidence of ideas being contributed not only by Shaw, but also by Edith Craig, and unnamed others, presumably from the committee. Shaw favoured casting Ellen O'Malley (who performed Vivie) as 'far the best, though not English enough' but was less keen on Mary Jerrold, 'not full blooded enough', or Nina Boucicault, 'not young enough'.[13]

Shaw seems to have been ambivalent about Edith Craig's production of *Mrs Warren's Profession*. In correspondence with Edith Craig, Shaw claimed provocatively that she only wanted *Mrs Warren's Profession* because someone else was going to produce it (23 February 1913; THM 384/9/5). He questioned the quality of the actors and difficulties with unlicensed plays. The production of *Mrs Warren's Profession* on 16 June 1912 at King's Hall, Covent Garden, came at a time when the Pioneer Players' planned production of Herman Heijermans's *The Good Hope*, a play that had been a reliable feature in Ellen Terry's touring repertoire, had had to be postponed because of Terry's ill-health. Shaw took the trouble to inquire about the proceeds from the production of his play and insisted that they should not go to the Pioneer Players:

17 July 1913 Why the Pioneers? They are not a suffragist body: technically, you might as well give it to Tree. I propose £1-1-0 to the AFL, and £1-1-0 to the Victoria St Society (Mrs Fawcett's), as they produced the play originally, and still consider it their property as far as it is anybody's but mine; but in any

case the money must go either to a suffragist body or to the poor starving author. GBS. (THM 384/9/6)

Following the success of the Pioneer Players' production of *Mrs Warren's Profession*, and endeavouring to develop all opportunities, Craig approached Shaw to become a patron of the society; this was an invitation he initially refused but then relented:

10 Jan 1913 GBS

I never patronize anything. It is the only way to escape patronizing everything. I have had half a dozen invitations to dress myself up and be a patron this year already. Only by refusing everybody impartially on the ground that I never do it can I avoid having to do it every night of my life.

Forgive a wretched victim of his own immoderate [?] vogue. GBS (THM 384/9/6)

Craig was persistent. In a brief note on a compliments slip, Shaw wrote to her on 28 July 1913, capturing his jocular begrudgingness to pay the subscription and performing the bullied victim as if an 'honble friend' on the same side in a heated parliamentary debate: 'very well, very well, very well. Maynt a man speak? How was I to know? Give it to whom you please, and don't bully your honble friend & well wisher' (THM 384/9/6). Through the Pioneer Players' secretary, Craig confirmed receipt of his postal order but crucially described the work of the Pioneer Players in *political* terms: 'Thank you very much for your Postal Order, value £1-1s (one guinea), which Miss Craig has handed to us. She asks me to say that it will be very useful to us in helping on our Propaganda Work. Yours truly, Secretary' (28 July 1913; THM 384/9/6). In reference to the purpose of the donation to the Pioneer Players, the highly significant term 'propaganda' is used. In the period during which the Pioneer Players was being formed, propaganda plays were advertised as a major feature in the headed notepaper Craig used following her work with women's suffrage drama and the productions of Cicely Hamilton's *A Pageant of Great Women*.

Charlotte Shaw's involvement with the Pioneer Players was invited from the earliest days of the society's development. Three letters from Edith Craig to Charlotte Shaw have survived. On 20

December 1910 Charlotte Shaw was invited to join the advisory committee and again on 18 December 1912 with a circular letter to members inviting contributions for a present for Miss Nordon the secretary for her voluntary work on *The Good Hope*. This correspondence seems to have prompted Charlotte Shaw to offer her resignation as Craig responded on 19 March [1913?] asking her to continue with her membership but to attend only when she was able to do so. In the event, therefore, Charlotte Shaw's involvement with the Pioneer Players' management was rather short-lived and seems to have reflected the low priority she placed on active engagement with the organization. She gave as an explanation, her difficulties in travelling to the city from her Hertfordshire residence (THM 384/9/3). However, travelling proved no obstacle to her husband when the Pioneer Players produced his plays.

## *Mrs Warren's Profession*, transatlantic brothel drama and the women's suffrage campaign

Edith Craig's production for the Pioneer Players of Shaw's *Mrs Warren's Profession* would have made sense to the membership as part of a series of plays that Craig had directed for the Pioneer Players concerning prostitution in the context of the women's suffrage campaign.[14] Debates about prostitution had changed significantly since Shaw's play had been shown to the Stage Society audience in 1891. As Lucy Bland (1995; 2002, 2nd ed.) has shown, the rights of women and the wrongs of men in the matter of prostitution and sexually transmitted diseases were suitably summarized in the provocative slogan of the WSPU, 'votes for women and chastity for men' and in their cartoon showing a female St George fighting 'the beast'.[15] The logic of the political arguments which supported the introduction of the Contagious Diseases Act and Amendments (1864–9) assuming that the female body must be controlled in order to prevent the spread of disease rather than any intervention in the business of prostitution itself was fundamentally rejected by the Pioneer Players.[16] Shaw's play had become highly relevant for the women's suffrage arguments about women's rights and the exploitation of women in prostitution. New research on 'brothel drama' in America in this period demonstrates that the Pioneer Players' approach to the dramatization of prostitution, and the 'white slave trade' in 1912–14 was a transatlantic phenomenon. Katie N. Johnson (2006) has established how the debates about dramatizations of prostitution were linked to other concerns about female performers and the display (imagined or actual) of parts of the body such that the panic centring on brothel drama and prostitution seems to have coalesced around the autonomy of the female performer herself. Olga Nethersole's performance in a transparent costume in Clyde Fitch's *Sapho* in 1900 had led to the closure of the theatre and an obscenity trial, a furore about which Ellen Terry became aware at that time, while she was in Canada; she wrote to her friend the American drama critic William Winter, alluding to his own review of *Sapho* and concluding: 'The outrageous Plays will soon keep all decent people away from The Theatre' (5 March 1900; *CLET* 4: 1076). Terry's observation was astute. The novelty factor was an issue but what became, over the next decade, a political agenda was the female body as a site of contested meanings. The exploitation of a displayed female performing body and the challenge posed by female performers themselves led to the development of an aesthetic of explicit bodily performance. This coincided with other debates about the female body as a knowable phenomenon rather than a mysterious vessel; for with such knowledge women might gain power over the deadly infections that were part of a silent battle exposed in militant suffrage debates in 1912–13. Edith Craig's staging of plays in this period engaged with the force of these cultural shifts.

At a rally on 12 October 1913 to draw attention to the position of women, Nethersole referred both to her own experience as a performer in *Sapho* and announced the forthcoming attendance of British militant women's suffrage leader Emmeline Pankhurst the following week at George Scarborough's play *The Lure* (Johnson 2006: 132). Johnson notes that oddly the 'white slave could only signify sexual purity' and the costumes of the prostitutes in *The Lure* did not depict nudity (Johnson 2006: 129). This furore was engaging female performers in the debates about staging female sexual autonomy as well as the topic of exploitation. One of the American authors working on this topic, not mentioned by Johnson, was Reginald Wright Kauffman. One of his novels on the subject namely *The Daughters of Ishmael* (1911) was dramatized by the Pioneer Players and produced in London in this period of acute attention to the political implications of prostitution. Kauffman published widely on prostitution and the white slave trade.[17] In January 1914 in New York, Cecily Spooner had staged *The House of Bondage* (according to the reviewer, known as *The Daughters of Ishmael* in England) and was arrested and charged with producing an immoral play (*The New Zealand Observer*, 7 February 1914, p. 22). Less than one month later, on 1 March 1914, the Pioneer Players staged an adaptation of the novel for their membership at the King's Hall. In doing so, the Pioneer Players followed the WSPU in foregrounding the double standard embedded in the treatment of prostitutes and highlighted in the sensational court case of a brothel manager, Queenie Gerald, in July 1913 and kept the topic in the public eye. In August 1914 Keir Hardie asked a question in the House of Commons about the apparent cover-up of the identities of the men involved, rumoured to have included cabinet ministers.[18] So the Pioneer Players' series of plays about prostitution, including *Mrs Warren's Profession*, was linked to a very specific *transatlantic* campaign about women's rights and fuelled debates resulting in questions in the House of Commons. The Pioneer Players were certainly not deterred by the threat of the Lord Chamberlain (as warned by Shaw) or the intervention of the police (as had occurred in New York).

## The Man of Destiny

The Pioneer Players usually staged a play for a single performance but many of these plays made an impact and occasionally they had a fund-raising function, as mentioned in Chapter Four. The Pioneer Players' production of George Bernard Shaw's *The Man of Destiny* in 1912 at the Savoy Theatre raised funds for the International Suffrage Shop (ISS).[19] Edith Craig had been planning this from March the previous year, at which point she sought permission from the author:

Dear Mr Shaw
I am very much interested in the International Suffrage Shop which is going to open premises in Adam Street. I am getting up

a Matinee for its benefit and want to know if I can possibly get permission to do 'The Man of Destiny'. Have you still the rights, or have I to apply for them elsewhere? In any case, could you say with an easy conscience that you would not mind my doing it, even if I have to apply to Barker or Vedrenne or Margaret Halstan?

If there is no chance of my getting this play, can you suggest anything else by the same Author? (17 March 1911 from 31 Bedford St; THM 384/9/4)

Shaw's reply emphasized the value he quite properly placed on retaining rights as author over his writings and that this needed to be explained:

My dear Edy,

I always have my rights unless people steal them from me. The Man of Destiny is impossible: Margaret Halstan can do The Strange Lady; but the difficulty is to get a Napoleon. The play is a ghastly bore unless the two people are quite out-of-the-way interesting, fascinating, and clever.

I enclose a subscription for The Pioneer Players.

Far be it from me to suggest any play of mine. Why don't you stand by your own sex, and produce a play by a mere female? (17 March 1911; THM 384/9/4)

Shaw seems to highlight Edith Craig's naivety in asking about authors' rights and provocatively reminds her of the political importance at the present time of promoting female authors. His former difficulties with Henry Irving seem to inform the reference to casting that role and perhaps suggest that Craig may have been insensitive in asking for this particular play as it had been part of a fraught and protracted period of negotiation for Shaw represented by Craig's mother at the Lyceum Theatre.

Shaw wrote to Sime Seruya at the ISS, Adam St, Adelphi, W.C. on 26 January 1912:

Mr Winston Churchill is anxious, he says, to see The Man of Destiny. As it may be useful to have a Cabinet Minister at the performance, I recommend his case to your consideration.

I could not tell him anything about it, as I am quite in the dark as to where & when the performance is to take place – if at all. G. Bernard Shaw.[20]

Shaw's suggestion was likely to be ironic. Winston Churchill's attitude towards women's suffrage was antagonistic and, as Home Secretary, he had been responsible for encouraging the robust police response to suffrage demonstrators in Parliament Square on 18 November 1910 which escalated into violence, resulting in several deaths and its designation as 'Black Friday'. Shaw's play, *The Man of Destiny*, was given at the Savoy Theatre on 28 January 1912 together with *The Coronation* by Christopher St John and Charles Thursby, by the Pioneer Players theatre society in aid of Sime Seruya's ISS. For the occasion the Pioneer Players formed the Coronation Society to protest about the censorship of the stage.

*The Coronation* is set in 'a hall adjacent to the cathedral Church of St Stephan on the Coronation Day of Henricus XVI', the scene directions describing a vast and formal setting with officer and nobles in uniform and robes. Two features are significant in this scene: 'A shrine containing a statue of the Blessed Virgin. A State chair.' When the King enters the hall after the coronation, the stage directions indicate the respect he pays to the shrine: 'He pauses for a moment before the shrine of the Madonna' (p. 22). Craig's decisions relating to the staging of the 'shrine of the Madonna' are not made apparent in the published edition. However, the publication of an autobiography has revealed an unusual and controversial aspect of Craig's production which may well have influenced the decision to withhold the licence.

Kate Parry Frye (1878–1959), an actor and suffragist, recalled the experience of taking a minor role in *The Coronation* in her diaries, which spanned over seventy years. She had a non-speaking role as the Statue of the Madonna, not listed in the character list in the published text and redacted from the play programme. Frye's diaries, as the editor Elizabeth Crawford notes, are valuable for the insights they provide on the women's suffrage movement from the perspective of a 'suffrage foot soldier' (Crawford 2013: 15). The details Frye provides of Craig's production of *The Coronation* are illuminating. The running time of the play was thirty-seven minutes. Frye describes the redaction of her name from the programme, but does not explain that this was related to the regulation of the stage and the effective prohibition of representing certain figures on stage. Frye described the preparations for rehearsal and for her own position on stage Craig's precarious arrangement, using a roll of carpet and boxes, which made for a 'rickety throne' (Crawford 2013: 89). Frye describes the process of Craig personally getting her into her costume as well as the intricacies of the costume itself:

> At last I was ordered out – my cloak was on the stage, simply gorgeous, all gold – the front a mass of jewels and coloured pictures. Miss Craig had arranged my head piece and crown, only the veiling net was not forthcoming till night and then I had three crowns set one on top of each other and fastened together by jewel. I felt very fine, but the dress fascinated me most, the top, stockingette and the skirt blue green crepe which hung most beautifully. (Crawford 2013: 88)

The multi-part crown and the overlaying of stockingette over a blue-green crepe suggests that Craig was planning to exploit the lighting effects in picking out the colours and was paying a great deal of attention to this costume which might in another director's hands have been treated as part of the background scenery and represented by a wooden prop. As a prohibited depiction on the stage, the figure of Madonna was also being given the utmost respect in the way it was decorated. Given Craig's practice of repurposing and restyling costumes she had in stock, this may have been the cloak used for Justice in *A Pageant of Great Women*. An extant newspaper photograph of the scene shows a robed and a crowned figure at the back of the scene likely to be Frye.[21] The timing of the production, just over six months after the coronation of George V on 22 June 1911, caught the wave of expectation of success for the reading on 19 February 1912 of the compromise legislation that designated the third Conciliation Bill (Mayhall 2003: 104). On the second reading on 28 March 1912, it was defeated by only fourteen votes, creating a devastating disappointment and set in motion many different responses from suffragists, most memorably a period of intensified civil disobedience.

## Press Cuttings

Edith Craig directed George Bernard Shaw's *Press Cuttings* in various venues. Shaw was concerned that the proceeds went to women's suffrage and was prepared to insist on this with the most determined of suffrage campaigners. This raises doubts about Philip Graham's claim that 'Shaw was never deeply committed to the suffrage cause' (Graham 2013: 12). The correspondence, referring to 'propaganda' work, is substantiated by her headed notepaper in the period leading up to the founding of the Pioneer Players, which lists fifteen plays including George Bernard Shaw's *Press Cuttings*. This is the only play in the list for which any detail is given about potential venues: '(Town halls and schoolrooms)'.[22] Shaw wrote to Edith Craig on 15 October 1909 about *Press Cuttings* and her request for right to put it on in Bristol, Loughton and Epping: 'I thought you were already doing it in villages and such like places; and I suppose the difference between an Actresses League performance and the others is only nominal. The fees can go to the cause' (THM 384/9/1). In 1916, in response to an enquiry from the American author, (Anna) Alice Chapin (1880–1920), about rights to perform *Press Cuttings* in New York, Craig wrote to Shaw, describing her past involvement with that play as well as other women's suffrage plays:

> She wants to arrange some performances in aid of the Suffrage movement there. She wrote to me because I have handled the arrangements for similar performances by Suffrage societies in America and am agent for most of the English suffrage plays which they have asked for. (THM 384/9/7)

This puts a new slant on Edith Craig's involvement, described here as 'an agent' and handling 'arrangements'. This is an additional role to that of her directorial role. It also clarifies her international dealings for women's suffrage drama.[23]

*The Coronation* was published by the ISS, the activities of which were described in the preliminary pages of the edition:

> Besides its own publications the International Suffrage Shop has on sale other Feminist Literature, including also Anti-Suffrage writings and the publications of all Suffrage Societies.

The I.S.S. is entirely independent of all Suffrage organisations. Its aim is to supply a common meeting ground for all Feminists, and act as Information and International Bureau, and at the same time to bring the Woman's movement 'before the man in the street. (p. 93)

The close association between the ISS and the Pioneer Players emphasizes the international outlook of the theatre society and the feminist dimension to that internationalism. The Pioneer Players had effectively identified for its plays a publishing and marketing outlet with an international agenda and with Edith Craig as Honorary Managing Director, an agent for its plays with an international network.

George Bernard Shaw's play *The Man of Destiny* seems to have been an odd choice for the Pioneer Players' fund-raising production for the ISS and it was not available free of charge. Shaw emphasized his rights as author and pointed out the difficulties of casting it. However, his postscript makes a barbed political point, drawing Craig's attention to the contemporary concerns about supporting female authors, an agenda which the Pioneer Players might be presumed to pursue: 'Far be it from me to suggest any play of mine. Why don't you stand by your own sex, and produce a play by a mere female?' (17 March 1911; THM 384/9/4).

The place of *The Man of Destiny* in the programme seems anomalous but, alongside *The Coronation* by Christopher St John and Charles Thursby, it drew attention to the gendered aspects of government. The notion that however inviolable a male leader might appear to be, he was susceptible to the persuasive arguments of a woman was likely to have been an incendiary force in the women's suffrage campaign and fuelled their numerous comic plays, including Shaw's *Press Cuttings*. *The Man of Destiny* shows Napoleon is subject to emotional influence and in *The Coronation* the new king is influenced by a woman petitioning him on behalf of the poor. Edith Craig had been part of the mass symbolic petitioning of the new king by designing part of the women's suffrage coronation procession in 1911. She had also become associated, with Cicely Hamilton and Christopher St John, with a virile, revolutionary aesthetic drawn from a composite of masculine historical costume, with tricorne hat and cloak, the floppy bow tie of Rosa Bonheur. Since Edith Craig's repertoire of nicknames included Boney after Napoleon as well as 'Matka', the Russian for mother,

her interactions with those closest to her signalled the international revolutionary context in which she imagined herself as a leader.

The response to the outbreak of war brought the Pioneer Players in sympathy with George Bernard Shaw at a time when his views were publicly condemned. In 1917, the year of the revolution in Russia, the production of his play *The Inca of Perusalem* was promoted by the Pioneer Players as if by an anonymous author, 'A fellow of the Royal Society of Literature', a joke which Shaw himself encouraged. Again he was heavily involved in casting, as his correspondence with Christopher St John demonstrates.[24] He expressed his gratitude for the production which persuaded him to cut some lines from the play in order to improve it:

> The lines got rather mangled on Sunday; but I think we were jolly lucky to get through so well: don't you? The performance was very useful to me. I have just cut out a speech of eleven lines which was all wrong and never ought to have been there. (19 December 1917; THM 384/9/4)

The significance of the Pioneer Players' interest in Shaw's drama at this time is therefore considerable although he omitted any reference to them in his account of the period.[25] His political response to the First World War brought him many enemies but Edith Craig and the Pioneer Players were predisposed to embracing the controversial and the stance of the Pioneer Players in relation to the First World War was a critical one. However, the Pioneer Players was also capable of perversely staging a play that refused to take sides on the topic of the Easter Rising in 1916, so a liberal embrace of diverse views could provoke controversy (Cockin 2001: 149). As I have discussed elsewhere, the Pioneer Players' first wartime annual report used aesthetic terms to describe the impact on cultural life in what had become a 'khaki-clad and khaki-minded world' (Cockin 2015). It was as if a militaristic wash had been painted over the fabric of daily life, colouring all possible perspectives and rendering every imaginative landscape uniform.

## *The Mask* and the theatre today

At a time when the Pioneer Players was providing Edith Craig with the opportunity to develop her work as a director for a London audience, her brother Edward Gordon Craig was using his journal *The Mask* to generate an international debate about the quality and direction of theatre. Gordon Craig and Edith Craig held extremely opposing views on the issue of women's enfranchisement, and an understanding of this conflict provides an illuminating context for reading *The Mask* in the period 1911–14. As Olga Taxidou has demonstrated, Gordon Craig used numerous pseudonyms in *The Mask* to disguise his authorship of many of the articles (Taxidou 1998). In November 1908 Ellen Terry wrote to her daughter suggesting that she respond to her brother in *The Mask*: 'Have you read Ted's article in The Mask? Very clever only he shd not then produce any Play!! – Why don't you (if you have time) answer him in the Mask?' (26 [November 1908]; *CLET* 5: 1547). Terry was presumably referring to Gordon Craig's recent article on realism and the actor; he had written to his mother in provocative terms, asking her to take a public stance on the topic. Instead, Terry delegated responsibility to her daughter to take on this challenge, encouraging her children to engage in what would have been a most fascinating public debate about the future of the theatre. Edith Craig had published an article titled 'Producing a Play' in *Munsey's Magazine* the year before Gordon Craig launched *The Mask* (June 1907, pp. 311–14) which provided numerous details about the practical aspects of theatrical production. By contrast, Terry notes the logical consequences of her son's argument as well as appreciating its sophistication. The challenge, as ever, was to achieve aesthetic excellence with the available resources and neither Terry nor her daughter regarded art as a simple reflection of reality and, typically, this is apparent from their deep understanding of stage costume. It was crucial, for instance, to know when planning a theatrical production, as Terry did, with regard to choice of colour for costume on stage that 'purple is brown' (26 [November 1908] *CLET* 5: 1547) and she could be confident that her daughter understood this too. Although Edith Craig was prepared for a fight in the women's suffrage campaign, to the extent that she undertook and passed the test of street newspaper selling, she was not going to take on her younger brother in a public spat expressed in the form of published articles.

*The Mask* launched a debate about the state of contemporary theatre in 'The Position of the Theatre. A Symposium', an attack on the criticisms levelled at *The Mask* in *The Referee*. The attack takes the form of a survey issued to named representatives in the theatre

(*The Mask*, 1911, pp. 124–32) with the following six questions being circulated:

1. Do you believe that the standard in theatrical work has risen since the days of Henry Irving?
2. Can you name any manager who has added more distinction to the stage since those days?
3. Have Sir Herbert Tree and Mr George Edwardes raised the Theatre in any way?
4. If so, could you say exactly in what way?
5. Do you think the Theatre never has aspired to a position among the fine arts and never can aspire to such a position?
6. Do you consider The Mask does wrong in asking everything of the Theatre as a Public Institution and as a Fine Art? (p. 126)

Gordon Craig's calibration is graded from the depths of Sir Herbert Beerbohm Tree and George Edwardes to the heights of Sir Henry Irving. As a questionnaire it presents itself as inviting free responses but it is explicitly partisan thus leading respondents to a particular range of answers. Gordon Craig also uses his pseudonyms to enable him to provide two of the eight published responses.

There were eight responses to the editor who supposedly issued the survey named as 'J.S.' [John Semar/Edward Gordon Craig] published in *The Mask*, from Sir Arthur Pinero, Ellen Terry, Martin Harvey, Gordon Craig, Walter Crane, Christopher St John, George Calderon and Allen Carric [Edward Gordon Craig]. It is noteworthy that in answer to question number two regarding any 'manager' of distinction, none of the published responses named Edith Craig. Walter Crane, who knew of Edith Craig's work from the days of The Masquers, replied 'Certainly not.' Even Christopher St John apparently answered negatively to the first five questions and concluded, with question number six, 'The Mask does right as usual.' Gordon Craig's use of the term 'manager' in question number two is somewhat misleading. His own ideas for staging were associated with the role of the producer but subsequently came to be described as the director but this in this period 'manager' could designate the organizer or backer of a theatre. The individuals named, all men, were actor-managers. On this basis Christopher St John answered the question in good faith. But it comes across as distinctly disloyal since she does not name Edith Craig.

The choice of a survey by *The Mask* seems to be an unusual technique to have adopted but it had been used recently on the topic of women's suffrage.[26] It seems clear that Gordon Craig was responding not only to the women's suffrage campaign but also to his sister's involvement with the Pioneer Players when *The Mask* published a number of articles, such as John Semar's 'A Word About Schopenhauer and the Feminist Movement' and Schopenhauer's notorious misogynistic 'On Woman: An Essay' (1914). Schopenhauer claimed that 'women's reasoning powers are weaker', arguing for the failure to be objective, accomplish anything original in the field of fine arts and untrustworthy with inheritances on the grounds of inherent vanity. *The Mask* also published a gleeful notice about the involvement of Lucy Terry Lewis,[27] Gordon Craig's cousin, in the women's anti-suffrage league. Edith Craig is the unnamed referent in the coy remark concerning the inference that Ellen Terry's commitment to women's suffrage was superficial: 'Miss Ellen Terry is supposed to be a keen suffragette but there are reasons why she is obliged actively to espouse the cause' (*The Mask*, 1911–12, p. 78).

There is one specific reference to his sister's activities with the Pioneer Players and this is indirect and serves to imply a lack of originality in her production of Hrotsvit's *Paphnutius* in January 1914. By way of an introduction to an essay on Anatole France's 'The Plays of Hroswitha', he mentioned that the Pioneer Players, under the management of Edith Craig, had recently *reminded* the public about the work of Hrotsvit. As Olga Taxidou has noted about a later essay in *The Mask*, originality 'acquires an almost metaphysical status' for Gordon Craig (Taxidou 1998: 65). In the autumn edition of *The Mask* (Vol. 4 No. 2, October 1911), Gordon Craig published what the reader takes to be transcripts of the accolades he received by means of letter and in person in speeches on the occasion of a dinner given in his honour on his return to England from Italy. He also included his own response, a short speech which positions himself in an 'English' and a 'European' art theatrical context. The appearance in print of Gordon Craig's self-promotion only five months after the inauguration of the Pioneer Players theatre society in London is particularly relevant for the purposes of my reassessment of Edith Craig's engagement with art theatre. Gordon Craig positions himself as in exile and neglected by an ungrateful nation but on a transnational mission, with the recent success of his designs for Stanislavsky's *Hamlet* for the Moscow Art Theatre.

> It is because of this fact that this dinner becomes one of the most significant honours which can be paid to a representative of the European Theatre…and it is as the English representative of the awakening European Theatre that I am here this evening. […] Art is not a national thing. It is far more than that. It is a religious thing. (*The Mask*, Vol. 4, No. 2, October 1911, pp. 94–5)

*The Mask* positions his supporters at this dinner as endorsing this account. Five years after his mother's jubilee production, Gordon Craig's dinner in honour of his return to England appears to solicit patronage whether individual or institutional. The construction of neglected and unemployable male genius contrasts with his sister's recent successes and prolific activity as a director. It is in this light that some of the contributions to *The Mask* which engage in misogynistic attacks on women generally and women in the theatre specifically will appear to make a different kind of sense in the sibling rivalry over definitions of the art theatre of the present and future.

## 'Kleptomania at the Russian Theatre': A manifesto against beads and bulges

In the same issue of *The Mask* in October 1911 in which Gordon Craig's great success with the Moscow Art Theatre production of *Hamlet* was foregrounded, he wrote pseudonymously as 'John Balance', an article entitled 'Kleptomania at the Russian Theatre'. Here he launched an attack on the Russian Ballet which is charged with 'artificiality' and 'a few tricks stolen from other lands and arts' (p. 98). The putative thefts were also from 'the only original dancer of the age, the American [Isadora Duncan], and another idea or two from the most advanced scene designers of Europe [Edward Gordon Craig]'. 'John Balance' condemned Bakst's costume designs for female performers who were presented as intoxicated and amenable to sexually provocative behaviour as a matter of routine:

Bakst is ugly on account of his clumsy sense of the sensual. All his women, (and he is never tired of putting them before the public,) are drugged and in a kind of sofa orgy. They seem to hate ecstacy [sic] and they adore a good wriggle. (*The Mask*, 4, 2, October 1911, p. 99)

The explicit body in Bakst's staging is exposed in a new way. 'John Balance' reacts to the *female* body, providing details in a banal list, itemizing the clothing that would otherwise have been customarily used by performers to conceal the body:

The costumes he [Bakst] puts them into are mute; they want to speak and cannot; they are the old refurbished wardrobe of the old Racinet and of Sarah Bernhardt, save that these two spoiled us often with stockings, underwear and sleeves, vests and pinafores.(*The Mask*, 4, 2, October 1911, p. 99)

The aesthetic mistakes perpetrated by Bakst are described by 'John Balance' in terms of applying specific ethnic features to bodies which are marked obliquely in orientalist terms:

Bakst has a passion for beads, and his evidently sincere devotion to thick lips and flat noses enables him to indulge in a ring or two now and again.[...] (*The Mask*, 4, 2, October 1911, p. 99)

'John Balance' makes casual reference to the aspects of nose and lips as if no further elaboration were needed; this is a short form intelligible to the implied reader. It is the hybrid cultural referents that trouble him about the Russian Ballet and these are coalesced in the body shape of the female performers:

The women he draws protrude therefore when he attempts to suggest something Indian or Chinese (and Russian Ballets are wedded to the East), he gets curiously confused. Indians and Chinese hate that which bulges. Bakst adores bulge...it helps his beads so much. In short Bakst is vulgar. He is like a decorator of the French match boxes on seeing these maidens of the French match box one is reminded of Bakst.(*The Mask*, 4, 2, October 1911, p. 99)

The inauthenticity visually evidenced by the *protruding* female performing body seems to imply a monstrous phallic woman with misplaced erections. This essay argued that the Russian Ballet lacked originality and was characterized by the vulgar costumes influenced by Bakst's love of the 'bulge' and draped beads.[28]

Although Gordon Craig, like Meyerhold, was concerned to reject 'the actor as flesh and blood' (Taxidou 1998: 164), it is clear that Bakst's pretentions to art are dismissed by Gordon Craig by means of an ideological move that relegates Bakst to commercial art; indeed Gordon Craig claims that Bakst's expertise would suit him to the decoration of the match box. In his attack on the Russian Ballet, the object of his critique is the female performing body in particular. His article in *The Mask* coincides with the context of Edith Craig's developing involvement with the politically incendiary staging of an autonomous female performing body. It is therefore highly relevant to note that the editorial position of Gordon Craig's magazine was to reject the involvement of women in the theatre: 'The Mask alone of all journals has said that woman is a danger to the theatre and that before the stage can lay claim once more to its art women will have to leave its boards' (p. 71). The phrase 'once more' alludes specifically to the turning point in theatre history when banishment of women from the stage had been enforced by Cromwell's Puritan government. Moreover, the return of women to the stage in the Restoration had only recently been celebrated by Christopher St John in her play *The First Actress*, one of the three plays staged by the Pioneer Players theatre society in London for its inaugural production in May 1911. As mentioned earlier in this chapter, Ellen Terry herself appeared in *The First Actress*. Although all of these details about his sister's production of *The First Actress* for the Pioneer Players' inaugural production are omitted from *The Mask*, it seems likely that Gordon Craig had them in mind in publishing these articles.

## *The Russian Ballet* to the rescue

The year 1912 was difficult for Ellen Terry and, consequently, for Edith Craig. Edward Gordon Craig's children had whooping cough and needed to be nursed. This became a problem which befell grandmother and aunt rather than the children's parents. In May and June 1912 Terry was discretely taking a rest cure and seems to have reached a point at which she could not function (ET-5,131; ET-Z2,277). Her marriage to James Carew was effectively over and her financial situation was again reaching crisis point, prompting a highly unusual publication project to emerge as a solution.

Edith Craig sent a telegram to Christopher St John, who was staying in Worcester, to ask her to write a 5,000 word article on 'dancers' for the following week (13 January 1913; ET-D2208). Christopher St John suggested that she wrote the text to Ellen Terry's *The Russian Ballet*, drawing on an earlier article on the same subject:

> Busy as you are, do try and help me about this bally [*sic*] article. I have long ago lost any impressions I had about the Russians – and I must say, but for the money, I never would have consented to undertake such a difficult job. If you can send my old ballet article I might get something out of it – but if Picky has a book on them I could perhaps glean something better from it. (Weds; ET-D2198)

The reference by St John to money is somewhat ambiguous. Ellen Terry needed the money urgently but St John was, as usual, carrying out the task of 'literary henchman' for the appropriate fee. In January 1913 St John asked Craig for her brother's article on the Russian Ballet from *The Mask* as she explained: 'I want your mother to quote it.' Her postscript, 'found very little of use in what you have sent – but thank you all the same', demonstrates some unease about the public reception of her ghosted article: 'The thing will be done all right – but no-one will think it's by Ellen Terry who knows her irresistible genius' (ET-D2199). In an undated letter she explains the difficulties in providing text which describes the accompanying illustrations. Such a process is not the usual procedure and 'besides as your mother is supposed to have written her sensations before she ever heard of the pics it surely wont be expected' (ET-D2200). Christopher St John's struggles with this piece of writing highlight the lack of input she had at the outset in the choice of the topic. This raises a question about exactly why the Russian Ballet had been selected as a topic and by whom.

In 1913, Sidgwick & Jackson published it in England on 8 or 9 February in a book form (with a more expensive special edition) but the sales were not high; the American rights were then sold to McClure to publish Ellen Terry's *The Russian Ballet* in *McClure's Magazine*. When it is suggested by Mr McClure that the article has already been published in United States, this was rejected. The protest needs to be considered in the context of the circumstances six years earlier when McClure's were indeed sold material by Terry which was not original. Hughes Massie & Co. responded with reassurance that the query was simply concerning possible pirating of the article (ET-D2191, 14 March 1913). There were strict deadlines for submission of book and illustrations and Ellen Terry's annotation to one letter suggests that at least she was taking the matter seriously and was aware of the potential litigious consequences of ignoring instructions: 'We shall have to keep now to "the letter of the law" I s'pose or risk deductions' (ET-D2302). This insight was evidence of Terry emerging from the period of profound illness that had incapacitated her and consequently dried up the extended family income, giving rise to this frenetic publishing project. Tragic events of 1913 added to Terry's introspection. In 1913, reflecting on the death at the Derby races of the militant suffragist, Ellen Terry mentioned the loss of 'that poor girl Emily Davison' (THM 384/1/38/4). In April the same year, Terry confided in her daughter the traumatic effect of the tragic car accident involving the children of Isadora Duncan and Edward Gordon Craig: 'I have been made quite ill by the terrible doing to death of those poor things in the Paris horror. I could not sleep for 3 or 4 nights for my dreams & I can't see how that poor Isadora can keep from going mad – for I'm sure she was the devotedest of Mothers' (THM 384/1/38/11). Ellen Terry feared a transformation into Ophelia for Duncan but also for herself.

## Ophelia's response and the problem of the fat *Hamlet*

The physique of the performing body that concerned Gordon Craig with the Russian Ballet became an issue for reviewers of the Pioneer Players' production of *Hamlet* on 9 March 1913 but this time it was the male body that was under scrutiny. Louis Calvert had published his own idiosyncratic interpretation, *An Actor's Hamlet* (1912), but reviewers were less interested in his theories than his physical presence on stage. The *Daily Express* reviewed the production under the heading 'Was Hamlet a fat man? Pathological Facts for Idealists'. If Gordon Craig was aware of these reviews he would have recalled his sister's admonishment of his own Hamlet in 1892 when she had commented on his costume: 'I liked your long cloak very much but the hood is either too small or it looks it & is not becoming also you look so fat in HI's clothes – couldn't you put them on a bit righter or neater or something?' (quoted in Auerbach 1987: 324–5). Edith Craig was acutely aware of her brother's sensitivity about his own body image and therefore anticipated his adverse reaction to McClure's having chosen 'the <u>fattest</u> pictures' of her and Edward Gordon Craig: 'Won't he be cross if he sees it' (n.d. THM 384/4/ 6). Gordon Craig may also have assumed that the Pioneer Players' production was a response to his own recent experiments at the Moscow Art Theatre which had also been promoted by means of his exhibitions and lectures in London.[29] This seems to have been anticipated by Louis Calvert and Edith Craig when they were interviewed about the Pioneer Players' production by *The Daily Chronicle* (8 March 1913).[30] Louis Calvert emphasized the Pioneer Players' deviation from the flashy modernity of recent productions:

'So far as scenery and costume are concerned', said Mr Calvert, 'Sunday's performance will be given in the simplest and plainest way, and I prescribe the excellent remedy of absence to anyone who may be expecting our presentation of Hamlet to amaze the eye with the expensive glitter of modern production.' (*The Daily Chronicle*. 8 March 1913)

Somewhat defensively Edith Craig added that the production aimed to present *an interpretation*. In 1912–13 there were three significant publications on Hamlet's character by S. M. Perlman, Georges Brandes and Louis Calvert. Craig emphasized the Pioneer Players' commitment to the play of ideas, anticipating comparisons that might be made with recent experimentations although she does not name them. There were three likely candidates. William Poel's cross-gender casting had Rosencrantz and Guildenstern played by women. The 'post-impressionist' production by Harley Granville-Barker of *The Winter's Tale* was described by *The Times* as having 'stage decoration' rather than scenery, with striking gold and white pillars and 'squads of supers have symmetrical automaton-like movements'. Her brother's Moscow *Hamlet* had a particularly glittering court scene. Edith Craig avoided commenting on specific comparators:

> 'We are not setting ourselves to do more than air a theory,' remarked Miss Edith Craig, 'and I echo Mr Calvert's warning to those who may be looking for anything scenically ambitious. It will mainly be a presentation in character and costume of Mr Calvert's analysis of Hamlet's brain.' (*The Daily Chronicle*, 8 March 1913)

Both interviewees imply some aspects of collaboration in this production but Calvert's name alone is recorded in the Pioneer Players' annual reports.

The production of a female Hamlet would have been entirely feasible for Edith Craig and the Pioneer Players. Janette Steer, a stalwart member of both the Pioneer Players and the AFL, had been a female Hamlet in 1898 (Howard 2007: 90) and played the role of a revolutionary assassin, Charlotte Corday, in *A Pageant of Great Women*. Instead *The True Ophelia* (1912), anonymously authored by Jess Dorynne, seems to have been a response to Gordon Craig's essay 'The True Hamlet', in *The Mask*, in which Gordon Craig focused on a two-dimensional image of Hamlet. Dorynne's response was fully three-dimensional, engaging with the acting potential for the character and its wider significance. Both attempts to conceptualize the 'true' nature of these characters reveal their reaction to the indeterminacy of the play. By foregrounding the female protagonist, generating associations of political debates about what Ophelia represented for the women's suffrage generation, Dorynne was not alone in her interest in the character. Israel Zangwill (1864–1926), author of *Children of the Ghetto* (1892), turned his talents to women's suffrage purposes and seized upon Ophelia's abject characterization to point to Hamlet's egocentricity, symbolic of the anti-suffrage temperament in his *Prologue*:

But Hamlet was so hard soliloquising,
He had no ear for feminine advising,
Ah, if instead of suicide-suggestions,

To vote or not to vote had been the question,
Ophelia had met, with mocking flout,
Hamlet's male insolence of sneer and doubt,
Nunnery forsooth! When she at Hamlet's fat form
Could thunder suffrage from the castle-platform! (Gardner
   1985: 9)

Zangwill's critique envisages a warrior-like Ophelia with a voice invigorated by the women's suffrage campaign perhaps not unlike Calvert's Ophelia who was played by Ellen O'Malley, previously Vivie Warren for the Pioneer Players' *Mrs Warren's Profession*. Zangwill's representation of 'Hamlet's fat form' seems particularly relevant for Calvert's performance.

Edith Craig did not use Calvert's production for the Pioneer Players to fight back.[31] Perhaps by staging the play at all she emphasized the diversity of interpretations. In the manner of the Pioneer Players' 'play of ideas' and the ISS's stocks of even anti-suffrage publications for sale, Craig supported the breadth of opinion and debate whereas her brother was singularly emphatic and uncompromising in his worldview.

However, in 1912, Craig and the Pioneer Players had staged Dorynne's very explicit response to Gordon Craig's life off-stage in her play *The Surprise of His Life*.[32] Edith Craig, like Ellen Terry, supported the mothers of his children with unpaid childcare and, in the case of Jess Dorynne, supported her professionally. *The Surprise of His Life* concerned the resilience and political agency of Emily, daughter of 'an ambitious greengrocer', who finds herself pregnant. She rejects the begrudging proposal of marriage (arranged by Emily's father) from the unworthy father of her child Alfred Williams, 'a journeyman painter; when the Devil drives', and claims the right to determine her own future. Alfred's insincerity is exposed with his relationship with another woman, Sally and his arrogant behaviour is rebuffed by both women; Sally boxes his ears and Emily extricates herself from his hold 'with a scientific jerk' (pp. 17–18) reminiscent of the martial arts popular with suffrage activists. Emily and her aunt, who regretted that she had married because she was pregnant, decide to leave the family home and follow the women's suffrage movement. The triumphant resolution leaves the family and the young man surprised indeed. The strength and confidence of

Emily seems to provide a rebuke to the scenario outlined earlier in the short story 'An Introduction', discussed earlier, and its performance on stage realized the potential for women to respond with physical force. The author of *The Surprise of His Life*, Jess Dorynne, had had a similar experience to that of Emily in the play, although Edward Gordon Craig, the father of her daughter Kitty, was already married.

## Edith Craig and the Shakespeare tercentenary

Several years after Edith Craig's involvement with Shakespeare in the Pioneer Players' production by Louis Calvert of *Hamlet* in 1913, she had the opportunity to get involved in Shakespearean productions and characteristically she got absorbed in the process of productions and eschewed the accolades. During the First World War she was involved in the Shakespeare Hut, set up by the YWCA to entertain troops in London in a specially designed Elizabethan style building.[33] In 1915 she directed *The Merchant of Venice* at the Bijou Theatre, Rye, with the Pioneer Players, reviving Edith Craig & Co. for the costumes; featuring among the 'magnificoes and Venetians' was Pamela Colman Smith and as 'clerk of the court' was Cathleen Nesbitt (EC-D495).

In 1916 the Shakespeare tercentenary was celebrated, in spite of the wartime restrictions on resources for theatrical productions. Edith Craig's production with the Pioneer Players at Rye may have influenced her arrangement of *The Merchant of Venice* section of the *Shakespeare Pageant* with Matheson Lang in which Lang appeared with Ellen Terry, Terry's grandchildren Rosie Craig as 'a reveller' and Teddy and Nellie as pages (EC-D505a). This took place on Friday, 7 July 1916, at 3 pm at the Royal Opera House Covent Garden as part of women's tribute week. More scenes were arranged by other distinguished directors.[34] 'The Shakespeare Pageant' was arranged in chronological order.[35] The pageant was followed by *The Women's Tribute*, an extraordinary general meeting reported by Louis N. Parker. The scene was set in a board room at which the members present themselves in the order of the roll-call: Britannia, Truth, Youth, Faith Hope, Love, Courage, Mother,

Wife, Sweetheart, Drama, Music, Art, Worker, Postwoman. This was followed by a variety entertainment concert in the evening by the London Symphony Orchestra.

Edith Craig lent the costumes for the Shakespeare birthday festival for St George's day at the Royal Victoria Hall in which Ellen Terry appeared as Portia. Scenes from various Shakespeare plays were presented in the very full programme typical of these wartime events. Teddy Craig played a page in *The Merchant of Venice* with his grandmother. Costumes were lent by Edith Craig, Matheson Lang, Tom Heslewood, and H. & M. Rayne (ET-D509).

## 'The Don't Care Girl' and its aftermath

Some twenty years before the Pioneer Players produced *Ellen Young*, the president of the society had performed a very different kind of carefree woman in *Madame Sans-Gene* at the Lyceum Theatre. In 1916 the Pioneer Players produced two plays in a matinee, one of which was a translation of Nikolai Evreinov's *A Merry Death* and the other was *Ellen Young* co-written by their executive committee members Gabrielle Enthoven and Edmund Goulding, produced on 2 April 1916 at the Savoy Theatre. These plays, together with a later production, based on Pierre Louys's short story The *Girl and the Puppet* (produced on 17 February 1918 at the Princes Theatre), caught the mood of the time and presented a challenge to Craig in staging the dancer's performing body. The diary entry of one member of the audience has captured an impression of Craig's effects of lighting through gauze to provide a suggestive image that did not shock the viewer. Lady Cynthia Asquith's description of the scenography demonstrates that the effect achieved a representation of nudity which remained within the bounds of what was interpreted as acceptable (Asquith 1987: 411). In attempting the staging of this scene, Edith Craig was taking a risk in various ways, not least in alienating her audience and generating associations with other productions of questionable artistic merit. Given the furore internationally over the staging of the explicit female body, this Pioneer Players' production was emphasizing its position at the forefront of controversial performance as well as the insistence on the symbolic consequences of the presentation of the autonomous female body on stage. In the context of the debates which ranged from Olga Nethersole's performance in *Sapho* and the dramatic critique of prostitution, the political agenda of female practitioners committed to women's equality was being extended into women's rights to a free stage. In this respect *The Girl and the Puppet* and *Ellen Young* were productions which challenged Gordon Craig's manifesto against the 'bead' and the 'bulge' of Léon Bakst and the Russian Ballet.

In 1916 a different generation had its own version of the 'don't care girl'. A cultural and chemical shift had taken place. A different tone and scope for the behavioural spectrum of the carefree and careless was in evidence. The significant features of Ellen Young's character relate to her frenetic approach to her performance career as a dancer who was dependent on morphine to fuel her brilliant but self-destructive performances. The setting of the play moves geographically and signifies the rising fortunes of Ellen Young as she moves from the family home in Peckham in Act I to her a flat in the West End in Acts II and III. Gabrielle Enthoven (1868–1950) was a leading figure in the management of the Pioneer Players, acting as unofficial archivist, and became a pioneer theatre historian and collector whose own theatre archive is now the basis of the V&A Theatre Collection, London (Dorney 2014). Enthoven had worked in Belgium for the Red Cross during the war and her co-author Edmund Goulding (1891–1959) had returned from America where he had briefly worked as a baritone in 1915 (Kennedy 2004: 18). Their play, *Ellen Young*, was put on for the Pioneer Players without scenery at the Savoy Theatre as it was available only shortly before the performance. Ellen Young is a wild music hall dancer with a morphine addiction, expected to die within the year but a happy marriage at the end (implausibly) cures her of consumption and morphine addiction. A real counterpart, Billie Carleton, died of a drugs overdose after the London ball that marked the end of the First World War (Kohn 1992: 96–101). There were several associates connecting Carleton and the Pioneer Players, and it is likely that the wider association of the Pioneer Players with dramatizations concerning the female dancer may have affected the reputation of the society.

# James Joyce rejected but Susan Glaspell's dangerous women reach the London stage

The Pioneer Players' advice 'To Authors', discussed earlier in this chapter, made it clear that authors were invited to submit their plays for consideration. It is clear from the extant correspondence in the Edith Craig archive that some authors did so but Craig was also generally alert and used her network for news of relevant material. Ellen Terry's letters reveal that while in the United States Terry was searching for a particular American play on behalf of her daughter to whom she reported on her progress: 'I cannot find the little American play you ask me for but I have told Percy McKaye & Miss Crothers – perhaps they'll turn up something.' (6 March 1915; CLET 6: 1784).[36] Craig's search at this time predated Glaspell's *Trifles* and also *Suppressed Desires*, which was not performed until 15 July 1915 but it may well be that Terry's contact with McKaye and Crothers opened up a transatlantic route for suggestions including Glaspell's drama (EC-H708). In Craig's archive is a copy of *Berenice*, annotated by Glaspell, proving that the author was directly in contact with the Pioneer Players to offer her play for production.

James Joyce contacted his agent on three occasions between 1917 and 1920 to instigate contact with the Pioneer Players to offer his play *Exiles* for production: 'Have you any relations with the Pioneer Players, or the other theatre I spoke of the Manchester Repertory Theatre or do you know any actor or actress who would read the play?' (8 August 1917). Joyce prompted Pinker nearly a year later: 'And have you any news from Miss Horniman or the Pioneer Players? (29 July 1918). Two years later, presumably exasperated by the prevarication, he reiterated the question: 'Exiles, production: has this been offered to the Pioneer Players, Abbey Theatre or other management?' (13 March 1920). If Pinker ever sent it, the Pioneer Players seems to have declined the opportunity. Of the two plays by American author Susan Glaspell that were directed for the Pioneer Players, it was *The Verge* in 1925 which received the most extreme response; Claire Archer's bid to create new plant life provided a role in which Sybil Thorndike explored performance elements which she later used in her launch into Grand Guignol.[37] In 1919 Craig directed *Trifles* with three other plays at the King's Hall, Covent Garden.[38] Craig's production of *Trifles* appears to have been the first production of the play in Britain. She directed *Trifles* again in 1934, two years after Nancy Price staged it at the People's National Theatre. Publicity for these later productions carelessly overlooked the Pioneer Players' most pioneering earlier production of the play.

In the history of women's writing, Susan Glaspell's short story 'A Jury of Her Peers' and the dramatization *Trifles* have assumed an unquestionable place. Elaine Showalter foregrounds it in the title of her survey *A Jury of Her Peers: A History of American Women's Writing from Anne Bradstreet to Annie Proulx* (2009). For the Pioneer Players in 1919, *Trifles* would have spoken to the audience as they ventured into a postwar era with the franchise extended to the already privileged female members of a certain age. At the time of the Pioneer Players' production of *Trifles*, women in England were still excluded from juries but this was under discussion and rectified in January 1921. By 1927 only nineteen states in the United States permitted female jurors and the exclusion of women was on the basis of a 'defect of sex'. Glaspell's story has been of great interest in the field of law and literature for its depiction of the women who work in concert to read the crime scene, identify relevant evidence, interpret it and arrive at a possible motive for the crime. Thus Minnie Wright's neighbours and acquaintances use their insights to understand her circumstances and arrive at the position of withholding their shared knowledge from the authorities. In this sense Minnie Wright is unofficially tried by an unofficial 'jury of her peers'. The play dramatized and rewrote details of the true crime that Glaspell had reported on as a journalist. Significantly, Glaspell's version has the female perpetrator, Minnie Wright, presented as an abused but childless wife. The Pioneer Players' regular audience members would have interpreted *Trifles* in the context of the society's earlier plays about women's suffrage.

One hitherto overlooked aspect of Craig's production of *Trifles* for the Pioneer Players is worthy of examination. The casting of *Trifles* required three men to play the county attorney George Henderson, the sheriff Henry Peters and a neighbouring farmer Lewis Hale; two female characters were Mrs Hale, and Mrs Peters who is married to the sheriff. The casting of the Sherriff is significant in different ways. It seems odd that Ellen Terry's estranged husband James Carew is listed as the sheriff given the supposed

# CHAPTER SIX
## 1915–25

# Postwar recreation and the nativity play

Edith Craig's fearless response to war was confirmed by George Bernard Shaw. When Ellen Terry was still out of the country but on her way back from her Australian tour, Shaw reassured her in terms reminiscent of his play *Heartbreak House*: 'If Germans drop bombs on London, Edie, over whom I have no control – for the mere fact that I adore her mother and ought to have been her father gives me no rights – will possibly rush out with Christopher and post herself on Waterloo Bridge to see the fun' (17 January 1915; Laurence 1985: 283).[1] According to Margaret Webster, Edith Craig's reflex response to wartime danger was creative improvisation. Bedford Street, Covent Garden, which was 'well in the line of fire', offered an excellent view of the V-shaped formations of the bombers in the sky. During this terrifying spectacle, Craig co-ordinated some improvised performance that transformed the child's fear into joy:

> Edy Craig and her friends joined us, clad for a peaceful evening in a colourful assortment of turbans, sandals, corduroy pajamas [*sic*] and charades. Edy was splendid as an elephant. I enjoyed it all tremendously, including the Big Bangs, and was only sorry when the Boy Scouts came tootling down the street with their bugles to announce the all clear. (Webster 1969: 269)

Webster recalled Craig as an inspirational figure: 'She was no religion, but in her work she was religious' (Webster 2004: 269). In this observation Webster may have sought implicitly to distinguish Craig from her Catholic partner, Christopher St John, but she also captured the commitment and creative transformation that characterized Craig's theatrical productions. This informed Craig's approach to the newly emerging field of religious drama and the nativity play, inspired by her fascination with the historical development of drama from the earliest Christian didactic performances in church based on the 'Quem quaeritis?' dialogue.[2]

The nativity play has a surprisingly volatile history, within which Edith Craig played a significant part. In the interwar period and in the context of a powerful reconstruction of Englishness, the organization of productions of the nativity play became part of the rebuilding of communities configured as village life, driven by a utopian aim for a lasting international peace. The nativity play phenomenon has endured and become an over-familiar part of British contemporary culture often transforming into a hybrid, secularized end-of-term play. Embedded as it is in popular memories of childhood, nostalgia for the nativity play has forestalled critical analysis or historical examination. The nativity play is an international phenomenon with significant local variations.[3] Elements of the nativity play have been subjected to parodic revision.[4] The nativity play has often become a nexus of cultural anxieties about the school curriculum, freedom of speech and civil rights. The amenability of this form to manipulation and renewal has led to situations in which it is consequently met by the impulse to censor it.[5] The nativity play's connections to pageantry, both civic and dissident, and the development of art theatre earlier in the twentieth century in Britain have been forgotten along with Edith Craig's involvement as its leading director.[6] This chapter examines Craig's productions of *The Shepherds* (1915), *The Early English Nativity Play* (1919–25) and *The Great World Theatre* (1924), locating the phenomenon of nativity plays in the context of interwar Englishness, the Little Theatre movement and the conceptualization of drama as an educational force in *The Teaching of English in England*, known as the 'Newbolt Report' (1921).

## Nativity play precursors

The publication and performance of the nativity play in Britain was influenced by literary historical research on the medieval drama.[7]

For audiences it would have appealed to those with antiquarian as well as religious interests and those who had travelled in continental Europe and experienced the Oberammergau Passion Play, which had been performed by villagers in the open air as a traditional event in Bavaria almost continuously since 1634. Edith Craig seems to have referred to the Oberammergau Passion Play in preparation for her nativity play productions in York, an English city historically rooted in the ministry of Christianity. The focus on the period leading to the crucifixion and the ways in which characterization and dialogue were presented have led to charges of anti-semitism, exemplified in 1934 when the Oberammergau Passion Play was appropriated for Nazi propaganda. The nativity play, by contrast, lent itself to a reflection on the circumstances of the birth in a manger and, relatedly, humility and homelessness, social justice and democracy.

Although Edith Craig had experience of religious drama earlier in her career, those productions had had a secular context. In 1901 she and her brother staged Laurence Housman's *Bethlehem* in a production which has been discussed widely in relation to Gordon Craig's developing theories of the art of the theatre but not as a 'nativity play' as such.[8] The published edition (1902), which includes *The Pageant of Our Lady* and also *Christmas Songs*, makes it clear that the subtitle to *Bethlehem* is 'a nativity play'. Although there is extensive and strategic use of illumination and shadow to enhance the atmosphere and accentuate the reactions of those who welcome the newborn, crucially the stage directions indicate that the Christ child would be visible to the audience: 'Mary rising, stands in the cradle under shadow of the canopy displaying the Child in her breast, still partly covered by her veil' (Housman 1902: 46–7). This was sufficient to invite scrutiny from the Lord Chamberlain's office. In his autobiography, Housman recalled that Gordon Craig cut much of the script and Joseph Moorat's music. However, consequently there were no problems about censorship:

> In cutting the Virgin's lines, [Gordon] Craig curiously anticipated the scruples of Mr Redford, the censor, who, when in later years he granted the performing licence which for the original production was refused, allowed it on the condition that the Virgin was not to speak nor the Holy Child to be seen. On both those points Mr

Craig, the apostle of art, was of the same mind as Mr Redford; and as he made the play quite beautiful without those small and unimportant details, I did not too greatly complain. (Housman 1937a: 188)

When Gertrude Kingston, manager of the Little Theatre, applied for a licence to produce the play some years later, Housman recalled that she 'was met with the old traditional answer that Holy Families could not be allowed upon the stage' (Housman 1937a: 251). The circumstances of Housman's nativity play therefore locate it firmly in the history of challenges to stage censorship. Laurence Housman persisted for decades in writing plays which embodied forbidden individuals including the royal family, notably a collection of plays in a genre of play cycle of 'dramatic biography' which Housman claimed to have invented (Housman 1937a: 371). These were published as *Victoria Regina* (1934), and first produced by the Glastonbury Players in 1927–8.[9] *Bethlehem* may have inspired Edith Craig to include the unexpectedly transgressive element in a scene for *The Coronation* (1912) by Christopher St John and Charles Thursby: the embodiment of the statue of the Madonna. The published stage directions did not require this treatment and there is evidence that this interpretation was concealed in the play programme, where the role of the statue and the performer's name were redacted. It also drew on the dramatized ceremony and ritual that had appealed to The Masquers in 1903 (see Chapter Three). In the development of the theatre work of both Gordon Craig and Edith Craig, it fixed the nativity play as the foundation in their pursuit of the 'art of the theatre'.

Christopher St John was an influence on Craig's productions of several plays related to Catholicism. In January 1914 St John's translation from the Latin was used in Craig's production of Hrotsvit's *Paphnutius*. This was remarkable in many ways, including its rendition of appropriate music, with the use of plain song and antiphons. Rev. G. B. Chambers from Hove, Sussex wrote with advice on plain chant and his intention to send the play programme to his friend, a Belgian monk (EC-3, 137). The Pioneer Players' productions by Edith Craig of Hrotsvit's tenth-century play *Paphnutius* (1914) and Christopher St John's *Macrena* (1912) appropriated the warrior nun as a political force in the context of women's suffrage. Informed by St John's expertise as a historian and translator and her Catholicism, they foreground heroic struggle in the face of sexual temptation and sexual violence, as discussed in Chapter four.

St John had been working on a new novel exploring ideas of religious struggle and redemption as well as self-discovery. When in 1915 St John's novel entitled *Hungerheart: The Story of a Soul* was published, Ellen Terry assumed that it was autobiographical. In the period when Terry was suffering greatly from advanced cataracts and awaiting surgery she nevertheless set about reading *Hungerheart* and reported on the experience to her daughter:

> I only began yesterday to read Hungerheart[.] It – is – just – too wonderful – most beautiful – & I suppose it is Christy herself! of course = beyond being interesting. It is absorbing – I've just come to Part III. & am almost blind for reading it myself – & now I can't let anyone else – [...] I can't speak of C's book yet but I know how I'll delight in it – I am doubtful as to what I can do with it – it seems to be in Massie's hands – he directed it shd be sent to me – Am I at liberty to send it to Scribners (via Mr Halch – a friend of mine who is there –) or to let Appleton see it – or Century, & other Publishers? I was too ill just before leaving N.Y. to read, or do anything at all – but in 3 weeks (about) time I return to N.Y. & am to have my eyes done – which means 3 weeks at least shut up in Hospital –.(Saturday, 9 January [1915]; *CLET* 6: 1773)

St John sought assistance from Ellen Terry in the marketing of the novel as she had done with *The Crimson Weed* (1901). St John's fortunes in publishing suffered during the First World War and so she asked Terry to help her use contacts in United States:

> My little glimmering star is very much in the <u>descendant</u> – as my Paphnutius & my Methuen novel are both postponed indefinitely. If you do meet a <u>publisher</u> or publisher's man in New York, do try & get him to read attentively my Methuen book 'Hungerheart' by name. I cant get any-one to take it in America. Ask him if you see him (a publisher in N.Y.) to send to Hughes Massie for it – <u>He has it</u> but wont send it about any more. (THM 384/7)

Terry's priority, having left Britain for a short lecture tour, was to travel back safely from the United States. The dangers at sea and the zeppelins in the skies loomed in her imagination. She did, however, report to her daughter, with characteristic generosity, that she was promoting St John's book and added that she was also 'very glad you are producing a Nativity Play – & at The Cathedral Hall too' (Monday, 21 December [1914]; *CLET* 6: 1764).[10] There was no further comment necessary; as a project it received parental approval and was entirely consistent with Craig's current theatrical interests.

On her return from the United States, Ellen Terry, with her daughter Edith Craig, met Sister Laurentia at Stanbrook Abbey where she was introduced by Madame de Navarro, the American performer known as Mary Anderson; this took place in 1916 shortly after the tercentenary event at Drury Lane Theatre (Corrigan 1985: 20). Sister, later Dame, Laurentia had a wide circle of friends, including George Bernard Shaw. Christopher St John was already known at Stanbrook Abbey, where she had been staying in January 1913 when *The Russian Ballet* project materialized.[11]

The Catholic sentiments underpinning Paul Claudel's drama and the miraculous event in *The Tidings Brought to Mary* locate it as a relevant precursor to Craig's productions of the nativity play. Craig's production of *The Tidings Brought to Mary* in 1917 was part of the Pioneer Players' brief to bring internationally significant drama to a London stage and was cited as a landmark performance by the leading proponent of religious drama (Browne 1932: 44). Craig's production included Lady Maud Warrender's performance of 'Salve Regina' with unaccompanied plainchant (Warrender 1933: 233). The play was produced by a number of other directors in Europe in this period suggesting, according to Roberta Gandolfi, 'a vibrant network of cosmopolitan exchange' (2011: 109). Gandolfi argues that the production of Claudel's play in particular was evidence of Craig's interest in medievalism as spiritual rather than historical, and a 'small-scale', 'evocative', 'poor theatre' (pp. 117–18), in a new phase distinct from her earlier militant suffrage work. However, medievalist references were much in evidence in women's suffrage cultural engagement and Craig's involvement in improvisation and the appropriation of the Jonsonian masque form suggests a number of aesthetic continuities, transformations and reappropriations.

# Nativity plays as a response to war: *The Shepherds* (1915) and *The Child in Flanders* (1917)

Although the nativity play had a recognizable place in Craig's career in the field of religious drama, the wartime nativity plays had a specific resonance with the potential to inspire a reverential mood, to instil hope and spiritual reflection. The medieval origins of the nativity play lent additional gravitas and invited some comparison with the aesthetic and iconography of war memorials. War memorials in Britain and Germany were diverse in their representation of death in battle and, as Stefan Goebel has demonstrated, in some cases they featured medievalist references to sacrifice and heroism that were hard to categorize as either traditionalist or modernist (Goebel 2006: 185–6). Aesthetic continuities in this period can be discerned most obviously in the visual arts in the medievalism of the Arts and Crafts movement, in the little magazines and book designs with which artists such as Laurence Housman, Charles Ricketts and Walter Crane were familiar. The nativity play therefore provided a complementary example in the performing arts, an opportunity for a communal experience of memorialization but with a focus on rebirth and redemption of the new generation rather than sacrificial death.

At the outbreak of war, London theatres were significantly affected by the material restrictions on investment and audiences changing their spending habits on entertainment. The staging of unknown and experimental drama was hardly viable and rarely attempted, save for the stalwart Pioneer Players. The energies of women's suffrage campaigners were redirected to pacifism or patriotism but the principles of the suffrage were apparent, especially for those who ventured into the military support services. The bravery of these women signified a challenge to the anti-suffrage physical force argument based on the contention that citizenship depended on the ability to defend the country in time of war.[12] Some of those with theatrical skills organized theatrical entertainments for troops in the warzone, notably Lena Ashwell (1922). Hitherto reliable and available colleagues and companions were drawn to the warzone or war work. Laurence Alma Tadema (1865–1940) became a highly valued international campaigner for charitable aid with the Polish Victims' Relief Fund. Vera Holme gave up driving Emmeline Pankhurst and worked as an ambulance driver for the Scottish Women's Hospital in 1915 with her partner the Hon. Evelina Haverfield.[13] After a period of four months as a prisoner of war in Serbia, Holme returned to Britain in 1917. From 1919 to 1920 she acted as administrator in Serbia for the Haverfield Fund for Serbian Children, a charity which the Pioneer Players actively supported with their production of Saint-Georges de Bouhélier's *The Children's Carnival* in 1920.[14] Cicely Hamilton, one of Craig's closest collaborators, obtained a post as Chief Clerk at the Abbaye de Royaumont, which had been commandeered and transformed into a military hospital. Hamilton did not give up writing but she did change her priorities and political purpose. Notably in *William an Englishman* (1919), she depicted prewar English political activists as naive, idealistic and dangerously vulnerable. In 1917 she staged her own nativity play for troops at Abbeville.

## *The Shepherds* (1915)

Edith Craig directed the nativity play *The Shepherds*, written by Father Cuthbert OSFC, in 1915 at the Westminster Cathedral Hall, which had been used for liturgical services until 1903 when the Catholic cathedral adjacent to it was opened. So at the time that Craig produced *The Shepherds* there, it was not technically a church but was presumably a consecrated space. The production was widely reviewed (*Athenaeum*, 23 January 1915, p. 78) and was staged 'under the patronage of Cardinal Bourne' (*Referee*, 20 December 1914; EC-G1603) in aid of the Franciscans' Hop Fields' Mission. According to the *Sunday Times*, it was 'Father Cuthbert's first play and the first play, it is believed, by a Franciscan to be put on stage since the Middle Ages' (EC-G1601). The *Observer* reported that it was 'said to be written in a racy, colloquial style, precisely that style which the secular dramatist who associated religion only with church on Sundays seldom succeeds in achieving' (*Observer*, 20 December 1914; EC-G1602). The cast included Ellen O'Malley and Patrick Kirwan, who had appeared in numerous Pioneer Players' productions. The play was published in 1919 by Burns and Oates. Father Cuthbert was warden of the hostel for Franciscan students at Oxford University and a prolific author, renowned especially for *The Life of St Francis of Assisi* (1912).

The review of the production in the Catholic newspaper *The Tablet* noted that Father Cuthbert 'has expressed a preference for the word "representation" to "play"', suggesting perhaps some reticence about an association with the frivolity of the theatre. The reviewer provides valuable insights into Craig's staging which relied on simple curtains and involved the actors moving through the audience:

> The mounting of the piece, with the exception of the costumes, which might be described as models of costly simplicity, was of the homeliest kind. The back-scenes and the substitutes for dropscenes were almost entirely curtains. The shepherds threw their shadows on to the blue veil representing the starlit heavens. The old idea of the actors mingling with the crowds was retained by 'travellers', 'revellers' and suchlike passing through the audience to the stage.[15] (*Tablet*, 16 January 1915)

The simplicity and effectiveness of the lighting and the musical accompaniment created an appropriate mood, unifying elements of the scene in a manner suitable to the religious context of the venue:

> The musical effects were mostly very simple, though, it may be added, very charming, from the piping of the shepherds to the fine song of Nat the Minstrel (Mr. J. Rorke) and the 'Gloria in excelsis' of the angelic host. The climax, the vision of the Holy Family in the stable of the inn, was produced by the simple drawing aside of curtains. The epilogue, spoken by Mr. Charles King, thanked in a simple direct fashion those who had listened to their tale of these the first of evangelists, 'who came to thank Our Lord for His great gift to man'. (*Tablet*, 16 January 1915)

This report of Craig's production suggests that she achieved a staging which was aesthetically effective as well as sufficiently respectful that it was endorsed by the leading Catholic publication.

Edith Craig seems to have directed *The Shepherds* from the Chester cycle in 1923 at the Old Vic Theatre.[16] The play had a cast of eleven (Mary, Joseph, Gabriel [the three shepherds], Hancken, Harvey and Tudd, their servant Trowle and four shepherd boys) and a choir of angels. Some impressions of Craig's interpretation in the production are gleaned from the props listed as provisions for the three shepherds, Hancken, Harvey and Tudd. These would enhance the sense of their daily needs as shepherds to carry their food and drink with them. Each shepherd was suitably equipped. Hancken's bag contained 'pig's foot' and 'tongue'; Harvey's held a 'loaf of bread, onion, garlic, leeks, butter' and Tudd's included a 'flask of ale, a pudding sheep's head'. The use of real meat and other food items would have given a striking effect and reinforced for the audience the material circumstances against which the spiritual dimension would be enhanced.

## *The Child in Flanders* (1917)

The wartime resonance of the nativity story was, however, brought out more explicitly by Cicely Hamilton in her nativity play, *The Child in Flanders: A Nativity Play in A Prologue, Five Tableaux and an Epilogue*, which was performed in 1917 in Abbeville to an audience of soldiers.[17] *The Child in Flanders* consists of several very formal tableaux depicting the nativity, with the shepherds and the manger scene, as part of the dream vision of three soldiers, an Englishman, an Australian and an Indian, who have lost their way back to their unit in Arras and are staying overnight at the house of a French peasant whose wife has just given birth. The soldiers' thoughts of home are signified by the musical accompaniment of the song 'The Trail That Leads to Home', inspiring the English soldier to refer to his three-month-old daughter whom he has never seen.

Aligned with the three kings, the soldiers give gifts to the baby. The transition from the nativity tableaux to the realist epilogue, which shows the soldiers leaving the house to return to combat, is signified by the sound of distant guns. Although the baby has been brought out by the father, the mother and baby are depicted only by a stream of light from a doorway and are not visible to the audience. The audience understands that the soldiers do see the mother and baby and are noticeably affected by the sight. This scene elides the French mother and baby with the Madonna and child of the nativity. The nativity scene is used to unify differences, to render the alienating warzone bearable for the soldiers by invoking the prospect of rebirth. Hamilton's decision to draw attention to the difficulty of communication, with the use of French dialogue from the outset between the English soldier and the Frenchman, foregrounds difference in order to resolve it by the unifying power of religious and military discourses. The play was given a postwar production in London at the Old Vic theatre in December 1925.

Nativity plays, produced before and even during the war, have been overlooked in studies of the culture of the First World War. In particular, the staging of the nativity scene or moments of local historical significance in pageants served to foster a community spirit and revive confidence in religious faith. The nativity play provided a cathartic forum where traumatic memories of war could be indirectly mediated and resolved. This is evident in the wartime production for a military audience in 1917 in Abbeville, France of Cicely Hamilton's *A Child in Flanders* and in the nativity plays directed by Edith Craig during and directly after the First World War.

## The British Drama League (1919) and The Newbolt Report (1921)

The period immediately after the First World War was one of reconstruction, within which the arts were called upon to motivate, educate and inspire communities, notably at the level of 'the village' as part of the 'nation' with a view to building a lasting peace internationally. In this context, a national debate on the state of British theatre was launched at a conference at Stratford-upon-Avon from 15 to 29 August 1919 organized by the British Drama League (BDL) during the Shakespeare Summer Festival. The promotional pamphlet listed the official management structure of the BDL, the thirteen topics to be discussed with 'open discussion' to follow papers and announced that 'an exhibition of Scenic Models and Designs is being organized by a Committee, including Miss Edith Craig, Mr Norman Wilkinson, Mr Randolph Schwabe and Mr Norman MacDermott (Honorary Secretary) and will be held during the Conference'.[18] No specific reference was made to the Workshop Committee but such an exhibition was a matter of their discussion.

The conference was covered extensively in the press with reference to 'reform' and 'improvement' of the theatre and some reference to Ellen Terry's 'letter' or 'message' to the conference. Edith Craig presided over the discussion on 'Reform in Production' held on 21 August 1919. *The Times* gave a tantalizing impression of the discussion (22 August 1919; EC-G209) seeming to imply that Craig and MacDermott had disagreed on approaches to the roles of the actor and the producer. After a brief outline of the changing approach to historical costumes in the time of Charles Kean, Craig emphasized a less well-known innovation: 'One of the important reforms introduced by Charles Kean was the use of gauzes and limelight' (22 August 1919; EC-G209). The concluding summary of Craig's contribution addresses the relative roles of the author, the actor and, by implication, the producer: 'In a production Miss Craig said she would place first and foremost the author's intention as revealed by the play not necessarily by the author himself. The second thing was the actor's interpretation. That was his affair and should be left to him' (22 August 1919; EC-G209). Norman MacDermott argued for 'reform in acting methods' and asserted that the responsibility for the 'creative quality' of the play must lie with the producer.

A longer report of the discussion in the *Daily Telegraph* clarified who the main contributors to discussion were (Craig, MacDermott and Wilkinson), with additional details of Craig's arguments, and it does not suggest disagreement between Craig and MacDermott:

> Irving's reforms took the direction of correctness of detail, but this he did not hesitate to sacrifice if it did not help the play. The ideal of her own brother, Mr Gordon Craig, was that the play, the setting, the acting – the whole thing should be the creation of one mind. Herself she believed the theatre should be run entirely by the men and women of the theatre. Anything, irrespective of its being what was called artistic, that helped to make a play complete was right. First of all came the author's intention and then the actor's interpretation, which was his affair and should be left to him, the producer being the person in front to tell him the result of his interpretation. The essential think was to have one controlling mind. (EC-G216)

The *Daily Telegraph* report also summarized Christopher St John's contribution to the open discussion:

> [...] there had been too much of the introduction of the studio on the stage. Chelsea artists had invaded the theatre, and thought

production was quite an easy job. They did not bring about the reform that was needed. The people wanted were those who could develop the art of the theatre itself. (EC-G216)

The intriguing reference to 'Chelsea artists' may apply to Albert Rutherston (1881–1953, known as Rothenstein until 1916), member of the New English Art Club. St John, like many others in this period, was in pursuit of an elusive essence: 'the art of the theatre itself'. Edith Craig, however, made it clear in her pragmatic account that a producer should aim for a comprehensive and coherent interpretation of a play, involving the actors and anything that might contribute to its artistic effect. It was this openness and open-endedness, her welcoming of input from all 'men and women of the theatre' to enable the production to be 'complete', that contrasted with her brother's position although they shared the view of the producer's control of the overall effect. The fullest account of the conference was given in the *Stratford Upon Avon Herald* which provided more of a transcript of the talks, including Edith Craig's rejection of the word 'reform', her praise of Reinhardt's approach and explicitly quoting Norman Wilkinson as agreeing with her in rejecting the word 'reform' (22 August 1919; EC-G212).[19]

The BDL was founded to promote the 'little theatre' movement (which embraced children's theatres, community theatres in garden cities and the amateur dramatics sponsored by Women's Institutes) and amateur productions with the explicit purpose of securing peace and rebuilding communities. Sir Frank Benson supported the aims of the BDL: 'You will help to lead a blindly-groping and war-worn world into the old paths of peace.' (EC-G212) Thus Benson aligned the war with modernity and the route towards peace as obtainable through theatrical production. In 1919 the BDL had eight committees, each with a special remit.[20] Edith Craig was one of the BDL's original council (twenty-four members), and an active member of two of its eight committees: a member of the Workshop and Bureau Committee and Chair of the Foreign Drama Committee. Two documents in Edith Craig's archive give an insight into the issues of concern for the BDL Workshop Committee and Craig's working method. The BDL Workshop Committee aimed to set excellent standards in production as well as to provide the BDL's community theatres with samples of scenery, costumes and designs for carpenters to assist in set building. Albert Rutherston was one of the members of the Workshop Committee who wrote a memorandum proposing that miniature models be used in a permanent exhibition space to instruct others in the appropriate standards and as an incentive for further innovation and the Community Theatres Committee should refer to the Workshop Committee rather than work independently (23 December 1919, 4.5 pp; EC-B119). Rutherston's memorandum was not mentioned in the minutes of the Workshop Committee meeting on 6 January [1920?] at Edith Craig's flat at 31 Bedford Street, with Norman Wilkinson in the chair and six others present: Edith Craig, Clare Atwood, Lovat Fraser, Albert Rutherston, Randolph Schwabe. The minutes recorded one proposal, by 'Miss Craig' followed by a joint meeting of the Workshop and Community Theatres Committees, with reference to the forthcoming competition for stage set design to be announced in the journal *Drama* and organized by Penelope Wheeler and the resolution to arrange funding for the Workshop Committee's work. Edith Craig's proposal was resolved supported:

> That all work produced by the Drama League Workshop should be known as the Drama League Workshop work, and not that of any particular artist, but the names of the responsible directors and designers of the workshop should appear (as a guarantee) on the note paper heading etc. and all work should be furnished with the trade mark for purposes of standard. (EC-M76)

Craig's proposal may appear at first to be a routine bureaucratic matter of ensuring consistency of practice in the workings of the committee. In light of her tendency to avoid naming her own work, her proposal to the Workshop Committee appears to carry more weight and wider significance, suggesting an egalitarian approach.

The conference had provided a national forum for discussion about the stage of the nation's theatre and the work of its committees demonstrated the ensuing activities that were needed to build up an infrastructure capable of supporting theatre work nationwide and acting in an advisory capacity. In 1920 the BDL had entered into discussion with the Board of Education regarding the place of drama in education.

Two years after the BDL's conference, the government report on *The Teaching of English in England* (known as the 'Newbolt

Report', after Sir Henry Newbolt) included a section entitled 'The Drama as an Educational Activity', which cited the BDL's proposals for the training of school teachers in 'dramatic methods' (p. 322). The report associated the popular engagement in performance with the early modern period,[21] and therefore its promotion in education in the 1920s was expected to signal a revival of such communal pleasures:

> It was in no inglorious time of our history that Englishmen delighted altogether in dance and song and drama, nor were these pleasures the privilege of a few or a class. It is a legitimate hope that a rational use of the drama in schools may bring back to England an unshamed joy in pleasures of the imagination and in the purposed expression of wholesome and natural feeling. (p. 319)

The report focused on the educational institutions and their relationship to drama in teaching. Universities were identified as potential leaders in the study of this field, exemplified by Liverpool:

> The University of Liverpool has recently taken the important step of appointing Mr. Granville-Barker to a lectureship on the Art of the Theatre. We hope that there will be other similar appointments elsewhere. In the country where the plays of Shakespeare and Sheridan were written and acted, there should be University Chairs of Dramatic Literature. Professor Brander Matthews, who holds such a Chair at Columbia University, New York, has brought together models of theatres, from the days of the Greeks to our own, scenery of all kinds, and a large dramatic library. Similar collections would be of great value to students of the literature of the stage in this country. (p. 324)

The report briefly referred to the popular theatre which most closely resembled the Little Theatre activities with which Craig was engaged:

> But the whole tenor and spirit of the Report will, we hope, make it evident how warmly we welcome that revival of the popular stage which bids fair to restore to town and countryside in the twentieth century something of the spontaneous theatrical

energies of the mediæval craft-guilds and the Tudor village players. This popular dramatic movement is educational in the wider sense of the word, and has thus fittingly been brought within the survey of the Adult Education Committee. (p. 324)

Such activities were distinguished in the report from the 'professional stage'. Examples such as the Everyman Theatre, with which Edith Craig had also been involved in 1920–1, were given:

The work of the Everyman Theatre at Hampstead and of the Repertory Theatres at Manchester and Birmingham (the former of which has unfortunately had to close); the Phoenix Society productions of Seventeenth-century and other classic plays; and the successful revivals of *The Beggar's Opera* and *The Knight of the Burning Pestle*, all deserve appreciative record here. (p. 324)

Lena Ashwell was specifically named in recognition of her wartime theatrical productions:

And we note with satisfaction that Miss Lena Ashwell, who organized a remarkable series of theatrical and operatic performances for the troops during the War, is continuing in peace time her efforts to popularize good plays. By arrangement with the Mayors of some of the London Boroughs a repertory company under her direction, the 'Once-a-week Players' has given performances in various Town Halls. We hope to see this co-operation between the stage and municipal authorities extended to other parts of the country. In promoting such co-operation the recently founded British Drama League might well find one its most fruitful activities. (p. 324)

In the final chapter of her book *Modern Troubadours* (1922), 'Recreation and the National Life', Ashwell seems to be explicitly responding to Newbolt, picking up the term 'recreation', the organization of theatres and the relationships with communities as well as the dramatic canon.[22] Recalling her conversations with Henry Irving in 1905 about the decline in provincial theatre, Ashwell argued for the importance of a theatre engaging with the community such as the old stock companies and now replaced by the repertory theatres; overall she concluded, 'Let us have every kind of play' (Ashwell 1922: 225).

Ashwell did not refer to nativity plays at all in *Modern Troubadours* (1922) but the Newbolt Report (1921) did. It outlined advice on the selection of drama for different age groups and specified that advanced drama for older children may include nativity plays:

> With senior pupils the adventurous teacher may go earlier and later – earlier to such things as one of the Nativity plays, *Everyman* or some of the Tudor Interludes, and later to the printed drama of modern times. How far the translated drama should be used is a matter about which opinions may properly differ. (p. 315)

This establishes that the nativity play was a recognizable genre at this time and was expected to have a significant impact.

## The Newbolt Report, Englishness and the 'Art of the Theatre'

In *English and Englishness*, Brian Doyle has pointed out that the Newbolt Report assumed that 'only the state, in its cultural and even spiritual manifestation, is capable of overcoming the forces making for national disunity' (Doyle 1989: 49). That is, national organizations should be founded and take the lead. This is notable in the Newbolt Report's response to the growing amateur theatre movement. A section on 'The Popular Dramatic Revival' acknowledged rather anxiously the activities of drama organizations (such as the Glastonbury Players and a 'Plays and Pageant' committee in Birmingham) which were operating outside London and the educational establishments, and therefore were presumed to be outside the reach of the State. However, the Newbolt Report welcomed the potential that they offered 'to restore to town and countryside in the twentieth century something of the spontaneous theatrical energies of the mediaeval craft-guilds and the Tudor village players' (p. 324). The return to a medieval golden age and the cultural unification of town and country would be achieved by the imposition of and legislation for a specific kind of theatre practice from an organization based in London. The impulses of the BDL were, however, explicitly democratic. Its published aim was 'to encourage the Art of the Theatre both for its own sake and as a means of intelligent recreation among all classes of the community' (EC-C37).

The phrase the 'Art of the Theatre' recurs in these interwar debates about drama in education and in theatres designated 'popular' or 'professional'. It is noteworthy that the Newbolt Report associated 'art' theatre with the elite university institutions rather than the popular ones, whereas the BDL explicitly highlighted inclusivity in its address to 'all classes of the community'. The 'Art of the Theatre' was not only associated with Edward Gordon Craig but also affiliated with the promotion of theatre as a cultural practice of national interest which had informed Henry Irving's arguments for a national theatre in the nineteenth century. In the wider cultural landscape, literary forms such as the novel and poetry had infrastructural support in publishing and education to establish their status and social value. Theatre as performance and drama available for literary study were relative newcomers and undergoing arguments about their appropriate place in the national economy.

According to the categorizations used in the Newbolt Report, Edith Craig was at the forefront of promoting drama in education in a way which complemented the emerging national strategic plans for postwar reconstruction. The three categories used in the Newbolt Report may now seem to be not quite so distinct: drama in schools and other educational institutions; drama in the professional theatre; drama in popular theatre. The official promotion of the nativity play as suitable for 'senior' children gave significant weight to the wide dissemination of this kind of theatrical experience and explains why it became so familiar in the interwar period. The Newbolt Report effectively constructed a canon of drama and, alongside Shakespeare, the nativity play was presented as having a natural place within it.

Edith Craig herself was not mentioned in the Newbolt Report but one of the theatre enterprises with which she worked was praised, and she was a leading director of the nativity play. Her mother was mentioned in the role of Portia as having given an exemplary Shakespearean performance which would be ideally suited for educational purposes contrasted with the many mediocre performances that could do damage to youthful and still-forming sensibilities.

The role of drama in the development of English literature as a discipline in higher education in Britain in this period has been relatively overlooked. Chris Baldick and Brian Doyle have examined the relationship between the promotion of English literature and Englishness and its links with the First World War. Chris Baldick noted that 'English literary criticism [...] owes its own renaissance largely to the same catastrophe' (Baldick 1983: 86) and also identifies the religious discourse within which literature, especially poetry, was burdened with the spiritual rejuvenation of the nation. On this matter he quotes Professor Ernest De Selincourt's wartime lectures, published in the year of the Shakespeare tercentenary as *English Poets and the National Ideal* (1916),[23] which expressed concern for the German appropriation of Shakespeare and began thus:

> A time like the present, when we are in the throes of a great national crisis, affecting the lives of the most callous and indifferent of us, affords a clear test of the value that we really attach to literature, and, in particular, to poetry, the highest form of literature. Do we lay it aside as a pleasant pastime suitable enough for less hustling days but remote from our present practical needs and purposes, or do we turn to it with a keener spiritual hunger, feeling that it can give us not merely a pastime but in the true sense *recreation*? (quoted in Baldick 1983: 91; emphasis in original)

That recreation defined so carefully by Professor de Selincourt was most clearly evident in the amateur productions of plays which attempted to involve the whole community beyond the reach of any educational institution. To borrow Baldick's formulation, the 'social mission' of the nativity play within the Little Theatre movement was to humanize and pacify as well as enrich and unify communities. Its effectiveness in this regard is measured by the seamless way in which it not only became part of the fabric of school education and amateur dramatics but was also taken up by authors such as Richard Aldington (1924), Sheila Kaye-Smith and Dorothy L. Sayers (1939). Sayers's radio play *He That Should Come* was broadcast on 25 December 1938 and produced by Val Gielgud. In 1944, during the Second World War, the BDL published a brief history of its activities over the past twenty-five years. The interwar period had seen a general enthusiasm for religious drama in Britain: 'the movement for religious plays in this country was growing, not only in secular halls and theatres, but in churches' (BDL 1944: MCMXXXI).

## *The Early English Nativity Play* (1918–27)

Edith Craig directed at least eight nativity plays between 1918 and 1927, most of which were produced to raise funds for charities and one of which was performed in an educational context by drama students.[24] Craig's productions appear to have used the *Early English Nativity Play* text from E. K. Chambers but there were variations in the procession or tableaux of saints and martyrs which followed the play. The performance had musical accompaniment which was arranged and directed by others. Edith Craig was designated producer for each production but she was not always responsible for the costumes. Ellen Terry acted as the Prologue in several productions but the role was occasionally taken by others and in one production was possibly renamed.[25] There is inconsistent documentation of the productions but some points of comparison, difference and development are discernible that cast a new light on Craig's relationship with the nativity play.

Most of Craig's nativity plays were produced to raise funds for a charity with significant patronal and organizational support and ticket prices aimed at an elite audience. The first of three fund-raising performances was given at the Wigmore Hall, London formerly the Bechstein Hall in February 1918. A distinguished list of aristocratic patrons and programme sellers was used in the publicity for the production, tickets for which cost from 8s and rose to £2 6s and were obtainable from the secretary of the Women War Workers charity, Mrs Geoffrey Bowes Lyon.[26] Craig's involvement in this was consistent with her women's suffrage political campaigning.

Lady Maud Warrender was an active organizer of charity productions for which Craig directed the nativity play. The fundraising production at the Monastery, Rye, in January 1919, was organized by Lady Maud Warrender, a longstanding supporter of the Pioneer Players, and involved a number of the society's leading members. The production was in aid of the Borough Nursing Fund. Warrender was also involved in organizing the production at Daly's Theatre in a grand event to raise funds for the Children's Country Holidays Fund, 'under the patronage of Her Majesty the

Queen', with the central attraction being Edith Craig's production of an *Old English Nativity Play*. It was preceded by a musical
concert organized by Lady Maud Warrender featuring her partner,
Marcia Van Dresser.[27] Craig's production with the League of Arts
at the Guildhouse, Eccleston Square, in January 1923, was to raise
funds for a charity called 'The Home for Mentally Defective Blind
Babies' (EC-G1487). Each of these charities was associated with
health and welfare especially for the care of children and in this
regard there are continuities with Craig's involvement in women's
suffrage campaigning when these matters were clearly identifiable
as political issues affecting women and, in some respects, a key
indicator of the treatment of women in society. The educational relevance of the nativity play that had been identified in the Newbolt
Report is reflected in Craig's production for the Florence Etlinger
Dramatic School, Paddington St, London in December 1924. The
production was so successful that it led to Craig being invited to
teach classes at the school that month (*Referee*, 11 January [1924];
EC-G1435).

The Etlinger Dramatic School (1924) production gave the young
Peggy Webster an exceptional opportunity to read the lines of the
Prologue to the admiration of Ellen Terry, reported in the *Daily
Chronicle* (4 December 1924; EC-G1437). The nativity play had
a large cast with multiple angels, attendants, soldiers and pages,
offering the widest opportunity for participation and flexibility
to accommodate friends and family who wished to take part. In
the Daly's Theatre (1925) production, one of the pages was played
by Peggy Webster. Craig herself played second Monk, a role she
adopted in some of her historical pageants. John Gielgud was second Shepherd. He was twenty-one years old and at a point in his
career when he had only three years of experience as a professional
actor with Phyllis Neilson-Terry's company and before he established himself at the Old Vic Theatre.

Although superficially the productions of the nativity play look
similar, Craig made significant changes, developing and adapting
them to suit the context. In this regard, there are continuities in
her method with *A Pageant of Great Women*. At the Wigmore Hall
(1918), the nativity play was followed by a procession of saints and
martyrs, beginning with St Cecilia and ending with St George. At
the Guildhall, York (1925), a tableaux composed of thirteen 'saints
and martyrs' had a Yorkshire theme, with Saint Hilda of Whitby,
Saint William of York and Saint Robert of Knaresborough. In this

respect Craig's adaptation of the nativity play to the local region was similar to her approach in directing *A Pageant of Great Women* which she adapted slightly to include great women from history with a local relevance. This technique was also used in the Daly's Theatre (1925) production later the same year when the nativity play was followed by tableaux, presented as a vision, of mostly female saints with some association with children, education and the arts, explained in the historical glossary in the play programme. They appeared in sequence, ending with St Ursula, Patron Saint of Girls; St Nicholas, Patron Saint of Children; St Joan of Arc; and the Patron Saints of the Four Nations.

Craig's imaginative use of the performance space for the Etlinger Dramatic School (1924) production included unexpectedly breaking the frame of the conventional acting area: 'A couple of be-cowled monks occupied chairs either upon or just beneath the stage' (*The Stage*, 11 December [1924]). The strategic elevation seems to have created a sense of a separate perspective from the heavenly sphere: 'great skill was displayed in the portrayal of the Angel Gabriel, purple-robed, with huge aureole, and posed aloft on a sort of high pedestal' (*The Stage*, 11 December [1924]). Although the reviewer did not mention *Bethlehem* (1901), the lighting strategy of that production seems to have been adapted and developed further here: 'the shed irradiated by the Star of Bethlehem and guarded by Angels, was shown most effectively by means of illuminated transparencies, a double arrangement of curtains being used for this most artistic and reverentially presented production' (The Stage, 11 December [1924]).

Craig seems to have designed the costumes for most productions of the nativity play. At the Monastery, Rye (1919), an extant photograph of performers in costume, including Christopher St John as Herod, gives some sense of the careful grouping with a view to an effective presentation from a distance. At the Everyman Theatre production, Hampstead (1920), the costume worn by Dorothy Massingham as the Angel Gabriel gave the impression of great height, with long flowing robes hanging from outstretched arms (EC-G1438). The fabric appears to have been plain and sufficiently light to enable it to hang clearly in folds. The headdress rose above and behind the performer and appears to have been made of a metallic and reflective material. In the photograph reproduced in an unidentified newspaper, the costume bears some resemblance to those used for Woman in *A Pageant of Great Women*.

The costumes for the Wigmore Hall (1918) production were photographed in the press, giving a detailed impression of their style and construction. They were decorated with stylized motifs and borders which appear to be made of reflective material and symbolize a highly imaginative interpretation of the characters. The play programme unusually designated Edith Craig as producer and as 'Stage director Pioneer Players Society'. The play programme and the costumes were designed by Pamela Colman Smith,[28] with an acknowledgement of May's of Garrick Street for providing the 'gold armour' (EC-D202). A reviewer responded to Craig's Etlinger Dramatic School (1924) production by attributing the approach to others, as if it:

> might be styled the Reinhardt or the Elizabethan Stage Society manner, by processions of performers going along the centre aisle of the auditorium, and ascending by means of five steps up on to the stage, or reaching that by means of a side aisle in surprisingly expeditious fashion, as was show in the final groupings of the entire company after the flight into Egypt. (*The Stage*, 11 December [1924])

This exemplifies the often confused nomenclature critics adopt when faced with unexpected innovation.[29] The reviewer for *The Stage* did at least appropriately locate Craig in the company of William Poel and Max Reinhardt. Some of the productions of religious plays had developed a characteristic style which Craig had avoided. A review of Craig's 1923 London production of the *York Nativity Play* stated that Craig 'has kept her company free of the dismal practice of monotone, which threatened to become common in modern productions of religious drama' (*Times*, 19 January 1923; EC-G1487).

The impact of the nativity play on postwar community building, as promoted by the BDL and the Newbolt Report, is in evidence in the Everyman Theatre, Hampstead (1920) and most clearly in the Guildhall, York (1925) about which there is most documentation.[30] Craig's 1925 production in York was a landmark in the history of York and a precursor to the York Mystery Plays from 1951 onwards. The production of the nativity play at the Guildhall, York on 5 January 1925 was organized by the York Everyman Theatre, based in Coney Street, York with four directors: Edith Craig;

Charles F. Smith; Margery W. Patterson; and Herbert M. Duke. The chosen venue met with opposition and exposed a conservatism in York City Council, whose Estates Committee had originally recommended that the application for performance be refused. There may have been concerns about it being a public performance or its representation of Jesus: 'On taking legal advice, the council felt in a position to advise its members that so long as the play was of a biblical or a liturgical character, the question of stage licence need not arise.' (*Yorkshire Gazette*, 10 January 1925). The local paper, the *Yorkshire Gazette*, welcomed this change of mind: 'The Guildhall is unquestionably the desirable setting for such a play. A medieval atmosphere still clings to its structure and it is linked with the cyclic mystery dramas by reason of being the old home of the craft guilds which performed them' (*Yorkshire Gazette*, Saturday, 10 January 1925, p. 6). The reviewer emphasized the historical significance of the play and the authenticity of the setting:

> Dramas of this kind were a feature in the life of York during the fourteenth and fifteenth centuries, and the episodes of the Nativity Play were taken from the Miracle Plays performed between the fourteenth and sixteenth centuries by the Guilds of Coventry and York. The York text was written about 1430 and though alterations have been necessary for the adaptation of the play to a modern stage, no pains have been spared to create the atmosphere which must have surrounded the original performances. (*Yorkshire Gazette*, Saturday, 10 January 1925, p. 7)

The production had a great impact on the city of York and its developing Little Theatre movement was considerable. It was typical of Craig's directorial approach; it demonstrated her concern with the coherence of all elements of the staging, subtle lighting and historical authenticity. It was distinguished by 'unpretentious scenery, the gorgeous dresses, the admirable lighting which transformed their colouring and shed on them an almost mysterious brilliance' and 'the use throughout of an archaic simplicity of speech, in keeping with the simple Nativity legend' (*Yorkshire Gazette*, 10 January 1925).

Some distinguished members of the local community were cast in the nativity play, reflecting the support for the York Everyman Theatre enterprise.[31] The production had the effect on the city of York of increasing its status and promoting civic pride and the effect on the audience of instigating a mysterious transformation. These aims were shared by several organizations which promoted theatre after the First World War. The obstacles to the production at the Guildhall were presented by the *Yorkshire Gazette* as potentially 'tarnish[ing] York's standing as a patron of the arts' whereas this specific production was 'helping to place a city with a rich historic past on a level with Bristol, Birmingham, and Bath as a protector of the dramatic art' (*Yorkshire Gazette*, Saturday, 10 January 1925, p. 6). This event contributed to the development of the status and civic pride of York, enhancing its historical association with religious authority and locating it along-side other significant provincial cities 'as a *protector* of the dramatic art' (my emphasis). The application of the concept of protection positions the provincial city in a paternalistic role as well as invoking the military discourse of the recent war. Those concerned to protect and promote the 'art of the theatre' implicitly identified the commercial theatre and film as an adversary. These anxieties concerned a defence of art located in the metropolis and mobilized against the popular culture envisaged as colonizing the provinces. The diffidence of the City Council towards this production may be a measure of their resistance to cultural interference from the metropolis.

Craig maintained her interest in the drama of Hrotsvit, producing *Gallicanus*, and *Dulcitius* at the Grand Garden Fete at Campion House, Osterley on 22 June [1927] to raise funds for young priests and the Catholic Women's League, Westminster Diocesan branch. The publicity material lists a number of other attractions including folk dancing, photography, side-shows and thé dansant as well as 'a big rally of Knights & handmaids expected'.[32] The event seems to have involved some kind of historically costumed pageant or procession, suggesting a reiteration of the procession of saints and martyrs that had followed the performances of *An Early English Nativity Play*.

# Drama in churches, 'bringing art to dull towns' and the Reinhardt comparator (1924)

Edith Craig had a longstanding interest in theatre history and religious drama. She had served her time, learning the skills of costume design, lighting, musical composition, as well as acting and directing. Before the First World War those talents were devoted to performances for the women's suffrage movement of processions and plays which exploited historical precedent and civic pageantry. Hrotsvit was an exceptional woman amenable to appropriation by suffrage propaganda but she was of interest to Craig in other ways, namely reviving the close connection between stage and church, a subject on which she was interviewed by national newspapers. She claimed that when a play was performed in a church, the church itself became an actor.

In a lengthy interview entitled 'Bringing Art to Dull Towns: A Chat with Miss Edith Craig by W. W. F.' (*Daily Chronicle*, 4 December 1924 [?], THM 384/33/1), Craig described how 'the little theatre movement, as I see it, stands between the commercial theatre and the amateur dramatic society or club'. She generalized about America being more welcoming to new ideas than Britain. She referred to the plans at York for a production of a nativity play and her previous productions at Leeds and York, including *Ambush, The Secret Agent* and 'a church play, which was produced by Reinhardt in Germany and we are giving a Nativity play at York'. This designation of *The Great World Theatre* invites comparison between her direction and that of Max Reinhardt. 'Little theatres, I believe (concluded Miss Craig) have come to stay [...]' (*Daily Chronicle*, 4 December 1924).

## The Great World Theatre

Craig's understated description of her forthcoming production of *The Great World Theatre* by Hugo von Hofmannstahl exemplified the 'laughing self-effacement' which characterized her work for the women's suffrage movement. The 'church play' she was to produce was one of the two internationally renowned plays by Hofmannstahl, the other being *Everyman*, which Reinhardt had directed almost continuously at the Salzburg Festival, and which he co-founded with Hofmannstahl in 1920. *The Great World Theatre* was adapted from a seventeenth-century play by Calderon, with six characters, King, Rich Man, Farmer, Beauty, Beggar and Wisdom. Craig's self-deprecating description of her project and brief mention of Max Reinhardt typically misses the opportunity to elaborate on her own talents, methods and ambitions. Reinhardt's name was offered as a citation that readers would recall in association with *The Miracle*, produced at Olympia, London in 1911 to great acclaim, as a spectacular event. Lady Diana Cooper was celebrated in the Madonna role when Reinhardt revived *The Miracle* in New York, United States in 1924 and at the Lyceum Theatre, London in 1932. Craig nevertheless, uncharacteristically, locates herself in the field of contemporary theatre, inviting readers to treat Max Reinhardt as her comparator. Reinhardt had established himself as an eclectic director and had extensive experience in numerous theatres in Germany including the Volksbühne (1915–18). By 1924, when Craig cited Reinhardt, he had successfully run the Salzburg Festival for several years.[33]

In preparation for Craig's production, Charles Smith arranged for performance rights of *The Great World Theatre* and, after considering venues such as St John's at Holland Park, Queen's Gate, St Mary Abbotts, Kensington, by the end of October 1923 St Edward's at Holbeck, Leeds, was fixed. According to the play programme, the play ran from Monday, 7 to Saturday, 19 January 1924 at 3.30 and 7.30 pm. It was an intense period for Craig away from home. On 22 January 1924 Tony Atwood provided Vera Holme with a detailed account of the success of *The Great World Theatre*:

> You know she has had an immense success at Leeds – They've been doing the 'Great World Theatre' there in a church at Holbeck & the papers have been very keen about it – The booking is immense the whole of the seats sold out a fortnight ahead. They can't go on longer because the people engaged are all busy in the day time & couldn't stand the strain – Mat of the London papers sent representatives & the 'press' has been immense. We have not seen Edy for nearly a month here but we were so keen about the show – that Chris got sent to Leeds by her paper & I felt I must go so I scraped the fare together & went to Leeds for two nights & saw it twice & most wonderful it was – She is still there working the lights & keeping her hand on the show – This last performance will be the Saturday matinee this week & then I suppose she will come south when the strike permits. (7VJH 4/3/48)[34]

Something of Craig's method as a director is revealed by Atwood's account. As demonstrated by Craig's personal involvement in the costume and elevated arrangement on stage of Kate Parry Frye in

*The Coronation* in 1912, she continued a decade later with *The Great World Theatre* when she was 'working the lights'. In order for the director to have aesthetic control over the whole production, Craig revealed her expertise with each of the tasks that contributed to the overall effect: costume, music, lighting.

## *The Great World Theatre* revived (1934)

Some insights into the performance space within the church are given in the press when *The Great World Theatre* was revived ten years later in 1934 in the same venue for a ten-day run directed by C. F. Smith and members of the former Leeds Civic Theatre to raise funds for the Leeds Maternity Hospital. *The Sunderland Echo* reported that the Princess Royal was to attend the opening night and described the rehearsal in some detail, noting the 'brilliant flood-lighting, which pours down on to a scarlet-draped stage with a lovely oaken rood screen and an exquisite altar-piece as a natural back-cloth' (3 December 1934; EC-G1408). The use of 'a hidden choir of boys' added to the mysterious atmosphere. The description of a transformation from inanimate to living figures recalls the device Craig employed in *The Coronation* where the Madonna statue is embodied by a performer: 'Statuesque figures gorgeously attired and framed in the panels of the rood screen come to life during the play and step out of their niches.' (EC-G1408) It is not clear whether Edith Craig was directly involved in C. F. Smith's production but there must have been some influence from the 1924 production.[35]

According to one review, which emphasized the personification by the Beggar of 'a desperate socialism in revolt against the ordered Conservatism of Rich-man', the performers 'preferred to remain anonymous' (*Yorkshire Post*, 11 December 1934; EC-G1411). The inference of a collective enterprise where attribution to any single individual would conflict with the principles upon which the creative work is produced is reminiscent of the proposal Craig had made for the BDL Workshop Committee in 1919. It also explains further the likely significance of the mode of 'laughing self-effacement' adopted by Craig; rather than a personality trait of self-deprecation or dif-fidence, it appears to have been an aesthetic and political strategy whereby the produced work of theatrical art took precedence over the individuals who collectively contribute to it. Craig came into her own in the direction of nativity plays and pageants; a hooded monk figure, she worked in the footsteps of those who created the early drama in the guilds.

## Henzie Browne, E. Martin Browne and the afterlives of the nativity play

Edith Craig's productions of nativity plays are an important link in the history of nativity plays and religious drama in Britain as well as an identifiable influence on E. Martin Browne (1900–80) and his partner, Henzie. E. Martin Browne led religious drama in Britain from 1930, and directed T. S. Eliot's *The Rock* (1934) and *Murder in the Cathedral* (1935) for the Canterbury Festival. In 1939 he founded the Pilgrim Players and in 1951 he directed the first modern production of a four-hour abridged version of the full cycle of the York Mystery Plays at York for the Festival of Britain, marking the beginnings of the annual productions at York.[36] Edith Craig features briefly in E. Martin Browne's publications on religious drama and in Henzie Browne's history of the Pilgrim Players (1945). Craig's productions such as *The Shepherds* (1915), *The Tidings Brought to Mary* (1917), *The Shewing-up of Blanco Posnet* (1921) and *The Great World Theatre* (1924) were relevant and influential in the work of Browne and possibly T. S. Eliot.

In reflecting on the developments in Britain in this field of theatrical production in the keynote lecture at the first Leicestershire Festival of Religious Drama, published as *Fifty Years of Religious Drama* (1978), E. Martin Browne identified two founding moments: 'Today, we stand midway between the two events which established Religious Drama fifty years ago: the performance at Whitsuntide 1928 of the first play in a Cathedral since the Reformation and the foundation in Spring 1929 of the Religious Drama Society' (Browne 1979: 1). Canterbury Cathedral was the venue in 1928 for *The Coming of Christ*, commissioned by Dean Bell from John Masefield, Gustav Holst and Charles Ricketts. The Religious Drama Society was subsequently founded and the BDL asked E. Martin Browne to set up the first Religious Drama School, held in 1930 at the Eastbourne Parish Church, Bournemouth where he staged the York nativity play (Browne 1979: 2). Browne briefly mentions others who were involved in nativity plays, such as Laurence Housman, John Masefield and Bottomley. With regard to his production of the York Mystery Plays (1951), Browne mentioned as early precursors Nugent Monck (1877–1958) and William Poel (1852–1934).[37] In this retrospective account, Browne claims that 'With *Murder in the Cathedral*, modern Religious Drama entered the professional theatre' (p. 3), revealing the vexed relationships between the amateur and professional that had featured in the deliberations of the BDL and the Newbolt Report.

Forty years earlier and at a time in his career when Browne had not yet produced the ground-breaking productions of T. S. Eliot's plays, *The Rock* (1934) and *Murder in the Cathedral* (1935), he published *The Production of Religious Plays* (1932) in which Edith Craig's work as a director makes a significant appearance. In that book he provides a detailed account of the challenges and achievements of practitioners in this field. Some of these included women such as Marjorie Gullan, 'the pioneer of choral speaking' (Browne 1932: 21), and Sheila Kaye-Smith and her 'attempts to adapt the mystery play method to modern Sussex' (Browne 1932: 15) and authors May Pelton (*The Gladdening Light*) and Mary Kelly (*Jacob and Joseph*) (Browne 1932: 21). Browne had returned to Britain in 1930 after a period in Pittsburgh, United States at the Carnegie Institute of Technology where he was an assistant professor. When given an opportunity to select a play for production, he was inspired by Edith Craig's production of *The Tidings Brought to Mary* by Paul Claudel, using the translation by Louise Morgan Sills, which Craig had used with the Pioneer Players. Browne noted that the play, 'written in 1910 had been seen briefly in Paris, fleetingly in New York and on a Sunday night directed by Edith Craig in London. The poet was at that time French ambassador in Washington' (Browne 1932: 44). Browne emphasized the play's fifteenth-century setting 'in and around a farmhouse, both practically as well as mystically connected with an enclosed order of nuns' (Browne 1932: 45). The contrast in Claudel's play draws its power from the location of profound religious experience in the unlikely setting of rural poverty. In religious drama, including the nativity play, the contrast between the material and secular and the mystical and spiritual sometimes made for an uneasiness of tone if the director lacked excellent production skills.

Most significantly, Browne presents Edith Craig's production of *The Great World Theatre* as a landmark production; an example of innovative use of the church building in staging the play, making use of different spaces and features, notably the rood screen:

> Miss Edith Craig produced 'The Great World Theatre' in a Leeds church which had a rood-screen. She had in front of it, not a single platform, but several small structures, each with its own approach; and she used the niches of the screen as houses for various characters. For heaven, she used the chancel, seen lighted through the woodwork of the darkened screen. (Browne 1932: 45)

Browne noted the difficulties of staging plays in a church with regard to sound and arranging the entrances and exits of the performers but specifically mentions a method, which was used in *The Great World Theatre*:

> [...] the 'Processional Method' of production. This method, by which the action of the play moves through the audience, is a return to the principles of liturgical worship, and is the furthest possible from that of the proscenium stage. It does away with all sense of locality, and with the idea that the actors are in another place from the audience; they become linked together in the one act of showing forth God's goodness in visible form. Hence the writer believes that in its development lies one of the chief hopes for the right use of drama in church. (Browne 1932: 46)

Edith Craig had another part to play in the theatrical career of E. Martin Browne and his partner Henzie Browne. The Brownes worked together with the Pilgrim Players from 1939 about which Henzie published a history (1945), in which E. Martin recalled Henzie was taken on in 1921 as assistant stage manager at the Everyman Theatre Hampstead. 'Another was for Edith Craig in George Bernard Shaw's *The Shewing-up of Blanco Posnet*; she gave Henzie hell all morning, then took her out to lunch and they became friends' (p. 24).[38] Shaw's play subtitled *A Sermon in Crude Melodrama* (1909) presents religious and moral arguments through the dialogue of a drunken, horse-stealing cowboy, Blanco Posnet. Challenging the audience to deal with its grotesque and absurd aspects, the play located the potential for spiritual redemption and human development even in the North American frontier country.

On 15 June 1935 E. Martin Browne famously directed T. S. Eliot's *Murder in the Cathedral* in the Chapter House, Canterbury Cathedral.[39] Browne became head of the BDL (1948–57) and in 1951 directed the first modern production (since 1572) of the full cycle of the York Mystery plays in the ruins of St Mary's in York which constituted York's contribution to the Festival of Britain. The report written by the York festival organizer Keith Thompson indicates that other dramatic productions had been considered for this important event, including the possibility of restaging Louis N. Parker's *Pageant of York* (1909), but he cautioned, 'Pageants have the twin disadvantages of attracting bad weather and – on occasions – of being the dullest things known to man' (p. 16). There had been an idea to stage the Corpus Christi plays about the city in the manner of the medieval 'pageant' cart, moving the stage and requiring the audience to follow. Instead the programme emphasized the unique aspect of Browne's production which lay in the full cycle of plays, of which the nativity was only one element: 'The Festival performances are the first to be given in anything approaching the original completeness since 1572. It is a unique event in the history of the English Stage'.[40]

The nativity play and tableaux had also become associated with amateur dramatics and the self-indulgent foray into performance by the elite. In Evelyn Waugh's *Vile Bodies* (1930), Mrs Melrose Ape, 'the female evangelist', has a troupe of 'Angels', designated variously Faith, Hope, Charity – female performers whose behaviour off-stage provides the necessary comic contrast and their exit from the plot provides an allusion to the European influences on British religious drama: '[Mrs Ape] left the country with her angels, having received a sudden call to ginger up the religious life of Oberammergau' (Waugh 1930: 92). As Martin Stannard (2004) has noted, Muriel Spark's career was launched when she won an *Observer* competition for a Christmas story, with 'The Seraph and the Zambesi' (1951).[41] In Spark's story, a nativity masque written for performance on a makeshift stage in a garage, is gate-crashed by the real thing: 'the Seraph', a winged and mysterious being. The uneasy tone and potentially absurd contrast between the secular and sacred, the sombre and banal, the artistic and what Waugh calls 'bogus' in *Vile Bodies* (1930), render the nativity performance by amateurs on stage and represented in narrative as the material for satire. In the hands of the devout and expert, whether religious or theatre practitioner, the nativity play had the potential for recreation even in the garages in the dullest of towns.

Edith Craig's production of *An Early English Nativity Play* in York's Guildhall in 1925 has been the missing link in this history. Although no explicit reference was made in 1951 to Edith Craig's single earlier production, it was one of the partial productions of the cycle which had, nevertheless, promoted peace and civic pride and promised community regeneration following the First World War. In 1951 E. Martin Browne walked in Edith Craig's footsteps. Craig's productions exemplified the remarkable invigoration of theatre by the BDL and others. The appropriation of the nativity story for England and the restriction to the staging of the birth of Christ lent itself to a more indirect engagement with the necessary rejuvenation following the First World War. The regression in the narrative of the life of Christ to his birth in the nativity play therefore dwells on innocence and life, repressing the insistent traumatic memory of death which the First World War had imposed on many guilty survivors. The residue of this guilt accumulating after the war was resolved in various cultural outlets. The numerous war memorials which were erected signified the need to remember the dead and to close that memory by consolidating the identity of the community. Jay Winter has argued that, 'After August 1914, commemoration was an act of citizenship. To remember was to affirm community, to assert its moral character, and to exclude from it those values, groups, or individuals that placed it under threat' (Winter 1995: 80). It seems, therefore, that the interwar production of nativity plays provided a secular *and* religious event which, through association with the apocalyptic wartime religious discourse, constituted a ceremonial, ritual commemoration of the war. Its organization by a former militant suffrage activist symbolized the inclusion of women as citizens in postwar British culture.

# CHAPTER SEVEN
## 1919–46

# The Little Theatre mission: Pilgrims and pageants

A turning point for Edith Craig, as for most of her contemporaries, came towards the end of the First World War. For Craig other circumstances coincided to compound the upheaval. The Pioneer Players had lost momentum and financial pressures mounted as Ellen Terry became increasingly unable to work. Opportunities for Edith Craig to organize and direct plays abroad for J. T. Grein had been dashed by the sensational libel litigation in which he became embroiled. However, the British Drama League (BDL) provided her with a role in active leadership work at a national level. Her aim was to obtain a more permanent salaried position in a theatre and, in working to achieve this goal, Craig was active in the direction of many single performances for various organizations and charities. She made significant contributions to children's theatre (*Through the Crack*, *The Shoe*), Jewish theatre (S. Ansky's *The Dybbuk* and Israel Zangwill's *The Melting Pot*) and Restoration and early modern revivals (with the Phoenix Society and the Renaissance Theatre society). She directed several dramatizations from the literary canon (*Wuthering Heights, Pride and Prejudice, The Secret Agent*) and as an actor appeared in one (*Fires of Fate*) which took her on location to Egypt in the new medium of film. She enhanced her reputation for working with the latest plays, whether new writing or revivals, informed by her innovative and distinctive style and with a collaborative and supportive approach, fostering a new generation of theatre practitioners. The prolific theatre work Craig undertook in the interwar period in different theatres and regions was informed by her involvement in leading the work of the BDL.

This chapter will therefore explore some of these single, remarkable productions, considering their impact and significance and how they were located in relation to the various Little Theatres with which Craig had held (ultimately short-term) posts as a director: the Everyman Theatre, Hampstead (1920–21); St Christopher's Theatre, Letchworth (1924–5); the York Everyman Theatre (1924); The Leeds Art Theatre (LAT) (1922–4) and the Leeds Civic Playhouse (1930–1). In order to establish a sense of the complex circumstances facing theatre practitioners such as Edith Craig in this interwar period, a broadly chronological approach will be followed although Craig's prolific output complicates this to a certain extent. This investigation raises questions about the relevance of the Little Theatre movement in Britain and the United States and in the development of 'middlebrow' culture in the interwar period.

When Edward Gordon Craig published a short satirical article in *The Mask* (1918) on the Little Theatre movement, he highlighted a tension that the BDL had not quite addressed. On the front page he juxtaposed a translation of 'Little States' from the ancient Chinese philosopher Lao-Tzu with his own adaptation entitled 'Little Theatres and So On', written in a similar style:

> And then, 'said Yu-no-whoo, picking up the thread the Master had dropped as he fell asleep,' and then, were I your prime minister I would do so much to divert the people a little: do you know, Master, I would have tiny little Theatres every two miles – I would have them on the hills and down near the shore…one on the road once in away…but most of them dotted here and there along the hills…under olives if in Italy, under oaks if in that strange country about which you have so often threatened to speak to me…here in bamboo groves…it would be so pretty.

Work done, I and my son would stroll across the valley around the broken path. We might stop at the little church. (*The Mask*, 1918: 1)

Gordon Craig ventriloquizes the problem, mediating it through a Chinese perspective to highlight the national identity being constructed through the Little Theatre movement. The proliferation of Little Theatres 'in that strange country' and their embeddedness in a particular place would inevitably give rise to questions of identity and competition, creating tensions in their pursuit of an audience and sustainability. How would these theatres operate without government funding and without a commercial remit? The engagement with the community, drawing on local expertise from volunteers and financial support from local businesses and benefactors, seemed to be the favoured, if not necessarily a carefully planned approach. Inevitably conflicts arose when the leaders in the theatre were not collaborating with individuals with commercial expertise. These questions became particularly pressing in the new theatre announced by Norman MacDermott at the BDL conference in August 1919.

## The Everyman Theatre, Hampstead (1920–1)

In *Everymania* (1975), Norman MacDermott (1890–1977) recorded the details of the Everyman Theatre, Hampstead, which he founded and ran from its opening on 15 September 1920 to 1926. It attracted supporters who were so enthusiastic that Edith Evans referred to the 'mania' exhibited there; it inspired MacDermott's references to the 'Everymaniacs' and the title of his history of the theatre. Edith Craig was actively involved as director of many plays at the Everyman Theatre from 1920 to 1921 and contributed to its success, notably providing informal mentorship and training for MacDermott himself, who was an expert in scenic design and manufacture rather than direction. MacDermott announced the aims of the Everyman Theatre in a prospectus (reprinted from his article in the *Nation*), quoting Jacques Copeau of the Théâtre de Vieux Colombier as 'beginning by the beginning'; MacDermott highlighted the importance of the audience and the aim to recapture the Greek understanding of the theatre as 'a place of seeing' and to avoid an '*over emphasis* of social problem drama' (EC-C73). In 1975 the account MacDermott gave of the construction, development, operation and decline of the Everyman Theatre illuminates the difficult circumstances in which Edith Craig worked. At times appreciative, at others disingenuously exploitative, MacDermott records his method of leadership and management, using volunteers and paid assistants and moving towards a period in which he was solely in control. The Everyman Theatre had many successes but a highlight was the 1921 spring season of George Bernard Shaw plays directed by Edith Craig and Noel Coward's *The Vortex* (1924) directed by the author.

After a difficult wartime experience of conscientious objection, MacDermott was totally committed to the new call to revitalize postwar theatre. Although he knew no one in London, his pacifist position may have gained him some acquaintances. When he approached George Bernard Shaw, he received support as well as a warning about the financial obstacles to such an endeavour:

> In so far as your scheme seems to me a move in that direction it has my blessing and that of every playwright who wants to do first rate work. I cannot answer for the details of your particular scheme, which will require good business management and adequate capital as well as artistic inspiration and capacity. But I can answer for the thing being wanted and badly wanted. (22 January 1919; Laurence 1985: 588)

MacDermott additionally managed to secure the support of authors and critics, such as Miles Malleson, Ernest Rhys, Gilbert Cannan, William Archer and St John Irvine, holding a timely public meeting on 15 May 1919 to discuss the new theatre, only three months before the BDL's Stratford conference. MacDermott had established his own aesthetic position in a public lecture at the Aeolian Hall on scene decoration. In emphasizing the practicalities of this aspect of production, he consequently criticized Gordon Craig's designs. This provoked a threatening deputation of Albert Rutherston, Norman Wilkinson and Lovat Fraser. MacDermott consequently attributed their absence from the Everyman Theatre to this difference of opinion (MacDermott 1975: 9).[1]

In spite of this, MacDermott had affinities with Edith Craig; they both appreciated the incorporation of the useful with the beautiful in everything they did. MacDermott anticipated the use of the Everyman Theatre building as a social space and therefore transformed the foyer into a gallery with exhibitions of paintings, posters and glassware. For all printed publicity he used Garamond, reflecting the revival of interest in this font that suggested the elegant craftwork of early modern printing and he mentioned briefly in the early days of his interest in theatre having helped Edith Craig to set up an 'exhibition of theatre material' at the Shakespeare birthday celebration at Stratford (MacDermott 1975: 9) MacDermott knew that his skills were in the design and building of sets and so, for the first couple of years at the Everyman Theatre, he arranged for others to produce or direct the plays and provide assistance in coaching actors in voice and choreography.

It is in this early period that he relied heavily upon Edith Craig, whose many skills enabled her to take on several jobs at once and who could be trusted to provide what Shaw had identified as a crucial ingredient for the success of the scheme: 'artistic inspiration' (Laurence 1985: 588). He explained in the epilogue to his book: 'Money for the supplemental assistants became hard to find and, eventually, with the engagement of Miss Edith Craig with her all-round talent, these appointments were allowed to lapse' (MacDermott 1975: 90). In 1920 he involved her as the 'assistant producer' for *Romeo and Juliet* and referred to a formal announcement that was made in the play programme: 'The play produced by Miss Edith Craig under the general direction of Norman MacDermott' (MacDermott 1975: 30). This reflects some discussion that must have taken place about the question of acknowledgement for her work but oddly, although MacDermott records this remedy in his history of the Everyman Theatre, he repeats the omissions elsewhere in the book. He fails to acknowledge her as director of *Through the Crack* or the nativity play and in his 'Calendar of Plays' all of the other producer/directors' names are omitted.[2] However, he explained the arrangement whereby Craig and other producers (naming only Milton Rosmer, Nicholas Hannen and Komisarjevsky) were engaged by the Everyman but worked under his overall direction (MacDermott 1975: 94). Given the clear position Craig had given at the Stratford conference in 1919 about one person – the producer – having overall control of the production, it is not surprising perhaps that her time at the Everyman Theatre was fairly short. MacDermott's 'general direction' or supervisory role was also pedagogical, as he recalled that he 'spent part of each day, silently in the darkened auditorium, watching Miss Craig at work with the company and, both now and later, other producers I engaged when a fee was available' (MacDermott 1975: 94). It was therefore in 1922, after which point he felt he had learnt enough from Edith Craig's example and, driven by the exigencies of taking on sole financial responsibility for the entire theatre, he assumed the role as sole director of the plays. This required some caution in the scheduling and consequently the plays staged in the summer periods of 1922 and 1923 were produced by the actors as a collective, presumably at their own financial risk, as 'commonwealth' productions.

Craig's significant achievements at the Everyman Theatre, Hampstead include her productions in the spring of 1921 of Shaw's plays which were responsible for reviving Shaw's reputation: 'Several of the critics were certainly seeing them for their first time. Some found it still difficult to write of the author without wartime prejudice but the standard of the performances won over practically all' (MacDermott 1975: 31). These eight plays are listed in MacDermott's 'Calendar of Plays [...] under the management of Norman MacDermott', beginning with *You Never Can Tell* on 24 January 1921 and concluding with *Major Barbara* on 30 April 1921 and *Major Barbara* and *Man and Superman* being staged again in May and June. It is widely known that for the first six months of 1921, Everyman Theatre audiences could see George Bernard Shaw's plays, raising his profile as a dramatist but Edith Craig's involvement as director has been somewhat marginalized, partly as a result of MacDermott's methods of presenting himself as the 'director' of the theatre at the expense of the assistants he employed. Dan Laurence has noted that MacDermott 'founded in 1920 the Everyman Theatre, Hampstead, an experimental arts theatre, in which Shaw's plays were re-introduced to the London area, after long neglect, in a series of Shaw seasons' (Laurence 1985: 587) but Edith Craig's direction is (understandably) not mentioned.

Shaw approved of the staging of his plays at the Everyman Theatre. He challenged St John Irvine about the accent of Douglas Jeffries in the role of Burgess in *Candida* which Irving had criticized in his review in *The Observer* on 13 February 1921 (Laurence 1985: 710). Shaw wrote to William Archer in 19 June 1923:

> But you may have noticed that at the Everyman, where there is a conventional stage adapted by a few mere hints to the three scenes of *Major Barbara*, the effect is just as good, and in the last act distinctly better, than it was at the Court Theatre, where there were three scenes solemnly painted with views of East Ham, Perivale, and Wilton Crescent. The four scenes of *The Doctors Dilemma* are played in that same conventional scene, and are equally and sufficiently effective. (Laurence 1985: 835)

As part of the intense correspondence between Archer and Shaw at this time, in response to Archer's collected lectures *The Old Drama and the New* (1923), Shaw made continued reference to the excellent interpretation and staging of his plays at the Everyman Theatre:

> Mrs Warren's Profession is a crude melodrama; and The Philanderer is a tragi-comedy (exquisitely put together, as I perceived when I saw it at the Everyman lately) on the very subtle subject of the operation of the Ibsenist changes in feeling about marriage and sexual relations in a society mainly quite impervious to Ibsen, even when it tried to be fashionably advanced in his name. (Laurence 1985: 838)

Craig's production therefore was alert to the tone and meaning of Shaw's play in a way which others had not achieved. Unfortunately, because neither Shaw nor MacDermott drew attention in their letters to her name as director, the attribution of Shaw's approval of this excellent interpretation has been overlooked. The impact of Craig's season of Shaw's plays at the Everyman Theatre in 1921 was so profound that, followed by Shaw's production of *St Joan* in June 1923, Shaw would write discouraging Madge McIntosh from pursuing a production of his plays in 1925 because so many others were attempting them: 'Shaw is becoming a monomania with all of them especially since the success of St Joan' (Laurence 1985: 901). Edith Craig's productions at the Everyman Theatre had been the catalyst.

# Restoration and Renaissance revivals: *All for Love* (1922), *The Faithfull Shepherdess* (1923) and *The White Devil* (1925)

Edith Craig's productions for the Phoenix Society and the Renaissance Theatre Society brought rarely seen plays from the Jacobean and Restoration stage to London. T. S. Eliot and Virginia Woolf attended the Phoenix Society production of *Love for Love* (1921) at a time when Eliot was working on his essays on Metaphysical Poets as well as *The Waste Land* (1922), with its staging of ventriloquized voices in a landscape of scenery lifted from Webster, Shakespeare, the local pub and possibly the kind of middlebrow amateur dramatics on offer in those Little Theatre movement enterprises directed by Edith Craig. Clive Bell described Eliot's self-fashioned 'cadaverous' appearance by means of green face powder (quoted in Ackroyd 1984: 136), which would have been at home in the Phoenix Society. This was organized by Montague Summers (1880–1948), a Catholic priest, scholar, editor and translator with interests in literature and witchcraft. By the time Edith Craig was involved in the Phoenix Society in 1922–3, Summers had published editions of Aphra Behn and Congreve, studies of Jane Austen, Ann Radcliffe, Lourdes, St Catherine of Siena and his own collection entitled *Antinous and Other Poems* (1907).[3]

Edith Craig's interests in theatre history and historical costume would certainly have drawn her to these organizations and their productions. Since the BDL Workshop Committee had been planning to devise model sets and costumes for period drama, it is possible that Craig's involvement in directing these productions had a pedagogical function. The production at the Shaftesbury Theatre in March 1922 of Dryden's *All for Love* was associated with both the Phoenix Society and the Incorporated Stage Society, with Craig's work in production supported by scene designs by Norman Wilkinson, (one of the angry deputation to Norman MacDermott). Costume designs were provided by Tom Heslewood and B. J. Simmons (SC16-D21). A similar team was reconvened, just over a year later, when Craig directed John Fletcher's *The Faithful Shepherdess* at the Shaftesbury Theatre in June 1923 for the Phoenix Society, again in association with the Incorporated

Stage Society and with the scene designs of Norman Wilkinson. For this production there was a musical accompaniment, conducted by Sir Thomas Beecham and personal significance for Craig in directing a play in her father's footsteps.[4]

Craig's production in October 1925 of *The White Devil* for the Renaissance Theatre Society was praised in *The Observer*, which singled out Laura Cowie's excellent performance as Vittoria. By contrast, a couple of months later, in December 1925, Cowie played the Angel Gabriel in Craig's production of the *Early English Nativity Play* at Daly's Theatre. Other actors in *The White Devil* were Esme Percy and Cedric Hardwicke. Reviews were headed 'Horrors at the Scala' in the *Star* and 'Wicked Duchess' in the *Westminster Gazette*, noting the emotionally difficult material that was alienating to the audience, and concerns about the extent to which the text had been cut. However, J. T. Grein wrote to Craig, as 'my dear friend', to praise her production (EC-Z3, 308). This production of a Jacobean revenge play and two other revivals, John Dryden's *All for Love* (1922) and John Fletcher's *The Faithfull Shepherdess* (1923), followed the strategic guidance offered by the Newbolt Report as the ideal repertoire for the modern audience.

## Forays into film: *Fires of Fate* (1923)

The new medium of film became a commercial threat to theatrical production but it was embraced by Ellen Terry, James Carew and Edith Craig, all of whom experimented with film work. Craig brought her expertise of lighting and composition on the stage, and working with tableaux as a means of thinking about film as moving pictures. Before the First World War, Craig performed in *Her Greatest Performance* (1916) as the dresser, in a supporting role to her mother. She appeared in several films, including a documentary about the invasion of Britain and claimed to own a section of this forgotten film. As a member of the Film Society, interested in the artistic and experimental potential of film, she had access to the lectures and workshops on film-making as well as screenings of films at the New Gallery Kinema, Regent Street, London.[5]

In February and March 1923, Craig's film work *Fires of Fate* took her on location to Egypt at probably the most exciting of times. It was only four months after the discovery of Tutankhamun's tomb

FIGURE 3 *Edith Craig riding a camel in Egypt (1923) (reproduced with permission of The V&A Theatre Collection); Edith Craig using her wheelchair (1933) (reproduced with permission of The National Trust).*

by Howard Carter in November 1922. Craig was in Egypt at the time of its sensational opening on 16 February 1923, publicized worldwide and generating a fashion for Egyptian aesthetic characterized by ebony and gold. *Fires of Fate* was directed by Tom Terriss (1872–1964), son of actor William Terriss. The film was made for Gaumont Films, starring American performer Wanda Hawley (1895–1963), who had performed with Rudolph Valentino in *The Young Rajah* (1922), one of his least successful films but renowned for the costume designs. Hawley's sensational divorce case off-screen attracted the attention of some journalists covering the filming of *Fires of Fate*. At fifty-three years, Craig played the character-acting part as the elderly aunt. The press coverage in Britain provided an account of the film production but it also revealed the national standing of Craig such that readers would be interested in her departure from Victoria Station, London, witnessed by Ellen Terry; her daily rides on a camel, said to be the fastest in the country; and even the sadness of her pet cat while she was away. Journalists associated Craig with intrepid adventure and eccentricity.

Craig's private letters home give an impression of the extent to which Egypt had become an attraction to tourists on a mission to see the wonders of the world. Craig took care to remember her mother's birthday with an early telegram, one on 15 February 1923 and another from the Continental Hotel. She wrote just before setting off on an eighteen-hour train journey to Luxor and reported, 'Yesterday I rode on a camel for the first time and loved it', but did not appreciate the other hotel guests:

> This hotel is simply crowded with cackling Americans of the worst type. They move round the world in batches for a sun down & then work to a set programme of sight seeing. Most of this lot are now off to the Holy Land as they say 'With doo reverence & a bible in my hand I will do the Lake of Gallilee [*sic*] in two day[s] & then on to the next place.' They talk a lot about 'God's own sunshine & Ocean breeze etc' but they are the worst lot I've ever met. (Sunday, 11 March 1923; THM 384/4/5)

In mimicking these Americans, Craig involves her mother in a shared criticism of the brash consumerist approach to travel but in so doing there would have been some risk of sensitivity concerning Terry's marriage to James Carew. Craig found time off from performing in the film to explore the landscape and the new experience of camel-riding:

> I spend my days now on a camel. I get fearfully stiff when they trot but I like riding across sand & sand & nothing in sight & seeing the wonderfull [*sic*] white sunsets[.] I like them better than the red & orange ones. The sun goes down white & the clouds are violet & blue & purple & the Pyramids are first pink then blue then black = I'm off now (on a camel) to look for mummy bead in the sand heaps the other side of the pyramids [...] I hope I won't be sick on the way home as I have to share a cabin with the leading lady! You must meet her she is a scream. (30 March 1923; THM 384/4/5)

These experiences probably provided her with excellent research for her performance in the film, which was based on Arthur Conan Doyle's imperialist novel *The Tragedy of the Korosko* (1897), about a hazardous journey up the Nile. Doyle's depiction of Egypt would not have enhanced the idea of an independent nation freed from colonial rule. The film locations mentioned in the press included a mosque, a battle scene in the Nubian desert and a banquet hosted by 'the Sheik of Mena'. The staging of the battle scene was given a great deal of attention as having been observed by representatives of the British military, still based in Egypt after independence had been declared in 1922: General Herbert, who was Resident Commissioner, and General Hunter, head of the Camel Corps in Egypt. The reviews described 'The battle scenes included a reconstruction of a famous Dervish charge upon a British square' (*Daily Graphic*, 17 April 1923; EC-G1571). When Tom Terriss was interviewed in September 1923 by the influential American film critic Louella Parsons about his experiences in Egypt, he claimed that scenes of 'whirling Dervishes' had made Wanda Hawley faint (1923: 4). Louella Parsons envisaged that 'one of the wonderful things about the film is to be able to see the pyramids, the desert and all that land around Cairo, Alexandria and Luxor, without actually going there' (1923: 4). The film exploited an orientalist voyeurism fuelled by the archaeological discoveries of Lord Caernarvon's English expedition which created tensions for the newly independent Egypt in this highly volatile political period.

Most of Parsons's interview concerned Terriss's account that Harold Carter had invited him to be one of the twenty-four witnesses at the opening of Tutankhamun's tomb. Terriss is not listed in Carter's published record, which refers to named witnesses who are included in the party 'of about twenty individuals' but it appears not to have been an exhaustive list; Carter does mention that Lady Evelyn Herbert witnessed the opening (Carter and Mace 2014: 169).[6] Edith Craig had probably only just arrived in Cairo at the time. She is not mentioned as one of the witnesses at the opening of the tomb but it is unlikely that she was spared Terriss's account of it. The film work brought Craig a much-needed income of £7 a week from 8 February to 1 April (EC-B118) and an unforgettable experience of Egypt at the time of the discovery of Tutankhamun's tomb.

# Leeds Art Theatre (1923–4), the middlebrow and modernism in the north

A few months before Edith Craig set off for Egypt, she received a letter from the Vice Chancellor of Leeds University, M. E. Sadler, thanking her for having agreed to give an informal talk in early March [1923].[7] Since his appointment to the position of Vice Chancellor in 1912, Sadler had been at the centre of the promotion of the arts in Leeds. He was a patron of many Leeds organizations and individual artists, including Jacob Kramer (1892–1962) whom he encouraged to apply to the Slade School of Art; Kramer's work was subsequently exhibited at the New English Art Club and was promoted by Augustus John (Steele 1990: 205).[8] Sadler's son, Michael Sadleir [*sic*], translated *The Art of Spiritual Harmony* (1914) by the Russian artist Wassily Kandinsky. Kramer lectured on post-impressionism with illustrations of the interpretation of colour with sound. As Tom Steele has noted in his study *Alfred Orage and the Leeds Arts Club 1893–1923*, Leeds had been the centre of a highly active arts debate since 1903 when Alfred Orage, editor of the radical journal *The New Age*, founded the Leeds Art Club and personally gave its first lecture on 7 November 1903 on Nietzsche. The weekly lectures covered a wide variety of topics, and were underpinned by the pursuit of art and cultural experiment, considered to be ennobling, and a development of an individualism which could be compatible with collectivism in this avant garde led by an intellectual elite. Steele observed that 'the medieval and Celtic past became the inspiration for social reform and signified a rallying call to women's consciousness' (Steele 1990: 95). Steele identifies several phases of activity in the Leeds Art Club: in 1903–11 there had been numerous lively debates and in 1912 two individuals, Michael Sadler appointed as Vice Chancellor of Leeds University and Frank Rutter as director of the Leeds Art Gallery, became leaders of a new direction in its activities. I suggest that Edith Craig became a third leader of the arts in Leeds in 1923 when she organized the LAT. She inherited a significant and knowledgeable community from which to build an audience.

Tom Steele has proposed the reconsideration of Leeds as a significant but overlooked centre of modernist art, in the visual arts with Jacob Kramer, Henry Moore and William Rothenstein, and the cultural and theoretical debates about art promoted by Michael Sadler and Frank Rutter. In a chapter entitled 'Making It New: Modernism and the North of England', Michael T. Saler notes, 'Indeed, prior to World War One, Leeds was arguably the modern art capital of England' (Saler 1999: 46). Saler examines the phenomenon of medievalist modernism in the visual arts but overlooks drama. Ezra Pound's interest in the medieval period characterized him as 'a living archaism', according to Laurence Rainey, but it appears to be engaged with the latest trends when examined in a wider cultural context which extends to include theatre.[9] Oddly, given the active interest of canonical modernist authors in the writing of drama and their active participation in performance or attendance at theatrical productions, there is a significant omission in studies of modernism of theatrical enterprises, whether established theatre institutions or the numerous theatre societies operating informally or inter-mittently. The case of Edith Craig, her theatrical productions and leadership in the organization of Little Theatres and significant single productions of plays, reveals the wide interest in theatre in this period and its influence on the development of thinking about modern art in an interdisciplinary context. This invites a new con-sideration of the impulse to organize the Little Theatre movement and how this influenced and had an impact on modernist art forms in narrative, music, poetry, periodical and visual cultures. Although literary critics have tended to overlook drama, theatre and the new medium of film in modernist studies, the authors themselves were inevitably aware of, immersed in, and often directly contributing to theatrical innovations in this period, given the dominance of thea-tre in cultural practices. Instead of considering theatre and perfor-mance as an afterthought, its relocation as a central focus reveals new, hitherto overlooked spheres of influence and activity.

Edith Craig became a leader of theatrical innovation in Leeds and York, notably becoming Art Director for the new LAT. As Tom Steele notes, William Rothenstein (1872–1945) was a highly influ-ential artist in this period, having studied at the Slade, exhibited in Paris and was known to Degas, Pissaro, Whistler, Oscar Wilde and Verlaine; he promoted Yorkshire artists, such as Henry Moore and Barbara Hepworth, as well as art in the north of England to combat a metropolitan bias. Rothenstein was actively involved in several art clubs and became Professor of Civic Art at Sheffield University (1917) and Principal of the Royal College of Art (1920–35). In 1897 he had produced a portrait of Ellen Terry. In 1916 he was in correspondence with Edith Craig, mentioning that he was studying her costumes and advising her on relevant shops in London from which to obtain props for an unspecified production:

> [...] the man who sells their precious stuffs you will find in the left hand side of Camomile St, Bishopsgate (just past Liverpool

St Station). He is a Parsee from Bombay – I forget his name &
you will see Indian pots & figures in his window. His shop is less
than 100 yards up the street before you get to Francks, whose
Eastern emporium you probably know. (Sunday, 4 June 1916;
EC-3,577)

Craig's acquaintance with Rothenstein and his respect for her theatrework made him a significant contact in Yorkshire when she
worked with the LAT.

One of Craig's early LAT productions was *The Boatswain's
Mate*, the opera by Ethel Smyth in 1922, when Smyth improvised
by singing the part of the missing cello. Craig and Smyth corresponded about the production, and Smyth wrote a detailed review
of the production for the *Yorkshire Post*.[10] The plot concerns a
scheme with romantic aims but with features associating it with
women's suffrage. Boatswain Harry Benn tries to persuade Mrs
Waters, the innkeeper, to marry him by means of a ridiculous
plan to rescue her from a burglary which he has himself staged
using his friend, the ex-soldier, Ned Travers. Benn's plan casts Mrs
Waters in the role of vulnerable female victim and himself as patriarchal saviour. The romantic plot engineered by Benn is undercut
structurally and aurally by the overture, where the sound of 'The
March of the Women' would recall armies of suffragettes. Equally
it is undermined by the quick-witted retaliation of Mrs Waters,
who pretends to have killed the burglar and asks Benn to help her
bury the body and, notably, the fact that she is armed with a gun.
Mrs Waters is shown to be no match for Benn; she is indeed far
superior in intellect, courage and the ability to defend herself.[11]

In a very long and detailed letter to Edith Craig, Smyth described
research for an unnamed production (presumably *The Boatswain's
Mate*) and debating various techniques for lighting and production.
Smyth emphasizes the physicality of performance, the embodiment
by actors on stage and the need to acknowledge the dramatic effect
of this on an audience:

You say 'how can a man light the actors if he doesn't know
what they are going to do?' Why – of course not –! That is why
he must (& gladly would) first get at the producer's intentions
then build, and, far later on, light accordingly – in collusion
with her.

But much as I agree with what you say about mechanism ever replacing brains, it is true, isn't it?, that in this particular case you have to make the public rise to *the thrill of a physical situation* [my emphasis]. At the end of the Walkure you wd not deny, (would you?) that the actual springing up of flames round that rock-bed is an essential? The music crackles & spurts – just as my music gives the oncoming roar of a wave (it happened just 3 times...the 3rd behind the Curtain) the crash of its impact against the rocks, the swish of the spray & so on.

Once a work has been really launched into people's imaginations, such things can be very perfunctorily done; the audience jumps to the intention. (2 August 1924; EC-3, 651)

On 10 March the *Yorkshire Post* printed Ethel Smyth's unsigned article entitled 'A Leeds Chorus', which is more of a report on her experiences of working with amateurs and the value of the enterprise than a review of Craig's production of *The Boatswain's Mate* itself (EC-G1391). She was surprised by the high quality of the amateur singers and noted the general musical education now widely available from Gilbert and Sullivan operas and the forgiving nature of such familiar pieces which tolerate singers coming in at slightly the wrong place: 'It is like stepping off the asphalt path across a municipal common – no fear of losing your way! Perhaps too, there is someone at the piano with a finger ready at any moment to strike the note that calls home a lost sheep.' (EC-G1391) Smyth endorsed Rutland Boughton's argument that amateurs were 'a valuable asset' and she set out ten rules, as if for the training of a new army: 'along the lines of a soldier's drill book, for the guidance of both officers and men' (EC-G1391). She concluded with an emphasis on the role of the conductor, with 'the first and last piece of advice to give amateurs, it would be "Mind the stick".' (EC-G1391) The metaphors Smyth uses to emphasize the value of amateur productions draw on the discourse of the pioneers of military and other exploration where new territory is being encountered and the endeavour requires careful planning and organization.

The LAT was so successful that plans were made for a new venue. Edith Craig advised on the adaptations to the building for the new theatre, which was based in the Blue Triangle Hall in Cookridge Street, Leeds. There was input and support from Lascelles

Abercrombie (1881–1938), Professor of English at Leeds University 1922–9, who is credited for his summaries of the plays in the LAT programmes. The LAT operated as a cultural centre by organizing talks by invited speakers, such as Clemence Dane, Barry Jackson, J. T. Grein, Henry Ainley, Viola Compton and William Armstrong. The *Morning Post* described the LAT's claim 'to be the only unsubsidised repertory theatre in the country' (11 August; EC-G1380).

The aim was to engage fully with the local community. The *Morning Post* commented on the forthcoming plays as 'undoubtedly high-class without being highbrow but there is nothing experimental, however enterprising, in playing "John Gabriel Borkmann" or "The Inspector General" or "Merton of the Movies". Only about one in four of the pieces in contemplation is unknown' (*Morning Post*, 11 August; EC-G1380). The breadth of events on offer was deliberate but the *Morning Post* reviewer's disclaimer about the 'highbrow' suggests the LAT was perceived as locating itself within the newly developing, accessible category of the arts, designated by the derogatory term 'middlebrow'. This term was applied mainly to novels which were endorsed, mediated and promoted by a culturally informed elite for the consumption and edification of a mass market. In the context of interwar Englishness, this phenomenon took on a specific character after the Newbolt Report, which was focusing on the place of English literature and drama in education and society. In the theatre, the 'middlebrow' is an applicable designation for the amateur productions of the Little Theatre movement, in community and village theatres including those sponsored by the Women's Institutes. Edith Craig was at the centre of this national project to promote art theatre to a wide audience in the period of postwar reconstruction. The remit and audience encompassed by the 'middlebrow' had affinities with Craig's activities in the women's suffrage movement and Henry Irving's aims for theatre as a temple of art and offered to all. The promotion of literature in performance, as endorsed by the Newbolt Report, was evidenced in Edith Craig's production of a dramatization of *The Secret Agent* by Joseph Conrad for the LAT. The reviews were somewhat mixed on the feasibility of the dramatization of this particular novel, but the performance of LAT member Ruby Wigoder as Winnie Verloc was very well received.

The end of Edith Craig's involvement with the LAT was not quite as described in their publicity material. Craig was officially acknowledged in the prospectus for 1925–6 'to whose genius and devotion the Leeds art Theatre owes so much of its success' and 'she announced at the end of last season that she could not undertake any further work for the Theatre. She feels, as a pioneer, that now that the Theatre is firmly established, her work may be said to be complete' (EC-C133). The departure of Charles F. Smith, entrepreneur and supporter of the LAT, is not mentioned. He had resigned after conflicts with L. B. Ramsden, the business manager, about the LAT's management. Smith confided in Craig by sending her a copy of his resignation letter. Craig stayed with Laurie (L. B.) Ramsden's mother when she visited Leeds on at least one occasion. Craig was replaced at the LAT by F. Owen Chambers, who had assisted Bridges Adams at the Stratford Shakespeare festivals and in 1908 had organized the Winchester pageant. Twelve plays were announced for the forthcoming year and a new venture was announced: the LAT Green-Room Club for everyone who took part in their productions.

## 'Edith Craig: An informal interview' (1924): The article she never wrote

In the United States the Little Theatre movement was supported by *Theatre Arts* magazine but the contributions made by women have been somewhat overlooked, as Dorothy Chansky (2004) has demonstrated. In Britain, Norman MacDermott had started his own journal, *Theatrecraft* (1919–21). Following the tradition of their polar opposition in some aspects of life and work, Edward Gordon Craig had a magazine but little theatre work, and Edith Craig was immersed in productions and would not write about them. An article by C. F. Smith in the *Yorkshire Post* is entitled 'an informal interview' but it presents itself as a performance of the article that Edith Craig never wrote. Having arranged to meet her at a restaurant and broached the subject of her authorship of an article for the *Yorkshire Post*, he suggested that suitable topics might be 'comparative methods of production' or 'modern stage lighting' (EC-G174). He coaxed her into divulging her views on the theatre by proposing: 'let's pretend you are dictating an article' (EC-G174). She replied that her topic would be 'the duties of an audience' and those would be 'to come with a fresh and open mind'. She blamed the focus on only one kind of play as the reason for the failure of many theatres. Having cunningly drawn her into the performance of author-of-an-article-for-the-*Yorkshire Post*, Smith obtained the material he was after and quoted her at length in print. This is quoted at length here as it is a rare account of Craig's views on the theatre and it is, indeed, the article she would have written had she been a writer:

> To come with a fresh and open mind. The Repertory Theatre has accomplished wonderful work in educating audiences to demand dramatic sincerity, but as a regrettable backwash it has given birth to a certain amount of intellectual snobbishness. Shaw and Galsworthy and a few more of the giants have been accepted and acclaimed; but new work does not receive an unbiased hearing. A Repertory Theatre should not fall into the error of producing work of one description only. I know of many promising movements that failed because the organisers could only see value in one type of drama. It is right that social questions should be discussed on the stage, because the stage should be the reflection of life; but of the wholeness of life. And this means that fun, poetry, romance, should all find their place. I am glad to see for instance, that in our Leeds experiment you intend to produce farce, comedy, drama, romantic extravaganzas, and moralities. Indeed, a 'Little Theatre,' or an 'Art Theatre' might well be termed an 'Experimental Theatre'. Your playgoer should with enthusiasm and free from prejudices, accept the conventions of the type of play he is witnessing, and then judge whether it is good of this kind. That should be his sole demand. The Press could do incalculable good here. In any town where there is a serious dramatic movement, the criticism should be in the hands of a writer who has an adequate knowledge of the drama. In my own experience, I have known where important newspapers, scorning any but experts writing their commercial and racing intelligence, consistently delegate their theatre notices to juniors. The ideal critics should know something of the history of the drama, its philosophy, and its place in aesthetics; in fact, he should have an attitude to it, know what he likes, and why. His judgments should be respected, and his approval sought by local producing societies. Instead, we often have critics condemning a comedy of manners – in the direct line

of Sheridan and Wilde – depicting unreal people in an unreal world, indulging in unreal conversation, because it is 'talky' and not 'serious'. Who on earth wants a serious soufflé or an earnest omelette? Lightness is the essential requisite of both, and also of the artificial brilliant society comedy. One does not demand blank verse from 'Charley's Aunt,' or witty epigrams from Lady Macbeth. Many a promising play has failed because, although the author has conceived it in a comedic spirit, he has worked it out in terms of farce. Or the contrary. An English audience does not analyse its fare so closely, but becomes suddenly conscious of a jarring element. It feels that probability is being strained. But, really, the fault is that the conventions proper to that particular type of play are being violated. [...] (EC-G174)

At that point, Craig's dictation of the article-she-would-not-write is interrupted by coffee being brought to the table and C. F. Smith and Craig enjoy their coffee and cigarettes. Smith concludes his article with his own whimsical but insightful conclusion: 'And this is the history of the article that, like all history that matters, is never written' (EC-G174).

Craig's exploration of terminology is significant. In considering the different designations of 'Little Theatre', 'Art Theatre' or 'Experimental Theatre', she seems to favour the latter. This may be connected with her reference to 'a certain intellectual snobbishness' in the Repertory Theatre regarding new writing. She identifies a problem with the evaluation and understanding of dramatic form and conventions, attributing responsibility for the development of a community's understanding of theatre history to the critics. Uninformed junior reporters were writing reviews, propagating inappropriate expectations of different dramatic genres and such misunderstandings led to the closure of some productions. Craig's culinary metaphor appeals to the reader's knowledge of the omelette and soufflé; applied to drama, this draws attention to the aesthetic features that complement certain forms and structures. However, Craig emphasized not just the relevance of appropriate tone (an 'earnest omelette' or 'a serious soufflé'); she also argued for 'lightness' as applicable to both. The skill in creating and presenting these works of art is to know what is required and when to stop.

# York Everyman Theatre and the York Civic Playhouse

Charles F. Smith wrote an article for the *Yorkshire Herald* about Edith Craig as 'the inspirer' of the York Everyman Theatre, presenting her as having a nationwide brief: 'By this time her activities had extended to the north' which resulted in her founding of the LAT and the development of the actors who owed so much to her, 'Not only direct instruction but in unconscious assimilation' (20 September 1924; EC-G1376). The York Everyman Theatre produced at least three plays: *Everyman* in the Guildhall, York in April 1924, followed by *The Mollusc* by H. H. Davies at the Art Gallery, York, for three performances (25–27 November 1924) with the Between-Time Players (described as a temporary company drawn from performers from the LAT) and then the nativity play at the Guildhall. A planned production of Elmer Rice's *The Adding Machine* was postponed as a result of Edith Craig's ill-health but the production of *The Mollusc* seems to have been produced under her influence.

The programme for *The Mollusc* provides a great deal of information about the York Everyman Theatre, its aims and manifesto on the Little Theatre movement as well as an explanation of Edith Craig's involvement. Four directors were listed: Edith Craig, Charles F. Smith, Margery W. Patterson and Herbert M. Duke. The entire back cover is devoted to 'Our Aims', arguing for the need to recognize and support 'the Theatre as a Repository of artistic tradition and arbiter of a correct pronunciation of our glorious language' and the solution: 'The remedy for this lamentable condition lies with the Amateur Actor. Gone are the days when the title was a term of reproach. Some of the finest work accomplished in the Theatre to-day is the product of Amateur or semi-Amateur organisation.' (EC-D728) After summarizing the extensive nationwide activities of this kind of theatrical activity, it emphasized the centrality of the amateur to its success:

> The mainspring of all this activity is the Amateur who, too, it must be remembered was the foundation of what is now the Birmingham Repertory Theatre and the Abbey Theatre Dublin. It must be understood that the 'Little' Theatre Movement is not a 'highbrow' Movement. It is the intention of the Everyman

Theatre in time to present plays of every form including Comedy, Tragedy, Farce and Mime; all must pass one test only; they must be the best of their kind. Our one axiom is that Theatrical work of Art should enlarge the field of consciousness and stimulate the mental life. (EC-D728)

In this formulation, a claim is made for the social and perhaps even the psychological benefits of theatrical performance. The 'Theatrical Work of Art' which is simultaneously *not* 'highbrow' seems to position the Little Theatre movement, including the Everyman Theatre as middlebrow although that term is not used.

The York Everyman described the rationale for its methods of staging in such a way as to establish its niche in the varied approaches at work in contemporary experiments:

While disowning any doctrinaire spirit, the York Everyman Theatre will avoid elaborate staging and extravagant decor. Apart from financial considerations it is felt that scenic accessories should be sufficiently adequate to illustrate the intentions of the author, while allowing perfect freedom to the imaginations of the beholders. For the same reason there will be no music, unless it is an integral part of the play. Good music would be unworthily employed as an accompaniment to the animated discussions that it is hoped will be indulged in during our entr'actes, while indifferent music would be an impertinence. (EC-D728)

The York Everyman Theatre prospectus (1925–6) redefined its mode of operation, as developing 'on Club lines' for a subscription of £1 entitling subscribers to a seat at each performance, use of the Everyman Theatre Library and the Supper Club, 'at present known as the "Hot Pot Club"', providing 'light refreshments' and invited speakers who were 'interesting modern Dramatists, Critics and other persons connected with the Theatre to speak'. It is made clear that the enterprise was based on 'voluntary effort' although 'technical services' were paid for and it was affiliated to the BDL. On the basis of the success of the 'public performances in the Guildhall', the risk was taken to introduce free seats at each performance. The relationship of the York Everyman Theatre with its audience is reinforced in this prospectus by a mission statement which is capitalized for greater emphasis:

THE THEATRE IS THE MOST POTENT CULTURAL INFLUENCE IN MODERN LIFE AND NO COMMUNITY CAN AFFORD TO ALLOW IT TO BE NEGLECTED OR DEBASED. THE EVERYMAN THEATRE EXISTS TO PRODUCE THE DRAMATIC MATERPIECES OF OUR OWN AND OTHER LANDS AND TO PLACE WITHIN THE REACH OF ALL THE OPPORTUNITY TO WITNESS SUCH PRODUCTIONS. (EC-C62)

The aim to develop the theatre was expressed in terms of reconstruction but also civic planning, to make it 'an important feature in the life of the City and that it will be appreciated and supported by all classes of the community'. (EC-C62) The reference to social class is a salient feature of the democratic ideals of the Little Theatre movement in developing a community of citizens unified in the creative activity of theatrework for the improvement of society as a whole.

## St Christopher's Theatre, Letchworth (1924–5)

Three directors were associated with the St Christopher's Theatre, Letchworth: Edith Craig, Beatrice Wilson and Norman V. Norman. Craig's work in the south for the new theatre in the garden city of Letchworth was as eclectic as ever but significant in various ways. In addition to Lady Florence Bell's *The Fog on the Moor*, Craig directed Lady Gregory's adaptation of Goldoni's *Mirandolina*, with Ruth Bower in the title role.[12] Most intriguingly, she directed *Through the Crack*, reprised from her production at the Everyman Theatre, Hampstead in 1920 and subsequently repeated at the Apollo Theatre, London in 1925. *Through the Crack* was the St Christopher's Theatre's first production. Based on the novel *The Education of Uncle Paul* by Algernon Blackwood, it was co-written by Blackwood and Violet Pearn. Craig referred to *Through the Crack* as a children's play; there is some resemblance to *Peter Pan*, but it more explicitly deals with an imaginative interpretation of the death of a child. As Blackwood's biographer, Mike Ashley, notes, the play is similar to Blackwood's novels and stories about breaches in time and space and also such plays as *Pinkie and the Fairies* by Graham Robertson, in which both Ellen Terry and Edith Craig had performed. Ashley suggests that Craig may have met Blackwood in the 1890s when he interviewed Ellen Terry (Ashley 2001: 340).[13] Craig's production at the St Christopher's Theatre involved child performers and its nine consecutive performances put some strain on them.[14]

## Leeds Civic Playhouse (1930–1): *The Dybbuk, Back to Methuselah* and the Eyebrow Club

In the interwar period, Craig's productions took her from London, Kent and the suburbs to Yorkshire. Her production of *The Dybbuk* by S. Ansky (Solomon Rappaport, 1863–1920) for the Leeds Civic Playhouse at the Albert Hall, Leeds on 7 March 1927 was memorable according to C. F. Smith, who noted it in an interview with the *Observer* in 1934 where he reflected on the Leeds Civic Playhouse. *The Dybbuk* has a central place in the canon of Jewish drama; it was one of several significant productions by Craig for the Leeds Civic Playhouse and it should receive special acknowledgement as the first British production of the play. Ansky's play was subtitled 'Between Two Worlds', written c. 1914 and first produced in Warsaw in 1920. It concerns the possession of Leah by the spirit of her beloved and exorcism. The play had been produced in New York in December 1926 but Craig's production seems to have been the first in Britain.[15] The Robert Atkins production in London is the most widely known in Britain. Michael Sherbrooke, who had been involved in performing the monologue, 'Gymnasie', by Sholom Alecheim for the Pioneer Players at the St Martin's Theatre in 1917, wrote to Craig mentioning his forthcoming performance at the Royalty Theatre in *The Dybbuk*, directed by Robert Atkins on 4 April–26 May 1927 (EC-3, 622; EC-3, 625). C. F. Smith recalled Craig's 'wonderful production of *The Dybbuk* for about two pence halfpenny, and got magnificent Rembrandt effects with some old velvet curtains we had had in stock for years'

(*Observer*, 9 December 1934; EC-G1410). He also mentioned other Leeds Civic Playhouse directors, a group who could be regarded as Craig's professional peer group: Nugent Monck (*The Tempest* and his own play at Kirkstall Abbey); Norman Marshall (*Danton*, *The Twelve Thousand* and *Pilgrim's Progress* at Trinity Church); A. E. Filmer (*The Unknown Warrior*) and M. Komisarjevsky (*The Cherry Orchard*). It is noteworthy that Smith highlights several plays directed by others which were produced in churches.

Smith mentions the Leeds Civic Playhouse production of George Bernard Shaw's *Back to Methuselah* but does not attribute it to Craig.[16] Instead, he emphasizes its unexpected commercial success: 'we were the only repertory company ever to make money out of "Back to Methuselah". We made £300 before the curtain went up' (EC-G1410). The programme for the production (12–26 May 1930) described the success of the Leeds and Bradford Civic Playhouses over the previous five years, with nearly 5,000 and 2,000 subscribers respectively: 'It is this assured audience, however that enables us to venture on dramatic work of a definitely experimental nature, and will in time we hope, secure for the WEST RIDING, the most enviable name in theatrical annals.' Tom Steele notes that the Leeds Civic Playhouse was probably unique as a free theatre relying on subscriptions (Steele 1990: 249).

On 11 October 1931 the Leeds Civic Playhouse launched the Eyebrow Club, playing on the northern pronunciation of the word 'highbrow' and described in a play programme as 'the only Private Play Producing Club outside London', an exclusive club with subscription of 10s available only to subscribers of the Playhouse (EC-D12) and featuring Sybil Thorndike and Edith Craig, with Craig reading from her mother's letters to George Bernard Shaw which had just been published. Tom Steele describes the venue used by the club as a warehouse basement decorated with the paintings of Jacob Kramer and it 'immediately became the centre of Leeds Bohemia where distinguished patrons like Berkeley Moynihan mingled with artists and actors, watched risqué plays and indulged in the odd spot of illegal gambling [...] The Club saw itself as carrying the torch for minority experimental drama' (Steele 1990: 251). Nevertheless, the acting space had some sophistication, with a revolving stage and the latest lighting equipment.[17] It is not clear whether Craig used the Eyebrow Club as a social space; it is more likely that her involvement was in her appearance at the launch and the performance of her mother's letters. She had been involved in at least one production in January 1928 for the Cave of Harmony, a nightclub run by Harold Scott and Elsa Lanchester in Seven Dials with a reputation for 'Victorian cabaret' but described in judgmental and unambiguous terms by Vera Brittain:

> In spite of the still dominant Victorianism and pseudo-respectability of the period, clubs and societies existed where those believed to be specialists in the practices vaguely known as 'vice' were welcome. The greater their interest in sodomy, lesbianism, pederasty and kindred topics was thought to be, the more welcome they were as associates. Radclyffe Hall frequented one club known as 'The Cave of Harmony,' where Katherine Mansfield gave amateur stage performances. Frank Harris was also a member.

> The locked-cupboard atmosphere of these places gave them their attraction, and still does, in so far as they exist today. (Brittain 1968: 100)

Harold Scott invited Craig to repeat her production, staged at the LAT in 1924, of *Marion's Crime*, in January 1928 at the Cave of Harmony. The subversive and subcultural dimension attributed to clubs and societies by Vera Brittain may explain the wider context of the reading in April 1931 Sunday Performances (Regulation) Bill and the subsequent legislation, the Sunday Entertainments Act (1932). The effect was to restrict performances or screenings in theatres on a Sunday, the day usually made available to the low budget subscription societies, but the timing of this new and devastating legislation on cultural life had its political consequences too, with the demise of the new Masses' Stage and Film Guild, with which Edith Craig was centrally involved in their inaugural play production of Upton Sinclair's *Singing Jailbirds*.

## *Singing Jailbirds* (1930)

Craig's 'propaganda work' for women's suffrage and with the Pioneer Players occupied her for over a decade. She subsequently directed fund-raising productions for various organizations and charities as well as two that were politically opposed: the Independent Labour

Party (ILP) and the Ashford Conservative Association. The provocative agenda of the 'play of ideas' that had been promoted by the Pioneer Players may have influenced Craig's decisions to direct plays for these organizations. The support of the ILP's Masses' Stage and Film Guild with her production of *Singing Jailbirds* was consistent with Craig's known political views. However the production of *The Merry Wives of Windsor* for the Ashford Conservatives is likely to have been influenced by a desire to support her friend Edward Percy Smith (1891–1968), who was elected as Conservative MP for Ashford in 1943.

In November 1929 there was extensive coverage in the national press about the organization of a new 'socialist theatre' with plans to produce 'plays of democratic significance' (EC-G1696–EC-G1700). The organization had prominent support from Labour politicians. It was chaired by Rt Hon. Fenner Brockway MP and its distinguished supporters included four cabinet ministers: J. R. Clynes, the Home Secretary; George Lansbury; F. O. Roberts; and Sir C. P. Trevelyan (the latter having appeared in the Mount Grace Priory pageant three years earlier).[18] The aim of the Masses' Stage and Film Guild (MSFG) was 'to bring modern plays of democratic significance within the reach of working-class audiences' by pitching the price appropriately (1s subscription and tickets at the same price) and strategically building up interest and funds by staging plays in the West End with professional casts and screening selected films 'not usually to be seen at the commercial cinema' (*The Times*, 15 November 1929; EC-G1699).

The proposed plays for production included a suggestion from George Bernard Shaw: *Brain: A Play of the Whole Earth* by Lionel Britton (1887–1971), described as about 'the evolution of a dehumanised universal consciousness which finds a voice on the "wireless" and ultimately controls everything on the earth'; as well as Pudovkin's new film *Mother* at the Astoria (*Morning Post*).[19] In the event, as Ros Merkin notes, although it attracted 2,300 members by 1931, the MSFG produced only three plays, the second being Britton's *Brain* and the third namely *In Abraham's Bosom* (1927) by Paul Green (1894–1981), about a lynching in the southern states of America, was a Pulitzer Prize-winning play following its production by the Provincetown Players. The MSFG was closed as a result of legislation in 1931 to restrict theatres from performing on Sundays (Merkin 2000: 183) and following the application by the MSFG to screen banned Russian films: Pudovkin's *Mother*, Eisenstein's *Battleship Potemkin*, *Storm Over Asia*, *New Babylon*, *October* and *The General Line*. When the London County Council met on 11 March 1930 to discuss it, one MP, Sir William Ray, claimed that the MSFG's aim was 'introducing into this country propagandist films of Russian origin' (quoted in Richards 2010: 97).

It was Edith Craig, with her experience of pioneering Nikolai Evreinov's drama in London over a decade earlier, who directed the MSFG's first play at the Apollo Theatre. This was the first production in Britain of *Singing Jailbirds* by the American dramatist Upton Sinclair. *Singing Jailbirds*, set in 1923 and located in 'The Harbour Jail of a Californian City (All scenes outside the jail are the dreams of the prisoner)' is expressionist in form, representing the horrific imprisonment of political activists during a period of industrial action led by Red Adams, 'the Wobbly', played by Ben Weldon. Craig was assisted on the production by Audrey Cameron as stage manager and Mary Eversley and 'Edward Carrick' (Edward Craig, her nephew, as assistant stage managers. Carrick also played a minor part in the play as a waiter). When the central character, Red Adams, is assumed to be the 'leader' of the Industrial Workers of the World (IWW), he says that they do not have leaders, reflecting his political views and reminiscent of Craig's proposal that the BDL Workshop Committee produce work should not be attributed to individuals. The play programme provided a lengthy explanatory note detailing the poor ventilation of prison cells and the death of Paul Bourgon of the IWW in a similar way to that of Red Adams in the play.[20] The note also pointed out the relevance of the play to incidents in San Pedro and Los Angeles but also in Poland and even in England:

> Our own General Strike and other episodes (remember the 'trial' of the Cramlingham [*sic*] miners), show that if more clever and less crude, English methods are not beyond suspicion. We commend 'Singing Jailbirds' to our members as a courageous attempt to expose a very sinister side of capitalism the world over. (EC-D299)

During the General Strike on 10 May 1926, striking miners from Cramlington, Northumberland removed railway track to impede north-south traffic with the effect of derailing the Flying Scotsman.

The experiences of women's suffrage political prisoners are relevant too but not mentioned in the play programme note. It may have been that in 1930 the name 'Edith Craig' carried with it the provenance of the militant women's suffrage campaigns of 1905–14. With the MSFG, Edith Craig continued to play a part in the resistance to censorship of the arts whether in theatre or in the new medium of film, and she supported the exposure of injustices in the treatment of political prisoners. In 1910 she had reconstructed for the women's suffrage fair a prison cell and in 1930 for the MSFG in *Singing Jailbirds* she staged the appalling 'tanks' used for solitary confinement in United States.

## The pedagogical turn: Brighton (1933), Liverpool (1935), Cheltenham (1937)

Craig suffered periods of ill-health in the 1930s, heart problems in 1932 and near-fatal pneumonia in 1937. It was also a time of financial difficulties. She tried to build up resources to run The Farm as the Ellen Terry Memorial and she took on responsibility for her great niece, the daughter of Robert Craig, Robinetta, whom she adopted in 1932. In 1930 Christopher St John lost her writing jobs at *Time & Tide* and the *Lady*, prompting an intense period of publication projects that led to the Shaw-Terry correspondence, Ellen Terry's Memoirs and Ellen Terry's lectures on Shakespeare. In a letter to Edith Craig in 1932 Ethel Smyth referred to the active discrimination to which St John had been subjected by newspaper editors:

> I still lament Chris's disappearance from music criticism tho' I understand her point of view – & in a book of articles that may or may not appear shortly I am talking about her – & how she was kept out of the big dailies (a matter of which I know much). (14 February 1932; EC-3,652)

In *Female Pipings in Eden* (1933), Smyth writes a section entitled 'Where Musical Criticism Goes Astray', condemning the tendency of the press to encourage critics to dismiss new music. In 'Double Faults and Others', a talk she gave to a girls' school, she recommended 'directness' but warned of the 'slave-habit of mind' as a poisonous influence to avoid (Smyth 1933: 129):

> Meanwhile nothing is sadder then to see, as one often does see, some brilliant, fresh idea come bounding gaily forth from an enterprising female brain, to be firmly herded back into the pen by the inevitable conventional male, simply because this is 'not the sort of idea people are used to!' (Smyth 1933: 130)

Smyth's insights into the difficulties facing women in education and the workplace are all too familiar, several feminist waves later. In the 1930s, Smyth was writing on the crest of enfranchisement with all of the optimism of postwar reconstruction. This was a crucial time for leadership by women in the arts and in education, and it was also a period of international economic and political instability.

In response to this period of financial pressures, Craig diversified, with lectures and public speaking. She appeared in Brighton on a Women's Freedom League (WFL) platform in May 1933. In March 1933 the WFL newspaper *The Vote* interviewed her on the front cover, illustrated with her portrait under the heading 'Miss Edith Craig Actress and Producer (An Interview)'. It began with an emphasis on Craig's unorthodox optimism about the commercial theatre if West End theatre prices were reduced and good plays were made available. She regarded the Little Theatre movement as providing 'a valuable training school' with 'a valuable purpose in creating for professional productions an audience, keen and critical, because experienced in acting and producing. It is a great impetus to amateur societies to bring their plays to London' (EC-G118).

The local branch of the WFL hosted Craig's talk at the White Rock Pavilion and welcomed her with a bouquet of flowers from the garden of her mother's former house at Winchelsea. Craig's lecture examined the career of the female performer and the producer. She categorized the female performer into three types: great actresses, beautiful actresses and useful actresses, emphasizing the latter as most welcome in a theatre. She argued for the early training in performance, ideally from age seven since the consequence of training from age fifteen as constrained by the law at that time led to accomplished actors emerging at age twenty-two. She noted the relative lack of knowledge in performers in England as contrasted with America in the technique of bowing and curtseying, concluding that the Americans were 'more alive to such 18th century customs than in England'. Her own recent experiences may have prompted her reflections on the impact of ill-health on the career of a performer: 'They will be sorry for you the first time but the next time it is stamped upon your forehead for ever, and every manager knows it, and then you do not get jobs easily' (EC-G118). Thus branded as unreliable, the performer would find that opportunities for work consequently dwindle.

Craig recommended the role of producer rather than performer for women and noted the tendency for greater concentration by female performers in the performance when she worked for a female producer:

> A branch of the work which was specially suited to women was producing. As soon as a woman became connected with the theatre, she immediately wanted to act, whether she could or not. She might have no ability for it and yet have a great love for the theatre, and it was such people who made good producers because they had the ideas. A woman producer was better than a man where actresses were concerned because a man was often frightened of offending them, and thought they would burst into tears. With a man producer an actress was always trying to make the best of herself, but with a woman she was keen to get on with the job. (EC-G118)

This revelation suggests perhaps that Craig was unafraid of making her female performers cry and also that the (hetero)sexual tensions in the theatrical workplace were dispensed with when a woman was in charge of direction. She regarded her own abilities as a performer in the category of 'useful' but less accomplished than as a 'producer'. When asked by an audience member whether 'an actor resented a woman producer', Craig responded in a characteristically witty fashion:

> If you know your job there is no actor who will resent you because you are a woman. There are a lot of men who do not know their jobs and get away with it, but I do not think an actor would let a woman get away with it. (EC-G118)

In this context the term 'actor' would specifically designate a male performer. Craig's response on the issue of sex discrimination and gendered expectations is concise and reflects decades of experience in the theatre. Probably influenced by her mother's arguments from the position of an exceptional woman, it is also a meritocratic position that avoids consideration of the process of arriving in the position of producer as a woman in favour of whether performers reveal any gender bias in their behaviour in the workplace. The role of 'producer' was for a woman a minority occupation; it was an authoritative position to hold in a period when Craig and her contemporaries implemented it with complete control. So the audience member had touched on a highly salient point and Craig's response only briefly touches on the difficulties. It is noteworthy also that she was asked about producing pageants and responded very briefly: 'In reply to a question concerning pageant producing, Miss Craig said that it needed great organisation talent. She had produced one or two pageants but she considered it was difficult' (EC-G118). At this point she did not categorize herself principally as a pageant producer.

By 1933, five years after her mother's death, Craig had firmly acquired the designation 'Ellen Terry's daughter', as part of the concerted publicity campaign to promote the Ellen Terry Memorial. Nevertheless she was recognized in her own right as a theatre practitioner and had sufficient standing to be appointed to a prestigious lectureship. Edith Craig's Shute Lecture at the University of Liverpool on 28 February 1935 would have been walking in her brother's footsteps if he had fulfilled his promise to lecture there in 1932.[21] The lectureship was, founded by Lt Col. J. J. Shute one of the founders of the Liverpool Playhouse, a great honour and put her in distinguished company. The annual Shute Lectures (1921–59) had begun with Harley Granville-Barker, and his lectureship on the art of the theatre was given a special mention in the Newbolt Report as the one example of a British university leading the way in the promotion of drama in education. In 1926 the five Shute lectures had been given by Ivor Brown (1891–1974)[22] and were subsequently published as *Parties of the Play* (1928). The *Liverpool Post* reported on 1 March 1935 that Edith Craig 'gave at Liverpool University last night, the final Shute lecture on the art of the theatre' (EC-G134). The Liverpool University Calendar lists four individuals holding the Shute lectureship in 1934: Sydney Carroll, Edith Craig, John Van Druten and Paul Rotha.[23]

Craig's Shute lecture focused on the 'changes in the production of plays in England'. She identified the different 'component parts' as 'the dramatist, audience, theatre designer (by which she meant the producer) and the actor. The actor was usually left running wildly behind all the others. The designer controlled, but the basis of everything was the actor. The actor had been known to do without all the rest, though whether he could do without the audience she did not know (laughter).' (EC-G134) The introduction situated Craig in opposition to her brother, without explicitly naming him, by placing the actor at the centre of theatrical production. In overtly conflating the producer and the theatre designer she may have recalled the difficulties experienced at the Everyman Theatre, Hampstead where she was officially working 'under the direction of' Norman MacDermott. The record of laughter from the audience occurs several times in the *Liverpool Post*'s account of Craig's Shute lecture and in reports of her lectures on other occasions, giving an impression of the rapport she built with an audience.

Craig's survey of changes in theatre from the period of the Restoration onwards, identified changes in costume and lighting, the social context and its influence on theatre from the political challenges to the period when theatre became fashionable and respectable. She noted the shifting terminology and its effects: 'Then the producer appeared form America. To-day a "producer" might be organizing a play and getting in the money, or he might be designing the scenery and dresses or he might be training the actors. The term was very confusing'(EC-G134). She regretted the 'Stage Children's Act' [1933] and the impact on training actors at an older age, consequently 'the only trained actors came from Oxford and Cambridge' (EC-G134). The concluding section of the report of her lecture, with the sub-heading 'Fourth Wall Danger', focused on the undesirability of the proscenium arch and picture-frame for many plays:

We have in London an apathetic audience which is creating an apathetic actor. The actor wants all the time to avoid the audience, to think they are not there. We have this idea of the fourth wall. But if the actor is going to build a fourth wall, the audience will do the same, and what is going to happen? Your play has to be developed. Your actors have to be given every chance of creating something not a picture-frame play.

Lots of people say to me 'The moment you come out of the picture-frame you lose all illusion.' Actors have said it. I think that sense of illusion has nothing to do with picture-frames, but with the inside of the person who is looking on. I have experienced more illusion from the wings than from the front of any picture-frame.

The audience should be an integral part of the play, and feel that it is in it, and not merely looking on. (EC-G134)

The report of her lecture does not mention that, given the limited access to sufficient resources to build new theatres, Craig had sought out performance spaces that enabled her to experiment with productions that broke the fourth wall. These were inside churches and in outdoor spaces.

When she gave the first of the spring series of public lectures at the Cheltenham Art Gallery on 11 January 1937, it was entitled 'Theatres Good and Bad', focusing on the selection of suitable venues for performance (*Gloucestershire Echo*, 12 January 1937; EC-G170). She deplored the use of public halls although she made no reference to the suitability of the present space in which she was delivering her lecture. She especially mentioned church halls as the worst places of all for theatrical performance. She recommended a surprising variety of potential venues, even circuses and lorries, since in these performance spaces the audience would be able to see the actors and the best place for performance of religious plays was the church. She described how she renovated her own Barn Theatre, fitting it with a rostrum stage, dispensing with scenery and using motor lamps instead of candles for lighting. With regard to the future of theatre she believed that it would require new plays, new methods and a new theatre. She encouraged the audience to campaign for a local theatre. The WFL branch meeting concluded after Craig's lecture with a summary of the aims of the WFL in campaigning for 'free unfettered citizenship of woman' and the pursuit of equal pay for equal work and equality of opportunities in senior posts in public service such as the diplomatic service and the House of Lords (EC-G170).

## Honours and reflections (1937–9)

The Citizenship Group and the Hillhead Equal Citizenship group in Scotland held an annual dinner to commemorate the passing of the Representation of the People Act (1918). In 1937 their principal guest was Edith Craig, whose forthcoming appearance was reported in the *Glasgow Evening Times*. The report used two sub-headings to describe her achievements and to introduce Craig in relation to Ellen Terry: 'Daughter of a famous actress' and 'stage manager for her mother' but oddly Craig's contribution to the women's suffrage movement is referred to vaguely: 'Though Miss Craig devoted her life to the theatre, she also found time to take an interest in the suffrage movement' (20 January 1937; EC-G177).

In 1938 when Edith Craig celebrated fifty years in the theatre she was interviewed in the *Evening News*. She reminisced about working in the theatre at a time when gas limelight was used and stage hands would sleep on the gas bag containers backstage; when electricity became available she recalled backstage pranks when sparks were made on her metallic costume for *King Arthur*; and when laughing on stage at the Adelphi Theatre cost her her job (25 March 1938; EC-G179). That year she was honoured by a dinner at the Savoy Theatre organized by Lady Maud Warrender and presented with a scroll and a cheque. The report in the *Queen* several months later noted that messages were sent by Queen Mary and George Bernard Shaw and given in person by Cicely Hamilton, Sybil Thorndike, Edward Knoblock, Herbert Griffiths, S. R. Littlewood, Violet Vanbrugh, Irene Vanbrugh, Vita Sackville-West and Dame May Whitty (10 November 1938; EC-G176). The report gave some insights into the anecdotes that were shared, notably Cicely Hamilton's recollection of 'how Edith thrust her into impossible situations in a pageant, even making her conduct an orchestra when she knew nothing of the ways of orchestras' and Edward Knoblock, Herbert Griffiths and S. R. Littlewood 'spoke of her wonderful work with the Pioneer Players' (EC-G176). Under the sub-heading 'A Forceful Character', several comments were made about Craig's personality in the second section of the article: 'Edy Craig is a forceful character and, especially in the production of pageants, in which she excels, nobody is spared until she has got the effect which has been created in her mind.' (EC-G176) The reporter noted that Craig's friends regarded it as 'a tragedy' that she had not been properly acknowledged although she had become nevertheless 'a producer of the finest type' (EC-G176).

## Bridging the gap: From Henry Irving to John Gielgud's *Hamlet* at the Lyceum Theatre (1939)

In 1939 Edith Craig was instrumental in a single production which had political, historical and familial significance. In his survey of

Shakespeare in the 1930s, Tony Howard has examined the impli-cations of various Shakespearean productions and the political appropriation of Shakespearean stereotypes in a period of ris-ing anti-semitism which was also 'the Gielgud decade' (Howard 2000: 140). Under the direction of Harley Granville-Barker, Gielgud played Shylock in direct contrast to Irving's sympathetic portrayal in the period of the Dreyfus case. It seems significant, therefore, that it was Edith Craig, champion of Jewish and socialist drama in Britain, who brought Gielgud's exceptionally successful Hamlet to Irving's Lyceum Theatre. In 1939 John Gielgud directed *Hamlet* at the Lyceum Theatre on 28 June to 1 July in a 'Farewell to the Lyceum Theatre' commemorative event.[24] Gielgud had impressed audiences with his performance as Hamlet at the Old Vic in 1929–30 and then directed and performed in the play in 1934 at the New Theatre and a couple of years later in New York, for very long runs that established him as the Hamlet of his generation. The souvenir programme for the 1939 production of six performances, with John Gielgud and Fay Compton as Hamlet and Ophelia, included several informative contributions from W. J. Macqueen-Pope (1888–1960), who became known later as a theatre historian but had at this point worked in publicity and management roles. The other contributor to the programme was Edith Craig with a one-page article on 'Ellen Terry and Henry Irving'. She described Terry's first performance at the Lyceum Theatre as Ophelia, the much larger stage at the origi-nal Lyceum Theatre and at the end of the article revealed that she instigated this commemorative production:

> The present Lyceum, although not to be identified with the Lyceum where that epoch-making performance of 'Hamlet' took place, is still a link with it. When I heard that the link was going to be broken, I felt very strongly that some last and splendid use of it ought to be made, that a performance of 'Hamlet' should be given it he theatre on the eve of its demolition. The idea met with a warm welcome from my cousin, John Gielgud, the most popular 'Hamlet' of our time. So it has come about that the gulf between Irving's Lyceum and its successor is being bridged to-night by 'Hamlet'. (EC-D60)

Although familiar names are listed in the cast,[25] Edith Craig does not feature elsewhere in the programme and appears not to have been involved in the production. Craig must have been very proud of her cousin's success on the stage and especially in one of the most difficult roles in Shakespeare.

## Pageants: Mount Grace (1927), Tenterden (1935) and Chilham (1946)

In Britain in the postwar period, the production of historical pageants was widespread but surprisingly diverse, as Mick Wallis has demonstrated. Drawing on Robert Withington's *English Pageantry: An Historical Guide* (1918, 1926), Wallis has traced the impulse for the historical pageant, from the reactionary approach of Louis N. Parker, one of the most influential and founding pageant organizers, to the democratizing pageants of the Popular Front. In addition to the 'pageant masters' Nugent Monck, Frank Lascelles and Louise N. Parker, Wallis focused especially on Mary Kelly, who founded the Village Drama Society and published *How to Make a Pageant* (1936). He identified clearly discernible phases of the historical pageant; popular in 1907–11, they declined in 1911–14, tended towards the 'church and small-scale' pageants in the 1920s and revived in the period of the 'trade crisis' in the early 1930s and 1936–9 (Wallis 2000: 204). He noted that the pageant in the Parker tradition tended to avoid narrative and focus on history itself, implying a 'sedimentation', in embedding and distilling the local in the history of the nation with some similarity to what later became known as 'heritage' (Wallis 2000: 204).

It is into this account of the historical pageant in Britain that Edith Craig needs now to be located as one of the highly acclaimed pageant organizers in the interwar period but also one whose productions spanned the different impulses and periods, and who shared the longevity of Louis N. Parker. Craig's numerous productions of *A Pageant of Great Women* challenge Withington's account of the fallow pageant period of 1911–14 and introduce the women's suffrage pageant phenomenon into the historical frame. Craig's commitment to the principles of the Little Theatre movement and the BDL are demonstrated in her determination to work with local amateurs in her pageants. The setting of performances in the grounds of stately homes, abbeys and historic buildings created the opportunity to promote civic pride and community spirit which could be harnessed to different political movements. In a period of rising taxes, an unstable international economy, political conflict and nationalism, the historical pageant was a highly dynamic dramatic form which brought a community together to reflect on the past and experience its construction, re-enactment and recreation.

By the time Craig was involved in directing the pageant at Mount Grace Priory in Northallerton for Lady Florence Bell in 1927, she brought a wealth of experience to the enterprise: the women's suffrage pageants; her costumes for Louis N. Parker's the *Pageant of Freedom* (1918); the skills to work with large groups of people in community-building practices of the BDL; and Reinhardt-inspired nativity play productions. Her three major pageants, at Mount Grace (1927), Tenterden (1935) and Chilham (1946), shared a similar approach to costume, organization, designs, staging and involvement of the local community as performers, but they were informed by different circumstances. In 1927, Craig was fifty-eight years old and endeavouring to secure a more reliable income as her mother's ill-health and financial situation worsened.[26] When Craig directed the local Tenterden pageant in 1935, she had recovered from serious illness but was somewhat restricted in terms of travel. Tony Atwood reported to Vera Holme that Craig was 'very well if it were not for her irregular irregularity of heart' for which 'she is being dosed with that vile digitalis again' (7 February 1932; 7VJH 4/3/52). The Chilham pageant was effectively her last production and relied on practical assistance from others.

*Mount Grace Priory Pageant* (1927) was written and hosted by Lady Florence Bell, who invited Craig to produce it in the ruins of Mount Grace Priory in North Yorkshire on 7 September 1927. It involved a huge cast, with some distinguished individuals. The press coverage and official photographs of the production provide further evidence of Craig's skill in arranging large groups for dramatic effect and her ability to interpret and make best use of unusual performance spaces, in this case an outdoor performance in the priory ruins.[27] Her personal photograph collection shows that she was assisted by Vera Holme from an office based in a disused train carriage (see Fig. 5).

The surviving film of the pageant provides valuable evidence of Craig's incorporation of processions, group scenes and contrasting performances choreographed in a designated space. The long-shots

FIGURE 4 *Edith Craig directs the pageant at Mount Grace Priory, Northallerton, Yorkshire (1–3 September 1927) (reproduced with permission of The National Trust).*

FIGURE 5 *Edith Craig in her railway carriage office and dressed in costume as a monk, Mount Grace Priory Pageant (1927) (reproduced with permission of The National Trust).*

convey the fluid movement of groups contrasted with other static groups while other wider shapes are described by hand-holding performers.

Instead of considering the Mount Grace Priory pageant solely in the context of historical pageants it needs to be relocated alongside Craig's productions of drama in churches and as foreshadowing E. Martin Browne's production of the mystery plays in the grounds of St Mary's Abbey, York in 1951.

Tenterden jubilee pageant (1935) at Hales Place, in Tenterden, Kent presented a historical account of the town from the twelfth century to the year before the battle of Trafalgar, drawing on over 350 performers and with two speaking parts, one of which was performed by John Drinkwater (THM 384/33/2) and the other was to be the author, Edward Percy Smith, but prevented from performing owing to illness. The pageant combined military display and cultural heritage, involving local dignitaries and military leaders, Major Franklin Lushington, Colonel W. A. F. Findlater, as well as the trumpet band of the Kent Yeomanry. The pageant engaged with local history, with reference to the Austen family (Jane Austen's great uncle Robert is buried at St Mildred's Church, Tenterden) and family history, with a direct descendant of Cromwell performing in the pageant. In the manner of Louis N. Parker's method, Craig was assisted by numerous individuals, including 'episode managers', wardrobe mistresses and a mistress of the dance. The *Sevenoaks Chronicle* emphasizes its effectiveness in community building by involving the local community in these different ways. Having inherited The Farm and the Priest's House at Smallhythe on her mother's death in 1928, Edith Craig was in the dual role of landowner and pageant organizer when she produced the pageants at Mount Grace and Tenterden.

Craig's situation had changed by the time she directed the Chilham pageant (1946), as she had transferred ownership of the property and land at Smallhythe to the National Trust. At Chilham she was leading a significant postwar local event to harness the power of cultural heritage and site-specific historical performance on behalf of the new landowner. The pageant was held on 5 and 6 July at Chilham Castle, originally built in 1607 by Sir Dudley Digges and in 1946 was owned by Somerset de Chair (1911–95), who was Conservative MP for South West Norfolk and a prolific author. The castle had been occupied during the war by the army and de Chair had been on active service from 1944 to 1946 in Syria and Iraq. On his return to England, he celebrated the end of the war and the consequent reinforcement of British territory represented by his own corner of Kent with its Norman keep.[28] The staging in the grounds of Chilham Castle of the grand historical pageant by Edith Craig symbolized the power and responsibility of the landowner and the aspirations for a shared future with the local community. However deeply sedimented this historical pageantry appeared to be, it was indeed short-lived. Escalating costs and other circumstances led Somerset de Chair to sell Chilham Castle in 1949. As a tenant he moved to Blickling Hall, Norfolk; once the family home of Anne Boleyn, it had passed into the ownership of the National Trust since 1940, just one year after Edith Craig had handed on ownership of The Farm at Smallhythe. A new era of cultural heritage had begun.

# CHAPTER EIGHT

# Conclusion: On the theatres of art

In Edith Craig's research collection, some notes have survived to give a glimpse into the development of her ideas. Much smaller in scale to Walter Benjamin's 'theatre of all my struggles and all my ideas', as he described his observations about Parisian city life,[1] Craig's notes appear under scattered headings. They are difficult to interpret in places without context or references but a brief sample of these observations – about scenery, lighting, the work of other theatre practitioners – provide a means of reflecting on the development of her thinking about aspects of production. With regard to 'scenery' she noted two questions: 'What is important in the scene? And 'When & why should a permanent scene be used?' In the technique of lighting she advised against anything 'excentric [*sic*] or curious' and made a note: 'Lighting audience? They then enter into the stage picture = what about this & any sense of illusion or atmosphere?' (EC-M134) This removal of the Fourth Wall informs other notes. On 'acting and scenery' detailed notes include two statements or affirmations. One concerns 'emotional interpretation': 'New words, only: same things happen for the same reasons = materials alter & conditions dictate.' (EC-M134) The other is about the evaluation of performance: 'Actors are judged for loosing [*sic*] themselves in their parts, not on their capacity for losing their parts in themselves.' (EC-M134) There is contemplation too of what might be possible in scenography and costume:

> Can scenery be done away with & still keep the pictorial interpretation[?] Can the actor be done way with? See costumes

by Picasso [...] Scene of 'Pulcinella' [1920] by Picasso. I've seen the ballet. The scene was expressionistic but the people!? & the light? & the atmosphere?[2]

At the other end of the spectrum was what she called the 'classic': 'Avoid perspective & foreshortening (there is something grotesque about them: Perspective has a comic element such as large boots in a photograph – In a pose good for comedy [,] bad for anything else.' (EC-M134) Perspective and spatial arrangements affected what could be achieved in the staging of crowds: 'Inner stage [is] of use when crowds are used or effects with people required see [...] Reinhardt's circus production of Hauptmann's "Festspiel" 1912 where the audience helped to form the crowd.' (EC-M134) Craig used Reinhardt as a reference point in her nativity plays and pageants and shared his interest in the new medium of film.

## 'Gold tissue; something stimulating and unreal': Virginia Woolf and the women of Smallhythe Place

In 1922, the year most associated with modernism, Virginia Woolf witnessed Edith Craig's rehearsal of Beatrice Mayor's *Thirty Minutes in a Street*, a short play depicting passersby. Reminiscent of the opening scene in Woolf's novel *Mrs Dalloway* (1925) where Clarissa leaves her house with the preparation of her party on her mind is Mayor's scene in *Thirty Minutes in a Street* where the Rich Lady emerges:

> [*Stage empty for a while. Then slowly, stealthily, RICH LADY opens door. Still moans under her breath. Her bosom heaves. She looks both ways. Comes out.*]
>
> RICH LADY [*Looking everywhere on ground and violently dabbing her face with large powder puff.*] My glove. My rose. My mirror. Oh, my reception. (Mayor 1923: 100)

In her diary, Woolf recorded the rehearsal, appreciating the 'easy manners of the theatre' but also Craig's transformation of a scene of chaotic amateurishness into a spectacular artistic moment

(Woolf 1978: 174). Woolf saw at least one other production by Craig: M. E. M. Young's *The Higher Court*, a play questioning divorce from a Catholic perspective, noting in her review for the *New Statesman* that the audience at a Pioneer Players' production would expect to be 'scraped and harrowed' (Woolf 1988: 207–10).[3] The art of the theatre could challenge the audience in different ways. Woolf's biographical essay on Ellen Terry contemplated the ephemerality of performance which only leaves 'a verbal life on the lips of the living' (1941). Terry was the subject of her play *Freshwater* (1923; 1935), set on the Isle of Wight when newly married Watts and Terry visited the photographer Julia Margaret Cameron and the poet laureate, Tennyson. In Woolf's posthumously published novel, *Between the Acts* (1941), the organizer of the village historical pageant play, Miss LaTrobe, is probably modelled on Craig. LaTrobe embodied what Jane Marcus has called 'a sort of swashbuckling English eccentric spinster's style' (Marcus 1977), and as demonstrated in earlier chapters, Craig and her partners engaged with a revolutionary masculinity with Craig as Napoleon.

# The Ellen Terry memorial (1929)

When Ellen Terry died on 21 July 1928, Edith Craig was apparently present. Tony Atwood reported that Terry 'lay with her hand in Edy's saying, "happy, happy, happy – you and me". I think she suffered no pain' (27 July 1928; 7VJH/4/3/50). Terry's death united the women of Smallhythe Place to create an Ellen Terry Memorial. In various acts of memorialization concerning Terry's property, artefacts and publications, The Farm became a museum and an annual performance was staged in the Barn Theatre. Although the fundraising for the memorial was initially thwarted by lottery regulations (Warrender 1933: 225) it rapidly became an annual ritual, bringing the leading actors of the day to rural Kent.[4]

The upkeep of the Ellen Terry memorial was a continuing responsibility, even after 1939 when Craig had handed the property to the National Trust. Ever resourceful and inventive, Craig made use of her mother's collection of stage costumes to give an instructive fund-raising talk about her theatrical career.[5] In these public talks and demonstrations, Craig was involved in

implementing the Newbolt Report's strategy for theatre in education. In August 1934 Edith Craig and Laurence Housman ran
a theatre workshop at the University of Cambridge Extra Mural
Board summer meeting where Harley Granville-Barker gave the
inaugural address on 'masterpieces of drama and the modern
theatre', followed by a series of specialist lectures on drama in
different periods, and eight lectures on 'modern movements'.[6]
Additional events ensured that students were actively involved
as participants; they included productions of plays in college
grounds and a specialist series of ten classes ('lectures, demonstrations and practical classes') for amateur producers led by
Edith Craig and Laurence Housman at Cambridge (THM 384/
14/5).

## The Story of My Life retold: *Ellen Terry's Memoirs* (1932, 1933)

Income from the publication of the correspondence between Terry
and Bernard Shaw and Ellen Terry's Memoirs was directed towards
the memorial although it caused a rift with Edward Gordon Craig
and a battle of the books ensued. The circumstances of the revision and publication of Ellen Terry's life story after her death are
complex and fraught. The extent to which these publications were
strategic in different ways for the different parties involved needs
further examination.

   With a need to replace her income and the opportunities of Ellen
Terry publications,[7] Christopher St John was kept busy with the
editing of the correspondence between Ellen Terry and George
Bernard Shaw. Tony Atwood informed Vera Holme that the consequence of the publication was that 'the Farm will become a memorial in September if all goes well' (7VJH 4/3/54). St John published
*Four Lectures on Shakespeare* (1932), encouraging Vera Holme to
promote their sale: 'Do try & get people to buy the lectures. They
have had splendid notices so far. I enclose a leaflet for you to stick
into letters' (St John to Vera Holme, 14 April 1932; 7VJH 4/3/77).
In 1932 St John and Edith Craig co-edited *Ellen Terry Memoirs*
for G. P. Putnam's in New York but the London publication was
delayed and the complications must have reminded St John and

Edith Craig of the fiasco they were caught up over *The Story of My Life* (1908). St John refers to a sense of inherited misfortune:

> The English edition of the book (E.T. memoirs) was to have come out in February, but Carew objected to the reference to himself, and Doris Keane threatened a libel action. The publishers then had to cut out the offending passages, and haven't finished the job yet. It is all very annoying & discouraging. I seem born to trouble. (Christopher St John to Jacko [Vera Holme], 17 April 1933; 7VJH 4/3/78)

Edward Gordon Craig's Paris diary claimed both a lack of consultation and that he had been asked to revise their mother's autobiography. The strength of feeling is suggested by his wilful renaming of Christopher St John:

> I see a new edition of E.T's 'Story of My Life,' edited by Edith Craig and Lily St John, is to appear – Gollancz. When E.T. died, Hutchinson instantly wrote me, asking me to do the book 'up to date'. Edith C. (plus Lily) thought any further edition quite unnecessary, and said so, with the line marked clearly under each word.
>
> So I agreed to that. Now, having got it out of Hutchinson's hands, the ladies, 'festering together' (as W. J. Turner described the London 'girl' groups), proceed, without consulting me, having legal authority; Edith C. being an executor, takes every centimetre of her privileges in the response and goes it. I think that since E.T. died, I have not been consulted more than three times, and that was during the three days after her funeral. After that, it was, 'Oh, he doesn't count'; but I count, right enough. I begin 1, 2, 3, 4, 5, 6, and go on till the full sum of egoism displayed by Edith shall reveal itself. (28 June 1933; Franklin 1982: 105–6)

By contrast, reports of Edith Craig's lack of egoism dominate accounts by her contemporaries.

## The Barn Theatre

Edward Gordon Craig was also sceptical about the Barn Theatre but still open to reports about it from his son: 'He tells me that

Edith is very aged these last months. Also that the festival at the farm (commemoration of E.T.'s passing) is like nothing on earth. Something in heaven? No – "We call it the wake." He doesn't explain in detail, so I get no clear idea' (5 September 1933; Franklin 1982: 129). By contrast, Virginia Woolf was apparently keen to join. Craig's standing in the world of British theatre and her visibility in the national press contextualize Woolf's motivation for joining Edith Craig's Barn Theatre.[8] The leading actors of the day performed there. Craig's reputation at this time placed her very much in the public eye. In 1935 in February she had spoken at the Ellen Terry Festival Week at Coventry, given a formal public lecture at the University of Liverpool and in July directed Tenterden Jubilee Pageant. Craig's interview was front-page news in *The Vote*, the Women's Freedom League newspaper (still in print long after enfranchisement was achieved). In 1932 Sackville-West had read her prize-winning poem *The Land* at the Barn Theatre, attended by Virginia and Leonard Woolf. Although Woolf had written to Sackville-West in 1933 about her intention to apply to join and to send a cheque, there is a much later letter (June 1938) from Woolf in which she bemoans to Sackville-West 'that there was "No sign from Edie. There's a fate against my joining"' (quoted in Cockin 1998: 179). Woolf may not have considered her own association with Sackville-West as a possible reason for evasiveness on Craig's part.[9]

In order to understand Woolf's reference to Craig's failure to reply, it is worth noting Woolf's interpretation which casts her membership of the Barn Theatre – her inclusion in this desirable community of theatre practitioners and inner circle of Ellen Terry pilgrims – as having a predestined prohibition attached to it. There may be, Woolf seems to imply, an underlying reason why she would be denied access to the hallowed ground: the Delphic site of Ellen Terry worship.

It was only posthumously that Woolf made an appearance on the stage of the Barn Theatre: in 1941 Vita Sackville-West read Virginia Woolf's 'Ellen Terry' essay in memory of both Terry and Woolf; and again in 1947 when Edith Craig was added to the joint remembrance of Ellen Terry, Virginia Woolf and Edith Craig (Cockin 1998: 176).

The Barn Theatre productions were resilient even in times of war. Henzie Browne recalled the difficult circumstances in which they produced Morna Stuart's *England's Green*, a play about the Norman invasion:

> The opening had long been arranged for that Sunday, in the famous barn theatre attached to Ellen Terry's cottage at Smallhythe, where each summer in peacetime her daughter, Edith Craig, gathered all the shining lights of the profession for a memorial matinee. Now Edy, and her friends Christopher St John and Tony Atwood, were the village air-raid wardens; but they still wanted a bit of theatre, and welcomed us with open arms. A surprisingly large audience gathered, and the play of English country life fitted the barn's atmosphere and seemed to thrive on the primitive lighting given it by Edy and Tony with two motor headlamps from the front row! Martin was watching the audience come out when he saw a woman stop suddenly and then say to her neighbour, 'What's that noise?' 'The guns, my dear,' replied the other. 'Do you know,' said he first, 'I'd quite forgotten them.' (Browne 1945: 36)

Margaret Webster recalled Craig's achievements at the Barn Theatre and the environment in which she worked. The unlikely transformation of beauty from chaos depicted by Webster is also part of Virginia Woolf's diary account of watching Craig's rehearsal in 1922:

> Conditions were frequently chaotic; willing helpers fell over each other in their excitement, inefficiency and enthusiasm. Edy marshalled everybody, dragooned everybody, charged them with resolution. Suddenly, there was a beautiful, moving performance. (Webster 1969: 279)

Webster interprets the process she had witnessed in terms of an aesthetic of improvisation:

> The improvisation for which she had a real flair was partly thrust upon her, for the professional theatre in London at that time would never have accepted a woman doing the job, or jobs, she did. But in a sense I think she preferred it that way. She hated anything prefabricated, elaborate, solid, frozen. Faced with our union regulations and restrictions of the present day she

FIGURE 6 *Edith Craig, Christopher St John and Tony Atwood in stage costume in productions to celebrate the birthday of Jacko (Vera Holme) at the Barn Theatre (1930–31); and in* The Venetian Boat Song *(reproduced with the permission of The National Trust).*

would undoubtedly have exploded in a blinding flash. (Webster 1969: 280)

Birthday celebrations for Vera Holme were also staged at the Barn Theatre, with comical sketches revealing the shared humour of this community. Edith Craig appears in a gondolier in *The Venetian Boat Song* as a moustachioed villain with a dagger, reminiscent of Pipistrello in Max Reinhardt's film, *A Venetian Night* (1913).

Craig and Atwood performed as local dignitaries with the power and authority to award Holme with honours. The contrast is striking between the reality of cardboard props and scavenged costumes and the jocular posturing in asserting their claim to absolute power and authority over Smallhythe and Bedford Street, as if a mobile, putative Vatican City in Kent and Covent Garden. Some sense of these dynamics at Priest's House, with St John as a papal figure, are revealed in an ironic alteration of St John's headed notepaper from 'Christopher St John, 31 Bedford St' to 'The Holy Bedford Empire (not order)[.] The Lord profoundly shocked you should have misstated it' (7VJH/4/3/102)

# Avatars and 'a channel for the age-old "life-force" of the theatre'

In 1932 Edith Craig stepped into her mother's shoes to lead the annual Daffodil Day fund-raising event and became President of the Servers of the Blind League, the charity which her mother had founded (THM 384/14/4). Her contemporaries noted that Craig seemed more closely to resemble her mother as time went on. Others came forward to become Ellen Terry's avatar. Florence Locke secured performing rights from Edith Craig to Ellen Terry's Shakespeare Lectures to raise funds for the memorial.[10] Locke took these on tour, even to the very heart of Shakespearean scholarship at the Folger Library, Washington DC in 1934 when she gave 'The Romantic Women in Shakespeare'. Locke's partner, Eleanor Adlard described the Barn Theatre as 'a National Theatre made radiant by Ellen Terry's Shakespeare and Shakespeare's Ellen Terry' (Eleanor Adlard, *Everyman*, 8 August 1933, p. 173).

Edith Craig is for the most part omitted from Gordon Craig's publications. She features very briefly in *Index to the Story of My Days 1872–1907* (1957) when he notes her response to his performance in 1892 in Margate:

My sister Edy came down to see me play Ford in *The Merry Wives* and said later that it was pretty good in it. This from her, was high praise – though praise never got much further into me than the ears, and so never harmed me.

The intense significance his sister played in his life is suggested by these silences and omissions. The two followed parallel lines in their pursuit of the art of the theatre, aiming for an aesthetic coherence for the production, but they disagreed on the role of the actor in the enterprise and on the abilities of women. In the same year as the publication of Gordon Craig's *Index to the Story of My Days* (1957), a major event was held to honour his sister's theatre work.

Margaret Webster was the strongest advocate for Edith Craig in word and deed, recording her views in print and in devising, arranging and narrating *A Festival for Edy* on Sunday, 21 July 1957, a decade after Craig's death. This event included excerpts from plays that Craig had produced, including W. B. Yeats's *Purgatory* (Barn Theatre, 1939). In 1949 Webster could not resist adding a postscript to her mother's essay in Adlard's collection, to summarize the influence Craig had been on a generation of theatre practitioners in her commitment to work in the theatre as 'metier' and 'service' rather than motivated by fashion or a career. Craig's approach to production stayed with Webster at an unconscious level, when she regularly found herself with 'Edy's brains working through my hands!' (Webster 1949: 57). She generalized this influence: 'In ways like these Edy made herself a channel for the age-old "life-force" of the theatre' (Webster 1949: 57). Webster was aware that this concentration on the transmission of ideas through theatre practice contributed to the delay in establishing the appropriate historical place for Edith Craig's theatres of art. Craig's time has now arrived.

# NOTES

## A note on sources and more dramatic lives

1. For biographical studies of Ellen Terry, see Holroyd (2008), Auerbach (1987) and Melville (1987, 2006).
2. In addition to Edward Gordon Craig's own writings, see Walton (1983), Innes (1998), Eynat-Confino (1987) and Taxidou (1998) on his theatre work. In 2016, to mark fifty years since the death of Edward Gordon Craig, the Stevenage Museum and Stevenage Arts Guild have created a project entitled 'Who Is Edward Gordon Craig?' See www.whoisgordoncraig.co.uk, accessed 9 October 2016.
3. See the *Oxford Dictionary of National Biography* for my essays on the lives of Edith Craig, Christopher St John and Clare Atwood.
4. Hallett noted, '[Cockin] locates the relative balances in Craig's life, where sexuality and professional activity intersect, to present Craig's pioneer suffragism, theatrical innovation and sexuality as part of a life fabric which Craig herself had woven. The work gives due weight to the mutually informing elements of Craig's "dramatic lives"' (Hallett 1999: 66).
5. According to Saunders, 'Edy Craig's role in developing suffrage and community theatre has until comparatively recently been neglected. Julie Holledge's *Innocent Flowers* [1981] did much to give her the prominence she justly deserves, followed by other writers such as Joy Melville, Christine Dymkowski, and, most notably, Katharine Cockin. Cockin's research has helped not only to show Edy Craig's role as theatrical innovator, but also to test the parameters of the theatrical canon' (Saunders 2011: 825).
6. The AHRC Ellen Terry and Edith Craig Database project facilitated the National Trust's long-term loan of the majority of the archive to the British Library, London. See www.ellenterryarchive.hull.ac.uk. Further funding has supported my follow-on project, AHRC 'Searching for Theatrical Ancestors' (STAR) 2015–16, to enhance the online database for family historians, with a focus on Shakespearean productions.

7. The Ellen Terry Collection at the Victoria & Albert Theatre Collection, London (GB 71 THM/384) consists of 513 files in 48 series, relating to the period 1856–1976. http://archiveshub.ac.uk/data/gb71-thm/384, accessed 9 October 2016.

8. The papers of Vera (Jack) Holme at the Women's Library, London School of Economics, London (GB 106 7VJH) consist of four boxes, three albums and a folder relating to the period 1900–c.1962. http://archiveshub.ac.uk/data/gb106-7vjh.html?page=3, accessed 9 October 2016. For an outline of her life and work, see Kisby (2014).

9. They include the exhibition 'Ellen Terry: The Painter's Actress', the Watts Gallery, Surrey, 2014; Eileen Atkins's performances of Ellen Terry's Shakespeare lectures at the Wanamaker Theatre, London (2014, 2016); Ros Conolly's plays, 'Ellen: Her Triumphant Women' (2011), and 'Ellen: Her Life in Shakespeare', the Gordon Craig Theatre, Stevenage (15 June 2015).

10. Anna Birch's production of Cicely Hamilton's *A Pageant of Great Women*, Glasgow Women's Library (March 2015); Lesley Ferris's production of Christopher St John's *The First Actress*, Ohio State University and with Palindrome Productions, the Barn Theatre, Smallhythe Place (June 2014); Naomi Paxton's 'Knickerbocker Glories', the Union Theatre, London (2010), three one-act plays including *How the Vote Was Won*, and 'Suffragettes on Stage', the National Theatre (June 2013); and various women's suffrage plays at the Orange Tree Theatre, Richmond, including Elizabeth Baker's *Chains* (2007), Cicely Hamilton's *Diana of Dobson's* (2009), and scenes from *How the Vote Was Won* and other suffrage plays (2009).

11. Following the precedents set by Craig's productions of *A Pageant of Great Women* in Cambridge (1910), the production staged at Middleton Hall, University of Hull on 8 May 2011 included additional characters drawn from the great women in the local history of Hull and surrounding regions (Mary Murdoch, Hull's first female GP; Amy Johnson, aviator; and the authors, Winifred Holtby and Mary Wollstonecraft). The event programme is available online: https://hydra.hull.ac.uk/resources/hull:10738, accessed 9 October 2016. The staged reading, directed by Anna Birch, is available online https://hydra.hull.ac.uk/resources/hull:8562, accessed 9 October 2016 with the audience discussion https://hydra.hull.ac.uk/resources/hull:8563, accessed 9 October 2016.

# Chapter 1

1. As the work of the AHRC Middlebrow Network (2008–10) project has established, the middlebrow has been examined extensively in

relation to the novel, popular culture, social class, as a transatlantic phenomenon and in debates about taste, reading habits and intellectualism. See http://www.middlebrow-network.com, accessed 9 October 2016 for some relevant discussion of the theatre in this context, see Barker and Gale (2000); and D'Monte (2015).

2. In Britain, the Little Theatre movement developed from the independent theatre societies of the 1890s but it became institutionalized in 1919. The American Little Theatre movement differed in various ways, including scale; see Chansky (2004).

3. The Independent Labour Party (ILP) was founded in 1893 and its first Member of Parliament, Keir Hardie (1856–1915), was elected in 1900. In 1906 the ILP joined other socialist groups and trades' unions to form the Labour Party. See the Working Class Movement Library at http://www.wcml.org.uk/, accessed 9 October 2016. Extant correspondence (c. 1930) shows that Edith Craig was associated with the ILP's Masses' Stage and Film Guild whose patrons included Rt Hon George Lansbury (1859–1940), Member of Parliament for Bow and Bromley, in the East End of London, cabinet minister in 1929–31 during the first Labour government and leader of the Labour Party (1932–5). He had been a hunger-striking suffragette, and a pacifist during the First World War, as well as editor of the radical newspaper the *Daily Herald*.

4. Sheila Rowbotham (1973) conceptualized the way in which women were systematically 'hidden from history'. However, the case of lesbians such as Edith Craig, inconsistently hidden from the public record and omitted or minimized in the critical narratives of past events, was compounded by the selective destructive of parts of her own archive her own attitude towards publicity and the desirability of a collective enterprise rather than one foregrounding the personality of one artist.

5. Radclyffe Hall's biographers (Baker 1985; Cline 1997) have noted the significance of the stalwart support from Craig, St John and Atwood after the sensational trial. Baker quotes Radclyffe Hall's partner Una Troubridge to this effect: 'There is great consolation and gratification to me in the company of these friends who like us & want to be with us because they know us for what we are and respect what John [Radclyffe Hall] has done for her kind' (quoted in Baker 1985: 271).

6. Charles F. Smith was son of Sydney Smith, a skirt manufacturer in Leeds (Steele 1990: 142). His important role in Yorkshire theatre is briefly mentioned (Nicholl 1973) and recalled by the actor Sir Donald Sinden as Smith gave him his first opportunity in the theatre in Mobile Entertainments Southern Area (MESA) in 1941 (*Yorkshire Evening Post*, 27 March 2006).

7. Margaret Webster was a renowned director, with pioneering productions of Shakespeare on Broadway, United States, in 1943 casting African American actor Paul Robeson as Othello. She was subsequently ostracised as 'Un-American' during the era of political persecution under McCarthyism and, as noted by Webster's biographer Milly Barranger, Webster was interrogated in 1953 by the House Committee of Un-American Activities (HUAC) (Barranger 2004: 223–56).

8. The artist W. Graham Robertson (1866–1948), a close friend of Ellen Terry, was somewhat critical of Edith Craig in his private correspondence (see Preston 1953: 259–61).

9. Full biographical accounts have yet to be written about St John and Atwood, both stalwart supporters of Craig's theatrical productions and highly regarded creative women in their own right.

10. For a detailed study of the work of the Pioneer Players, see Cockin (2001). Essays and articles include a detailed exploration of Edith Craig's production of plays by the Japanese dramatist Torahiko Kori (Chiba 1996); George Bernard Shaw's *Mrs Warren's Profession* (Fisher 1995; Conolly 2004); Nikolai Evreinov's *The Theatre of the Soul* (Smith 2010); the plays of Paul Claudel for the Pioneer Players (Gandolfi 2011); and a new analysis of the Pioneer Players' activities during the First World War (Cockin 2015).

11. These include: the first British production of French dramatist Paul Claudel's play *Exchange*; plays by the Dutch dramatist Herman Heijermans, including *The Good Hope*, about maritime disaster and exploitative working conditions; and two plays by Japanese dramatist Kori Torahiko, who spent a decade in Britain (Rimer 2015: 37).

12. This was produced on 7 March 1927 at the Albert Hall, Leeds; MS 138/50 XMS 38, Cadbury Research Library Special Collection, University of Birmingham.

13. See four letters from Rosina Filippi (b. 1866) to Edith Craig, July to November 1917; EC-3, 239 to EC-3, 242.

14. Roland Barthes (1977 [1968]) argued for the necessary liberation of the reader to interpret the text unencumbered by concerns about the author having ultimate control over the meaning. In theatre production, the approach to the playscript and author(s) have varied considerably but it was Edward Gordon Craig who became associated with a redirection of control from the author or performer to the director.

15. Harold Nicholson reviewed Adlard's book in *The Spectator*, 6 January 1950, p. 15.

16. Irene Cooper Willis and Eleanor Adlard both use this orientalist discourse in their essays on Craig in Adlard's collection (1949).

17. De Bouhélier, a highly respected figure as an author and cultural
commentator, had been aligned with Émile Zola against the
anti-semitic trial of Alfred Dreyfus in 1894. He names as Craig's
comparators André Antoine (1858–1943), director of the Théâtre
Libre; Lugné-Poe (1869–1940), who led the Théâtre de l'Oeuvre and
its symbolist productions; and Firmin Gémier (1869–1933), who
founded the Théâtre National Populaire, Paris in 1920.

18. Henry IV, the *Marie* in 1410; for Henry V, the *Jesus* and the
*George*; and for Henry VIII, the *Great Gallyon* for Henry VIII;
'Smallhythe: A Deserted Medieval Shipyard', National Trust, n.d.
https://www.nationaltrust.org.uk/smallhythe-place/documents/find-
out-more-about-our-shipbuilding-past.pdf, accessed 7 August 2016

19. Sackville-West had a great sense of her own aristocratic heritage
as well as the influence of her grandmother, 'Pepita', Josefa Duran
(1830–71), the Spanish dancer

20. Michel Foucault describes heterotopias as 'counter-sites', operating in
a variety of ways but categorized according to six principles; they are
different and special places that are real rather than mythic; they have
a function; they may be separate but also accessible, conflicted or
overlapping and relating to time, ritual or crisis; 'Des Éspaces Autres'
(1967) translated by Jay Miskowiec as 'Of Other Spaces: Utopias
and Heterotopias', *Architecture/Mouvement/Continuité*, 1984. In
exploring heterotopian aspects of Sackville-West's description of
the women of Smallhythe Place, I am grateful to Holly Furneaux's
response to my paper at the Queer Manifestations conference, 2010.

21. Ellen Terry shared this opinion about the commercial control of
theatres by investors operating in syndicates with the American
campaigner and performer Minnie Maddern Fiske (1865–1932).

22. The daughter of her nephew Robin Craig (also known as Robert),
who was the first son of Edward Gordon Craig and May Gibson; see
Cockin (1998: 167). Robinetta's mother was the poet, Elza de Locre;
see Lindsay 1982. I am grateful to Helen Lindsay for this reference.

23. Virginia Woolf's argument for the development of female authorship
in *A Room of One's Own* emphasized the value of access to a
physical space in which to concentrate as well as undisturbed time
and for which she acknowledged the related economic costs. Given
the more complex and expensive infrastructure and personnel
typically involved in theatre production, the desire for a 'theatre of
one's own' was even more difficult to achieve.

24. When St John describes this period with Craig, she seems to allude
to the disruption created by Craig's involvement with Shaw: 'It
came near to being a tragedy. Of that Edy never spoke in after years.
I think our life together subsequently was all the happier, because we

did not break open the grave of a thing past which had threatened to separate us' (St John 1949: 22). Edward Gordon Craig also briefly mentions his sister's apparent involvement with Shaw and their mother's determination to thwart it; see Craig (1957).

25. Evans was at one time president of the Art Students League of New York and elected to the Society of American Artists in 1891. His membership is listed posthumously in the twenty-eighth Exhibition Catalogue of the Society of American Artists.

26. Satty Fairchild, also known as Sally, was a longstanding American friend of Ellen Terry and her daughter, described as 'Miss Sarah Fairchild, a member of a well-known Boston family' (*STC* 1931: 108).

27. Loyall Farragut (1844–1916) was a businessman, leading the Central Railroad Company and his father's biographer. Admiral David Glasgow Farragut (1801–70), the first person to be appointed Admiral in the US navy, had been distinguished in the American Civil War and given the honour of having his portrait used for a postage stamp and currency.

28. Ellen Terry rarely used this form but she used the same phrase when she signed a letter to Stephen Coleridge on 18 January 1884; *CLET* 3: 551.

29. For the impact on Gordon Craig of childhood memories of an atmosphere of conspiracy see Eynat-Confino (1987: 9) and Craig (1957: 48).

30. Elizabeth Rumball, née Bocking, was known as 'Boo'. For extensive correspondence from Ellen Terry to Boo, see *CLET*; see also the Polling Collection held by the National Trust and described at www.ellenterryarchive.hull.ac.uk.

31. Terry was sufficiently well connected to use her influence with newspaper editors in Britain but apparently not in Philadelphia; *The Philadelphia Press* article is held at Y.d. 458 6, Folger Library, Washington DC, United States.

32. Bram Stoker (1847–1912) acted as business manager for Henry Irving at the Lyceum Theatre company and was a reliable source of advice for Ellen Terry.

33. The first issue of *The Freewoman: A Weekly Feminist Review* was dated 23 November 1911; it had an estimated circulation of some 2,500 and was available in United States in 1912. Fernihough reproduces a facsimile of the first page of the first issue where Ellen Terry is named at the end of the first paragraph (Fernihough 2013: 14).

34. Irene Cooper Willis was a prolific published author, with several books on the First World War and idealism, including *England's Holy War: A Study of English Liberal Idealism During the War* (1928) and

several biographies. She was later entrusted as the literary executor of the author, Vernon Lee (1856–1935).

35. Claude Lévi-Strauss described 'bricolage' in *La Pensée Sauvage* (1962) translated as *The Savage Mind* (1966), as a way of thinking which refashions and recreates from available materials. A repurposing and recycling mode was adopted by modernist radicals and theorists such as Walter Benjamin who promoted serendipitous collection of objects and experiences in *Passagenwerk*, translated as the Arcades project (1927–40).

36. The agreement was witnessed by Christopher St John on 21 November 1939.

37. See Beasley and Bullock(2013); for Craig's involvement with a ground-breaking production of a Russian play in London in 1915 (see Cockin 1994, 2015; Smith 2010).

38. Grein was the backer for the production of Oscar Wilde's *Salome* (announced for April 1918) starring Allan. He supported her libel case against Noel Pemberton Billing and was discredited during the trial (see Hoare 1997; Medd 2012: 27–75).

39. Angela Woollacott has examined the case of Rose Quong, born in Melbourne, Australia, in a period when migration from China was banned. In 1924 Quong left for London where she presented herself as an interpreter of Chinese culture (Woollacott 2011). Quong corresponded with Edith Craig, sending her a copy of *The Western Chamber* (1935) by H. S. Hsiung (1902–91), the author of *Lady Precious Stream*, the first play to be directed by a Chinese person in the West End, London (Little Theatre, 1935–6); (EC-B153, EC-B165, EC-H435).

40. The motivation for the publication of *The Russian Ballet* (1913) was not for the benefit of her son (Holroyd 2008: 452) but instead decidedly commercial, resulting from the joint effort of Christopher St John and Pamela Colman Smith, as correspondence in the Edith Craig archive reveals.

41. For instance, see Brooker and Thacker (2005); Holledge (2008); Wollaeger and Etough (2012).

42. The National Trust's Edith Craig archive holds a collection of forty-nine newspaper cuttings (March–April 1925) relating to Craig's production of *The Verge*; see www.ellenterryarchive.hull.ac.uk For a brief discussion of Craig's production and its reception, see Cockin (1998: 150–1).

43. J. F. Chipp wrote on 6 March 1925 to Lewis Casson from Kew Gardens to explain that the laboratory space was insufficient and suggested Imperial College or University College, London; EC-3, 143. This letter was forwarded on 7 March 1925 to Craig by S. Holmes, Sybil Thorndike's secretary; EC-3, 347.

44. Linda Ben-Zvi emphasizes the difference between the short story and the play and the more radical aspects of *Trifles* (Ben-Zvi 1992: 160; see also Hallgren 1995).

# Chapter 2

1. According to Edith Craig's memoirs, this incident occurred in St Albans Abbey; Rachlin (2011: 2–3).
2. Christopher St John describes herself as Ellen Terry's 'literary henchman' (1932: 7), implying a relationship with Terry which was conspiratorial and adversarial to the rest of the world.
3. Ellen Terry married the renowned artist G. F. Watts on 20 February 1864.
4. Julia Margaret Cameron photographed Terry when she visited the Isle of Wight with Watts just after their marriage, events fictionalized in Virginia Woolf's play *Freshwater*.
5. In the familiar Earls Court area, the residence was south of the Cromwell Road where other members of the family lived and near to 33 Longridge Road, where Ellen Terry lived with her second husband, Charles Wardell.
6. Terry regarded *Jude the Obscure* as 'coarse' but 'finer' than *Tess*; *CLET* 3: 671.
7. This may have been the dramatization rather than the novel itself; Rachlin (2011: 74).
8. He was named in the notorious Beecher-Tilton adultery court case in 1875 and condemned by feminist activists such as Elizabeth Cady Stanton (1815–1902) and Victoria Woodhull (1838–1927) (Applegate 2006).
9. Laurence's controversial play about leprosy *Godefroi and Yolande* was championed by Ellen Terry and revived by Edith Craig for the Pioneer Players, complemented by a talk by H. B. Irving in a tribute to his brother Laurence, who had died in a maritime disaster in 1914. Henry Irving separated from his wife, Florence, apparently because she disapproved of the theatre.
10. When Watts and Terry separated, an agreement was signed to the effect that he would financially support her so long as she did not return to the stage and led a single life (Terry 1908: 59).
11. This lone journey, as documented in Ellen Terry's letters, took place a couple of months before Craig reached her tenth birthday. In Craig's memoirs, her age at the time is given as eight; Rachlin (2011: 12).

12. Terry supported a fund-raising production at the Metropolitan Opera House in New York on 27 February 1911, designed to support 'the protection of stage children'; ET-D2114.

13. In Edith Craig's memoirs, reference is made to her having been 'confirmed' (Rachlin 2011: 63). See also *Ellen Terry's Memoirs* (1933: 195) and *CLET* 1: 158.

14. William Cody (1846–1917), known as 'Buffalo Bill', was a scout in the American Civil War and subsequently an international performer with 'Buffalo Bill's Wild West' from 1883, touring Britain in 1887.

15. The third Lyceum Tour of America opened at the Star Theatre, New York, on 7 November 1887. For an insight into their social activities in United States, see Terry's letter to her son; *CLET* 1: 186.

16. See letters in the period October—November 1888; *CLET* 1.

17. The others were: the harpsichordist, Violet Gordon Woodhouse (1872–1948); the Princesse de Polignac (Winaretta Singer) (1865–1943), a renowned patron of the arts in Paris; Maurice Baring (1874–1945), a prolific author; and Sir Ronald Storrs (1881–1955), a leading official in the foreign service in Egypt, Cyprus, Palestine and Northern Rhodesia (now part of Zambia).

18. Edward Gordon Craig's essay asserts family genius but omits reference to his sister's achievements as a theatre director or practitioner.

19. Sir Arthur Sullivan (1842–1900) was composer and collaborator who worked with W. S. Gilbert in musical theatre at the Savoy Theatre.

20. This informed her later productions with the Pioneer Players, such as the plainsong that accompanied Hrotsvit's *Paphnutius*.

21. Henry Irving would have had confidence in Craig's skills having sent her on a mission to Paris the previous year to make a prompt book of *Cyrano de Bergerac*. Craig had also appeared in Cora Brown Potter's production of *Charlotte Corday* in 1898.

22. Terry arranged to pay her £16 monthly in between salaried work but also for Coleridge to give her book-keeping lessons (30 July 1899; *CLET* 4: 1009).

23. In June 1902 Terry wrote to J. M. Barrie giving the business address in recommendation (19 June 1902; *CLET* 4: 1242).

24. Jess Dorynne, an actor and author, with whom Gordon Craig had a daughter, Kitty.

25. This may relate to Martin Shaw's proposal of marriage and the relationship Craig had with Christopher St John.

26. Edith Craig's rheumatism was a lifelong health condition and had prevented her from pursuing a career as a pianist.

27. F. W. Fairholt, *Costume in England: A History of Dress* (London: George Bell & Sons, 1885); (Hardie 1999).

28. Terry was aware of Craig's appreciation of colour and ordered for her daughter's birthday Edith's favourite flower, being a carnation of 'a certain vivid red' ([11 May 1902]; *CLET* 4: 1234).

29. Cora Urquhart Brown-Potter (1857–1936) was a successful American actor who took to the stage, leaving a respectable marriage to a financier, from whom she divorced in 1900. Sarah Bernhardt (1844–1923) was one of the most famous actors of her generation in France, the United Kingdom and United States. Lillie Langtry (1853–1929) whose acting and theatre management career was launched in 1880 after her affair with Prince Albert had ended

30. Phèdre's *Isael Tosca*, c. 1890; Rachlin (2011: 100–3).

31. One of her early Lyceum Theatre roles in 1880 was Polly in *Olivia* (14 and 19 September 1880; ET-D418a) in which Terry's other children appeared too; Edward Gordon Craig was Moses and Minnie Terry was Dick; see programmes ET-D712 to D714.

32. Terry bought the play from Pearl Craigie and had performed the role of Lady Soupire at Daly's London on 5 June 1894.

33. Terry was concerned about her daughter's welfare and sought George Bernard Shaw's opinion on her acquaintances (*CLET* 4:846).

34. Max Beerbohm was a prolific author and caricaturist, drama critic for the *Saturday Review* (1898–1910) and half-brother of Herbert Beerbohm Tree, the actor-manager.

35. Vesta Tilley (1864–1952) was the stage name of Matilda Powles, who, from 1890, was married to Walter de Frece. She was a music hall performer known for her male impersonations (c. 1868–1920).

36. For an insight into the diversity of approaches to the classification of sexual behaviours in this period, see Doan and Bland (1998).

37. Pamela Colman Smith published collections of stories but she was principally an artist, a pioneer in the visual interpretation of music and illustrator of the most widely known set of Tarot cards; see Boyd Parsons (1987); Greer (1995: 405–9); Cockin (2015). Her other areas of interest were women's suffrage and the occult; see Tickner (1987: 247–8).

38. The play had provided a vehicle for Edward Gordon Craig to appear on stage with her. The eighteenth-century actress Anne (Nance) Oldfield (1683–1730), leading performer at Drury Lane Theatre and lover of politicians Arthur Maynwaring and Charles Churchill, had nevertheless been buried in Westminster Abbey. Terry therefore chose a stage role which fashioned her as an actress with a past who successfully achieved some social acceptance.

39. Officially they were the sole responsibility of Boo's niece, Bo (Catherine Elizabeth Powell, 1839–1946), who had married Joe Powell (1850–1937); I am grateful to John Boyes Watson for this biographical information.
40. This practice of renting out accommodation on a temporary basis is a central feature of the Mapp and Lucia novels (1920–39) of E. F. Benson (1867–1940), Terry's near neighbour in Rye.
41. Letter from Edward Gordon Craig to Edy [Craig], c. 1904, quoted in the Exhibition Catalogue of the Philbrick Collection (Stanford: Stanford University, 1985): 7.
42. When Irving's possessions were sold at Christie's on 12 December 1905, some of his books found their way into Terry's library.
43. For an exploration of the gothic dimension of the Lyceum Theatre company, see Cockin (1998: 49–53) and Cockin (2015).
44. Edith Craig & Co. is the only advertisement in the first issue; a further seven issues were published in 1903 and five in 1904.
45. Letter fragment from Christopher St John to Ellen Terry; one page extant, numbered p. 3; THM 384.
46. For further discussion of the relevance of this essay to Yeats's contribution to the *Green Sheaf*, see Cockin (2016).
47. Colman Smith and Jack B. Yeats collaborated on *The Broad Sheet* (1902).

# Chapter 3

1. The *Masque of Flowers* was produced in 1887 and designed by John O'Connor 1830–89 for Queen Victoria.
2. Programme ET-D475b provides credits for performers, the producer and others involved including the wardrobe mistress Mrs Evans and even the electrician and machinist..
3. These were Milton's *Comus*, Ben Jonson's *Hue and Cry*, Thomas Heywood's *A Woman Killed with Kindness* and Congreve's *The Way of the World* and *The Castell of Perseverance*.
4. The identity of Miss Wardell, who appeared as one of the three graces, is not yet known.
5. Oscar Asche was later to become famous for his role in *Chu Chin Chow*, the musical which ran for over 2000 performances from 1916.
6. See Cullingford (1997: 60); Joan Coldwell (1977) has pointed out that Colman Smith had freedom in designing the minor arcana and that Waite failed to notice that she had indeed adapted his designs in different ways. In any event, Colman Smith was active in the occult movement independently of Yeats.
7. Jane Ellen Harrison (1850–1928) had subscribed to The Masquers. This was the year in which she published *Prolegomena to the Study of Greek Religion* (1903). Mabel Malleson had accompanied both

Edith Craig and Jane Ellen Harrison, on separate occasions, on their individual travels to Germany (Beard 2000: 54).

8. Florence Farr (1860–1917), actor, author and composer, experimented with performances on the psaltery, an instrument of ancient design, similar to the zither. Farr was centrally involved in mysticism, at this point in the Order of the Golden Dawn and supporter of women's independence most widely as well as the suffrage campaign.

9. Granville-Barker organized the influential productions with J. E. Vedrenne at the Royal Court Theatre (1904–7).

10. Letters to Edith Craig from Fred Kerr, Alfred Drayton and A. Lanzerte [*sic*], concerning arrangements for rehearsals; V&A THM 14/20/33 & 34.

11. Her name is not listed in the Executive or General Committees in the brochure advertising Terry's tribute (THM 384/13/28) and it does not feature in the decorative souvenir jubilee programme which comprehensively lists the committees, the full cast lists for the various short performances and acknowledgements for design or arrangements. By contrast, Gordon Craig, for instance, is listed as arranging and designing the scenery and dances for *Much Ado About Nothing* with the assistance of the Honorary Stage Manager Lionel Belmore and Honorary Music Director Christopher Wilson; THM 384/13/29.

12. For a discussion of Terry's management of her brand, see Cockin (2011).

13. The association of Terry's performances with charm and 'pictorial effect' are analysed by Michael Booth (1986).

14. Irving's expertise in producing crowd scenes is examine by Chotia (2008).

15. See the article 'Ellen Terry Bossed by Autocratic Daughter', *Citizen*, 13 February 1907; EC-G178.

16. Craig understudied for her mother in Graham Robertson's popular play *Pinkie and the Fairies*.

17. For instance, costumes for her role in *Henry of Lancaster* (ET-D449) and *Captain Brassbound's Conversion*; ET-D453.

18. Christopher St John's correspondence on this matter has been carefully preserved; ET-D2270. For an account of this role see Cockin 2002.

19. See Cockin (2002).

20. This photograph is described as depicting (unidentified) members of the WWSL about to take part in the NUWSS procession on 13 June 1908 when it featured in an exhibition at the Museum of London; see Sparham (2015).

21. In 1908 Sir George Lewis wrote to Terry regarding the resolution of the matter with Miss Marshall with the payment to her of £283.0.5 (19 March 1908; THM 384/7/20).

22. Terry had investments in Grand Trunk, Buenos Ayres Pacific, Salvador Railway, Cordela Central Extension, St James and Pall Mall Electric. She had bought a cottage for £305 5s, had £200 in deposit account and £324 4s 4d in her current account and lent £50 to a Miss Mapson. See www.ellenterryarchive.hull.ac.uk, accessed 9 October 2016.

23. The play was produced at Lena Ashwell's Kingsway Theatre by Edward Knoblauch and featured Marion Terry.

24. See Cockin (2005).

25. In *Modernism and Cultural Conflict* (2002), Ann Ardis has shown how even the posing of the female model for an artist is taken as an opportunity for destruction in Wyndham Lewis's novel *Tarr*.

26. These conflicts relating to social class are fundamental to the British women's suffrage movement; see for instance, Tickner 1987; Mayhall, 2003.

27. Hon. Gabrielle Borthwick's automobile company was a regular advertiser in the Pioneer Players' play programmes and, according to Georgina Clarsen, Borthwick was a Royal Automobile Club agent, still successful in the late 1920s (Clarsen 2011: 40).

28. Farr was described by George Yeats as Yeats's sole confidante (Bax 1946: 33).

29. Mary K. Greer examines the role of the female members of the Order of the Golden Dawn and how, after the numerous conflicts, the intervention of Alesteir Crowley and charges of fraud which split the Order of the Golden Dawn, Florence Farr became its leader. See also Ellic Howe (1972).

30. Her examples also include the lines from *Cymbeline*, 'fear no more the heat of the sun', which became so meaningful for Virginia Woolf in *Mrs Dalloway* (1925). Farr's article was reproduced in a collection entitled *The Music of Speech containing the words of some poets, thinkers and music makers regarding the practice of the Bardic Art together with fragments of verse set to its own melody* published by Elkin Mathews.

31. The cast featured Archibald McLean as The Past, Lewis Casson as The Present and Gwendolen Bishop, The Future. Incidental music for the violin was played by Mrs Gwendolen Paget. The masque has three male characters in the published text although The Future was played by a woman in the Albert Hall production. The Present is sitting on a throne that is described by the Past as 'The Place of Truth' (p. 3).

# Chapter 4

1. Adelin Beatrice Connell, known as Lena Connell exhibited her portraits of Ellen Terry, Edith Craig and Cicely Hamilton at the Royal Photographic Society in 1910 and 1911 in costume in their roles in *A Pageant of Great Women* (Neale 2001: 63). Like Christina Broom (1863–1939), and Norah Smyth (c.1874–1963), Connell was one of the commercial photographers willing to support the political movement by doing business with them.

2. An album of photographs mounted on cardboard in a concertina format which would facilitate display was part of Sime Seruya's archive; author's own collection.

3. Sime Seruya (1876–1955) was one of the founding members of the AFL and a member of the advisory committee of the Pioneer Players in 1911–12; PPAR.

4. Charles Thursby was a renowned actor and dramatist, having performed for Sara Thorne's company at Margate and for Charles Wyndham; he appeared as George IV in *Pains and Penalties* by Laurence Housman and continued to be an acting member of the Pioneer Players up to 1915–16. His play *Broken Fetters* was produced in July 1897 at the Matinee Theatre. Mrs Charles Thursby (husband deceased in 1903) née Brisbane had her portrait painted by John Singer Sargent.

5. Letter from Holloway Prison from Sime Seruya to Edith Craig, 1910, written on prison lavatory paper and addressed 'For Miss Craig, Adelphi Terrace House, Strand'; 7EWD/F/1, FL555, Vera Holme Papers, LSE. Although Craig was not arrested, a journalist mistook Christopher St John for Craig: 'Playwright's Arrest: Miss Ellen Terry's Daughter Complains of Police Methods', *Weekly Despatch* [21 February 1909], 7VJH/1/51/01.

6. For a detailed biographical study of Robins and her prolific writings, see John (1995).

7  Sue-Ellen Case foregrounds Hrotsvit's episodic style, notes Craig's production and examines the exclusion of Hrotsvit's drama in a chapter entitled 'Women Pioneers' (Case 1988: 34–5).

8. Women's suffrage drama has been collected and published in: an appendix to Holledge (1981); Spender and Hayman (1985); Gardner (1985); Cockin, Norquay and Park, Vol. 3 (2007); Croft (2009); Paxton (2013); included in Nelson (2004) alongside fiction, non-fiction and poetry. My research on Cockin, Norquay and Park, Vol. 3 (2007) was supported by an AHRC Small Grant in the Performing Arts.

9. Julie Holledge's (1981) ground-breaking study on women's suffrage drama provides brief accounts of the AFL and the Pioneer Players

in the context of female performers. For a study of the Pioneer Players see Cockin (2001); for the AFL see Hirschfield (1985, 1987, 1991); and most recently a comparative study of George Bernard Shaw and the AFL (Dolgin 2015). According to Cicely Hamilton, there was some conflict between Craig and the AFL (Hamilton 1949: 40–1).

10. The photograph of Craig in a street procession with author-actors Christopher St John and Cicely Hamilton and the WWSL banner was used as one of several photographic images on the paper cover of Cicely Hamilton's autobiography, *Life Errant* (1935) and has recently appeared in the exhibition 'Soldiers and Suffragettes', Museum of London, 2015; see Sparham (2015).

11. For analysis of the complex relationship between women's suffrage campaigners and the press, see DiCenzo (2011).

12. Lisa Tickner, *The Spectacle of Women* (1987), provides a definitive and comprehensive, interdisciplinary study of the visual culture of the British women's suffrage movement, briefly featuring Edith Craig, Laurence Housman and Pamela Colman Smith.

13. Edith Craig's notepaper headed 'suffrage plays' (EC-N99) announced that she was 'sole agent' to whom application should be made 'for permission to give readings or performances' for: *How the Vote Was Won* and *The Pot and the Kettle* both by Cicely Hamilton and Christopher St John; Beatrice Harraden, *Lady Geraldine's Speech*; Leslie Morton, *Deeds not Words*; George Bernard Shaw, *Press Cuttings*; Cicely Hamilton's *The Waxworks* and *A Pageant of Great Women*; Bessie Hatton, *Before Sunrise* and Charles Thursby, *The Other Side*. Craig's name appears as publisher of several plays.

14. In Gertrude Colmore's short story 'George Lloyd' (*Votes for Women*, 16 May 1913), the new servant, a suffragette in disguise, is indispensible in the preparations for the government minister's visit.

15. Norah Smyth was a supporter of Sylvia Pankhurst, the East London Toy Factory and led the People's Army which paraded in Ford Road on 3 March 1914 before being arrested for assault; Taylor (1993: 22). Smyth was a member of the Pioneer Players from 1912 to 1914.

16. The position of working-class women in the women's suffrage movement was a site of tension since the campaign prioritized the enfranchisement of women on the same basis as men and therefore would not directly benefit working-class women.

17. Stowell explores the phenomenon of suffrage drama and the work of individual dramatists, Elizabeth Robins, Cicely Hamilton, Elizabeth

Baker and Githa Sowerby (1992a) and developed her analysis on Robins and realism further in 'Rehabilitating Realism' (1992b).

18. The Woman's Theatre prioritized the production of challenging plays rather than those authored by women; see (Holledge 1981: 92–3); Cockin (2001: 3).

19. Edith Craig's 'descriptive list of characters for *A Pageant of Famous [sic] Women*' describes Christian Davis and Hannah Snell as both 'tall – square – wears uniform, and must march well'; EC-N116. Norman MacDermott recalled the military costume routinely worn by Edith Craig, Christopher St John and Tony Atwood: 'we christened them "The Three Musketeers": they all wore the voluminious black *capa* of Italian cavalry officers, recently acquired on a visit to Italy and large floppy black hats' (MacDermott 1975: 30).

20. A contraction of 'spiffing', a colloquial term meaning 'excellent'.

21. See review 'Sir Arthur Sullivan's *Haddon Hall*', *Graphic*, 1 October 1892, p. 401; 'Sir A. Sullivan has publicly stated that he desired to steer clear as far as possible of the topsy-turvydom of Mr Gilbert.'

22. Advice on how to wear a 'Marquisse' or tricorne hat was provided in the *Manchester Guardian*, 30 November 1900, p. 9; large hats including tricorne hats are described for the readers of the *Lancashire Gazette*, 8 December 1888; a juvenile fancy dress ball included a child in a tricorne hat; *Leeds Mercury*, 19 January 1895, p. 7; a tricorne hat was worn by Katie Seymour in *The Run-away Girl* at the Gaiety Theatre; *Glasgow Herald*, 23 May 1898, p. 7; Ellice Beere in 'The World of Women' column reported that the new 'bicorne hat' provided more interest than the tricorne hat; *Penny Illustrated Paper*, 27 November 1909, p. 350.

23. In March 1911 Teresa Billington-Grieg had published a book interpreted as a critique of the WSPU; Mayhall (2003:102).

24. The programme for the event was held on Thursday, 6 March 1930, at Victoria Tower Gardens London, included unveiling by the Rt Hon. Stanley Baldwin MP, twelve items of music (directed by Captain Charles Hassall OBE), and ended with 'The March of Women' fanfare at the unveiling and chorale from *The Wreckers* followed by five other items after the speeches, including the Marseillaise; see programme; 7VJH 1/3/07.

25. A herald with a trumpet features on the poster for *A Pageant of Great Women* and 'A Herald' was listed in the cast for the Sheffield production (15 October 1910) where the organist from Rotherham Parish Church, Mr W. J. Maidment, performed three pieces: Polonaise in A Major, Chopin; Intermezzo, Holius; Triumphant March, Holius.

26. See Tickner (1987) for extensive evidence of anti-suffrage iconography.

27. See Gertrude Colmore's short story 'The Nun' (*Vote*, 26 June 1912, p. 175); reprinted in Cockin, Norquay and Park, Vol. 2 (2007a: 353).

28. According to Karen Blair it was staged at Mount Holyoake College, United States, in 1912 and may have influenced Hazel MacKaye, sister of Percy MacKaye, who had led many civic and several women's suffrage focused pageants: *Allegory* (1913); *Six Periods of American Life: A Woman Suffrage Pageant* (1914; 500 actors); *Susan B. Anthony* pageant (1915, 400 actors); in 1923 *Equal Rights Pageant*; Blair (1990: 39). Blair incorrectly attributes authorship of Elizabeth Robins, *Way Stations* to Edith Craig; Blair (1990: 34). Christopher St John's *Pageant of the Stage*, directed by Edith Craig on several occasions, developed her historical recovery of the female performer in *The First Actress* and adapted it to the pageant form; see Cockin 1998a: 90;92; 107; Cockin 2001: 86; and Hindson 2016:136.

29. In April 1912 *The Freewoman* held its discussion circle at the Eustace Miles Restaurant; Dicenzo (2016: 184).

30. For the introduction and implication of the Prisoner Temporary Discharge for Ill Health Act in April 1913, see Mayhall (2003: 104).

31. Florence Edgar Hobson American author of *Ideals True and False* (1912), a collection of poetry called *Verses Various* (1927) and short stories titled *Shifting Scenes* (1906). Her husband John Atkinson Hobson (1885–1940) was a renowned Liberal economist. Much of this material derives from Florence Edgar Hobson's *Ideals True and False* (1912).

32. Rebecca West was ideologically opposed to Hobson's attitude towards the poor and their education especially in the domestic sphere. This took up most of the review of the play and spilled over into the letters section of *The Freewoman* where West accused Hobson of perpetuating women's inferiority by endorsing housework as valued work; by contrast, West regarded this as the occupation of 'cow-like women' [*sic*]. One anonymous contributor to an earlier issue of *The Freewoman* had criticized London University's plans for a course on domestic work as appealing to the 'Womanly Woman' and distracting women from more useful courses.

# Chapter 5

1. *The First Actress*; reprinted in (Cockin, Norquay and Park 2007b). For analysis of the metatheatrical aspects of the play see Ferris (1995); and for its place alongside the other early plays of the Pioneer Players in relation to Edith Craig, see Dymkowski (1992). Alan Sinfield suggests that, for the Pioneer Players, 'Probably this militantly feminist work

translated, for some women into a sense that these theatres were lesbian space' (Sinfield 1999: 12).

2. The Stage Society was founded on 8 July 1899 and its managing committee, with no female members, at the outset comprised of Charles Charrington, Laurence Irving, William Sharp, James Welch, John H. Watts and Ernest E. S. Williams, and chaired by Frederick Whelen. When Craig and her friend Satty Fairchild had given feedback to Shaw on his play *You Never Can Tell*, this seems to have been informal rather than in any capacity on behalf of the Stage Society.

3. The Pioneer Players offered a favourably lower membership rate to actors but did not pay them for performances, although rehearsal expenses were introduced (Cockin 2001: 30).

4. Their financial terms, in the event of a production 'in the British Empire or the USA' within twelve months of the Pioneer Players' production, was 25 per cent of the royalties payable to the Pioneer Players until the costs of the production were refunded (EC-C67).

5. Terry's lecture to the membership was on 11 June 1911, a month after the society's inauguration and her extensive tour of United States the previous year.

6. See Hoare (1997); Medd (2012).

7. A detailed account of this final phase of the Pioneer Players' activities is explored in the context of wartime theatre; see Cockin (2015).

8. Ellen Young is a young performer with a drug addiction that enhances her performance. Billie Carleton's fatal drug overdose on 27 November 1918, the night of the Victory Ball at the Albert Hall, London, led to a sensational court case in which Reggie de Veulle who supplied the drugs was tried for manslaughter and resulted in the criminalization of cocaine use; see Kohn (1992: 96–101). Carleton's friend Malvina Longfellow, a Pioneer Players member, was a witness in court. The wife of the accused, Pauline de Veulle (née Gay), was a seamstress in Covent Garden and known to Craig (Cockin 2001: 161).

9. Meggie Albanesi seems to have died following complications after an abortion; Dean (1970: 218).

10. Ethel Levey was internationally associated with ragtime music and dance. Margaret Morris was trained by Raymond Duncan, brother of Isadora, and by this time had achieved some success and established her own theatre in London.

11. The commercial relationships involved in the production of plays are revealed by the purchase of advertising space including, for instance, the Indian musician Inayat Khan (1882–1927), the leader of Sufism in the West. His daughter, Noor Inayat Khan (1914–44), a special

operations agent during the Second World War, was executed in Dachau and the posthumous recipient of the George Cross.

12. The Pioneers was founded in 1905 by Herbert Swears. James Woodfield incorrectly states that the Pioneers was 'reorganised' as the Pioneer Players in 1911; Woodfield (1984: 69).

13. Seven letters from Edith Craig to George Bernard Shaw and five letters from George Bernard Shaw to Edith Craig between 21 February and 29 June 1912; and annotated cast list; THM 384/9/5, V&A.

14. See Cockin (2001, Ch. 5). These plays engaged with suffragists' campaigns about the abuse of women but one in particular namely H. M. Harwood's *Honour They Father* emphasized the agency of the prostitute and the consequence of inadequate education for girls.

15. A cartoon on the front page of *The Suffragette* (17 October 1913) depicts the dragon marked 'indecency' being led by 'The press' towards 'Purity', an armoured knight figure and captioned 'The forces of evil denouncing the bearers of light' (Bland 1995: 255).

16. These included H. M. Harwood's *Honour They Father* (15 December 1912, Little Theatre; reproduced in Cockin, Norquay and Park 2007b;), Antonia Williams, *The Street* (30 November 1913, Little Theatre) and an adaptation of Reginald Wright Kaufmann's novel *The Daughters of Ishmael* (1 March 1914, King's Hall).

17. Kauffman's novel *The House of Bondage* (1910) was compared with *Uncle Tom's Cabin* by some reviewers (Donovan 2005: 36). Chapter XXV of *The House of Bondage* is entitled 'The Daughters of Ishmael', the title of his 1911 novel, one of the books read by Olive Walton, an imprisoned suffrage activist at Aylesbury Prison in 1912 (Crawford 2003: 349) and even recommended by the *British Journal of Nursing* (6 July 1912, p. 15). For an appraisal of the political implications of the 'White Slave panic' and how it featured on the stage, see (Eltis 2013: 166–7).

18. Hansard; HC Deb, 6 August 1913, Vol. 56 (c. 1473–6).

19. The programme describes it as 'a dramatic at home in aid of the funds of the International Suffrage shop, feminist publishers & booksellers, 15 Adam Street, Strand'. Advertisements included the Pioneer Players and the Eustace Miles restaurant. The front cover of the programme bears two logos, ISS, and *Jus Suffragii* the title of the journal of the International Woman Suffrage Alliance, launched in 1906 and edited by Martina G. Kramers of Amsterdam.

20. Author's own collection.

21. The caption of the press cuttings emphasizes the context of censorship, politically positioning the play: 'the play advocates Socialistic doctrines, and for this reason was refused a license

[…] The censored play which was produced the other day "The Coronation" at the Savoy Theatre.' The play programme shows the redaction of the role and her name; production file; THM production file; V&A.

22. For analysis of changes in Edith Craig's headed notepaper during the period of the development of the Pioneer Players see Cockin 2001.

23. *How the Vote Was Won*, for which Edith Craig held the performance rights, was apparently a phenomenon on several continents according to the authors' preface of the 1913 edition published by Edith Craig: 'Since its production performances have been given not only in all parts of the United Kingdom, but in several European countries, in practically every State of the American Union, in the Dominion of Canada, and in numerous towns in South Africa. It has also been translated into German, Hungarian, Italian, Danish and Swedish' (reprinted in Cockin, Norquay and Park, Vol. 3, 2007b: 140).

24. Five postcards from George Bernard Shaw to Christopher St John and one letter from Christopher St John to George Bernard Shaw, 2 January 1917; THM 384/9/8; V&A.

25. Shaw may allude obliquely to Edith Craig and the Pioneer Players as the 'young adventurers' in 'The higher drama put out of action' in Preface to *Heartbreak House* (p. 41), dated June 1919, just before the British Drama League (BDL) Conference was held (see Chapter Six in this volume).

26. Huntley Carter published a survey on women's suffrage militancy with responses listed systematically for each respondent: 'The following pages contain the results of an inquiry recently undertaken to discover the opinions prevailing amongst a large number of distinguished public persons on the still vexed subject of women's suffrage. The questions were as follows:
   1. What, in your opinion, is the most powerful argument –
      a) For, or
      b) Against, women's suffrage?
   2. Is there any reasonable prospect of obtaining women's suffrage in the present Parliament, and this immediately?
   3. Have the militant methods, in your opinion, failed or succeeded?
   4. What alternative methods would you suggest? (p. 3)

   The responses included:
   Miss Florence Farr

   1. Fools, not women, should be voteless.
   2. No man can be expected to give the vote to anyone who visibly wants to keep him in order with it.

3. The vote will have to be taken by force, not given; that is what makes it worth having.

4. I should get rid of women's delusions about young girls and their education. The young could win the battle in a week if they would only try. (pp. 16–17).

27. Lucy Terry Lewis was a branch co-ordinator for the Women's National Anti-Suffrage League but lost her position after a conflict with Lord Cromer; Bush (2007: 179).

28. Gordon Craig responded in *The Mask* April 1912 to the furore concerning the regulation of costumes of female performers, arguing that commercial incentives informed the debates on the prosecution for obscenity of Adorée Villany for obscenity in Munich in November 1911 rather than art or morality.

29. Ellen Terry noted in a letter to Elizabeth Rumball that she, Edith Craig and Sarah Bernhardt were to visit Gordon Craig's exhibition in 1911; *CLET* 5: 1653. In October 1912 his sketches and models from the Moscow Art theatre were exhibited at the Leicester Galleries in London.

30. Edith Craig had known Calvert since his days with the Lyceum Theatre company and in 1899 she had acted in his production of *Othello*. It is not clear what Calvert's views were on women's suffrage politics.

31. In October 1913 Suzanne Després performed Hamlet to Lugné Poe's Polonius at the Théâtre Antoine in Paris, reported in the *Daily Chronicle* ('Hamlet in Paris: A Woman as the Prince of Denmark', 1 October 1913).

32. Edith Craig directed Jess Dorynne in Maeterlinck's *Sister Beatrice* at the Court Theatre (28 March 1909) and as an extra in Laurence Housman's *Pains and Penalties* for the Pioneer Players at the Savoy Theatre (26 November 1911).

33. Ailsa Grant Ferguson (2015) explores the operations of the Shakespeare Hut in entertaining troops from Australia and New Zealand. At the Shakespeare Hut on 20 April, Edith Craig directed her mother in *The Merchant of Venice* alongside Edith Evans, Acton Bond, Miss Potter, Miss Gabain, Fabia Drake and Audrey Cameron; ET-D517.

34. *The Merry Wives of Windsor* was arranged by Lady Tree; *Much Ado About Nothing* by Sir George Alexander, *As You Like It* by Dion Boucicault; *Romeo and Juliet* by Owen Nares and Fisher White.

35. The master of the pageant was Arthur Collins, and the music was arranged and conducted by Henry Geehl.

36. Percy McKaye (1875–1956) was an associate of Edward Gordon Craig and leader in the development of civic theatre in the United States. Rachel Crothers (1878–1958) had already written the plays for which she subsequently became renowned as one of the most

significant American female dramatists of her era: *Three of Us*
(1906), *He and She* (1911) and *Ourselves* (1913).

37. Clive Barker notes that in 1926 Clemence Dane initiated a 'female
version of the traditionally male form, Grand Guignol', with Sybil
Thorndike in the role of Judith (Barker 2000: 29).

38. The other plays were Constance Holme's *The Home of Vision*, Miles
Malleson's *The Artist* and Christopher St John's *Nell'Est*, a play
performed in Italian.

# Chapter 6

1. In *Heartbreak House*, Ellie Dunn in particular is exhilarated by the
prospect of aerial bombardment at the end of the play which both
dramatizes 'leisured cultured Europe before the war' and a disengaged
attitude towards wartime risks to life. I am grateful to J. Ellen Gainor
for pointing out this allusion.

2. 'Where are you going [Lord]?'

3. In the United States, the production of school nativity plays and the
installation of nativity scenes in public spaces contravene the secular
constitution which prohibits the promotion of any one religion. In
December 1997 a nativity scene on the lawn outside City Hall in
Jersey City, United States, was the subject of litigation (*American Civil
Liberties Union v. Schundler* 168 F.3d 92, 95; 3rd Cir. 1999), and
ordered to be removed by the US Court of Appeal.

4. In 2004 a Saatchi & Saatchi TV advertisement for Mr Kipling cakes,
depicting a woman in childbirth as part of a nativity play, was the
subject of complaints to the Advertising Standards Authority in United
Kingdom, and Ofcom judged that 'it breached the Code's rules on
offence'; ASA Annual Report 2004, p. 15; www.asa.org.uk, accessed 7
August 2016.

5. Fears provoked by the regulation of religious and seasonal festivities
have been satirized in the TV animation, *South Park*, where the
prohibition of the school nativity play leads to mayhem; 'Mr Hanky
The Christmas Poo' (Season 1, Episode 9; aired on 17 December 1997).

6. Other directors of nativity plays in this period include Rutland
Boughton whose *Bethlehem* was set to music and performed by the
Glastonbury Players; EC-D105.

7. Ernest Rhys popularized the plays in his Everyman's library series
in 1909, an edition that was so popular that it was reprinted eleven
times between 1909 and 1939. E. K. Chambers (1903) was the scholar
whose research and translations were used by Craig in most of her
productions.

8. Craig's archive holds a special illustrated supplement from the 1922 Oberammergau Passion Play from *The Sphere*, 13 May 1922, p. 175; EC-G1393.
9. The extent and precise details of Edith Craig's involvement are not yet clear. Christopher Innes refers to Craig assisting her brother (Innes 1998: 76) and the annotated promptbook for *Bethlehem* showing lighting instructions (Innes 1998: 75) has some entries that are similar to Edith Craig's handwriting.
10. Housman's single revisionary biographical portrait of Queen Caroline had been directed by Edith Craig for the Pioneer Players in 1911; Cockin (2012).
11. Edith Craig and Pamela Colman Smith were collaborating on another wartime creative project, making toys for sale and export; CLET 6: 174.
12. For a detailed account of wartime theatre, see Maunder 2015. St John sought spiritual advice from Dame Laurentia about what St John regarded as a problematic publication by Vita Sackville-West in *The Eagle and the Dove* (1943), her biography of St Theresa. Bernard Shaw consulted her on the advisability of the Shaw-Terry correspondence publication project, noting that theatrical people were always 'on the rocks' financially (Corrigan 1985: 98).
13. Hon. Evelina Haverfield was a member of the executive committee of the Pioneer Players from 1912 to 1915. See also Kisby (2014: 132).
14. Documents relating to the production include a poster, postcard handbill, press cuttings, a press release and letter from Margorie Gabain offering her services as a flautist. Vernor Grant provided the music.
15. I am grateful to the archivist at Westminster Cathedral Hall for this reference.
16. An annotated typescript of 'The Play of the Shepherds' (30 pp) stamped 'Old Vic Theatre'; (EC-H127) *The Spectator*, 22 December 1923, p. 9.
17. See Lis Whitelaw (1990). The public record office at Abbeville had no records of this production.
18. The topics listed were: The Ideals of the English Theatre and its Historical Character; Shakespeare in the Theatre; The Actors' Trade Union; The Repertory Movement; Selection and Stage Training; Reform in Production; The Art Theatre; The Little Theatre Movement; Plays and Playwrights; Endowment in the Theatre: National or Municipal; The 'Union Theatre'; Music in the Theatre; Dramatic Art in National Life and the Case for a British Drama League.
19. Norman MacDermott refers to having assisted Edith Craig in an exhibition for the Shakespeare Birthday celebration (MacDermott 1975: 9).

20. Drama and education (W. L. Courtney, seven members); professional acting (J. Fisher White, eight members); community theatre (Penelope Wheeler, eight members including Edith Craig); repertory theatre (John Drinkwater, six members); foreign drama (Edith Craig, seven members); workshop and bureaus (Norman Wilkinson; eight members including Edith Craig); plays and publications (Geoffrey Whitworth, eight members); finance (Robert Mond, five members).

21. For instance Richard Mulcaster, Headmaster of the London Merchant Taylors' School and Nicholas Udall, dramatist and head teacher of Eton. I am grateful to Dr Stewart Mottram for this information.

22. Lena Ashwell OBE was one of eight vice presidents of the BDL in 1919 whereas Edith Craig was one of the twenty-four members of the BDL Council.

23. For examination of the debates about Shakespeare's patriotic role in this period, see Holderness (2010).

24. *Enfield Gazette*, 9 January 1925, announced the York Mystery Plays to be presented in Enfield the following week by the York Everyman Theatre; EC-G1527.

25. Sybil Thorndike delivered the lines of the Prologue but the role is named 'Sibyl' in the programme.

26. Captain Geoffrey Bowes Lyon was first cousin of Elizabeth Bowes Lyon who married Prince Albert on 26 April 1923. On his accession to the throne as King George VI, she became known as Queen Elizabeth the Queen Mother after the birth of her daughter, Queen Elizabeth II.

27. The Children's Country Holidays Fund patron was Queen Alexandra; it was chaired by Dame May Whitty and Hon. Treasurer Lady Carson, both of whom had been involved in the Theatrical Ladies' Guild. Marcia Van Dresser was a renowned opera singer; see Warrender (1933: 249–51); Cline (1997: 288). Christopher Robin Milne (1920–96) was one of the child performers in this production at Daly's Theatre, London, 15 December 1925; EC-D205.

28. Craig and Colman Smith had collaborated on stage designs for W. B. Yeats and J. M. Synge for the Abbey Theatre in 1904 and during the productions of the Pioneer Players Colman Smith was on hand in the management committee.

29. Gertrude Stein wittily exposed the overlooked, undervalued and otherwise invisible genius of female artists in *The Autobiography of Alice B. Toklas* (1933).

30. Margaret Rogerson briefly notes Craig's York Guildhall production in 1925 (2009: 36).

31. Mary was played by Friede Rowntree Harris (1898–1951), daughter of Francis Henry Rowntree (1868–1918), a director of Rowntree

& Co. Ltd. The First King was played by Rev. H. T. S. Gedge, who was a former rugby player for Scotland. Friede had recently married George Harris, the highly successful marketing director and later the chairman of Rowntrees responsible for launching new brands such as Kit Kat and Aero. The Quaker family founded the chocolate manufacturers in 1862, one of the most successful in the city; http://www.rowntreesociety.org.uk/rowntree-family-biographies/, accessed 9 October 2016.

32. The event was organized by the Duchess of Norfolk; see EC-P73; SC20-M10.

33. An extant programme for a 1936 production of the St Hubert Mass in Aigen park, Salzburg, and a number of professional photographs of performers in costume suggests that someone in Craig's household, probably Christopher St John, attended the festival that year; EC-D34.

34. A railway workers' industrial dispute took place on 21 January 1924. Christopher St John reviewed Craig's production in *Time & Tide* under the heading 'Well done Leeds!' (1 February 1924, pp. 106–7; EC-G1415).

35. A photograph of performers in costume inside the church was published in the *Yorkshire Weekly Post*, 1 December 1934 (EC-G1409); *News Chronicle Manchester*, 3 December 1934; *Yorkshire Evening Post*, 3 December 1934 (EC-G1413).

36. John R. Elliot Jr briefly notes Craig's production in the Guildhall York in 1925; (1989: 63).

37. Both Monck and Poel were associated with Shakespearean productions and an interest in the Elizabethan stage. Monck was founder of the Norwich Players in 1911 and of the Maddermarket Theatre, Norwich in 1921 in a converted Catholic chapel. Poel founded the Elizabethan Stage Society (1895) and specialized in productions with little or no scenery and full text, notably Hamlet (1881) at St George's Hall, London.

38. It is likely that Henzie Browne would have been aware of Craig's production of the nativity play at Everyman Theatre, Hampstead in 1920 but she would have taken way experience of an Edith Craig production which informed her later work with E. Martin Browne.

39. Edith Craig seems to have attended the first London production of T. S. Eliot's *Murder in the Cathedral* at the Mercury Theatre, Ladbroke Road; EC-P3; EC-P28. According to Peter Ackroyd, T. S. Eliot 'went to the theatre often and regularly attended, for example, the Restoration and Jacobean revivals of the Phoenix Society' (1984: 105). It is likely that Eliot was aware of Craig's productions for the Phoenix Society of John Dryden's *All for Love* on 19–20 March 1922 and John Fletcher's *The Faithful Shepherdess* on 24–25 June 1923 both at the Shaftesbury

Theatre, London and for the Renaissance Theatre Society of John Webster's *The White Devil* in October 1925 at the Scala Theatre, London. However, her productions of the plays by Fletcher and Webster coincided with periods when Vivian Eliot and he were unwell.

40. Margaret Rogerson provides a history of the productions of the York mystery plays 1951–2006, briefly mentioning Craig's 1925 production, and reference to the nativity play in Evelyn Waugh's *Love Among the Ruins* (1953) (2009: 36–8).

41. Muriel Spark's poem 'Nativity' was published in *Poetry Quarterly* (1951–2).

# Chapter 7

1. Albert Rutherston was born Rothenstein, brother of the artist Sir William Rothenstein. Albert anglicized his name during the First World War. His brother William was in correspondence with Edith Craig and involved in the support of the arts in Leeds. Norman Wilkinson (1878–1971) was an artist and illustrator whose expertise was applied to dazzle painting of ships during the First World War. Claud Lovat Fraser (1890–1921) was an artist and designer, renowned for his work on Nigel Playfair's 1919 production of *As You Like It*.

2. MacDermott (1975: 25). In December 1920 she produced Israel Zangwill's *The Melting Pot*, praised by John Francis Hope as 'not only the best they have done, but is a really good show'; 23 December 1920, *The New Age*, Vol. 28, No. 8, pp. 93–4.

3. Montague Summers later published editions of Wycherley, Otway, Shadwell and Dryden as well as *The History of Witchcraft and Demonology* (1926), translated Kramer and Sprenger's notorious book on witch identification entitled *Malleus Maleficorum* (1928), several other books on vampires and witchcraft and a two-volume history of the gothic novel (1938, 1940). How Craig became acquainted with Summers is not yet known. She may have been introduced by Laurence Housman who was, like Summers, a member of the Society for the Study of Sex Psychology for which Summers had recently published *Marquis de Sade: A Study in Algolagnia* (1920).

4. Edward Godwin provided designs for John Fletcher's *The Faithful Shepherdess* in 1885 for the Pastoral Players.

5. The National Trust's Edith Craig archive holds numerous programmes of Film Society screenings from 1925 to 1936. See www.ellenterryarchive.hull.ac.uk

6. Over a decade later Tom Terriss exploited the experience by appearing in a radio broadcast on 'The Fleischmann's Yeast Hour' programme in 'Tom Terris: The Mysterious Mummy Case' on 7 February 1935.

7. Sadler proposed to put Edith Craig in touch with the Leeds University Dramatic Society; 8 November 1922, EC-B100. A. E. Randall writing as 'John Francis Hope' in *The New Age* had reviewed several of the Pioneer Players' productions and, in reporting on the BDL in 1919, included Edith Craig and the Pioneer Players in a reference to the select audiences of the 'coterie drama' (11 September 1919, p. 327). This situated the Pioneer Players with the 'highbrow'. Hope's criticism of Craig's Pioneer Players' production of *The Good Hope* revealed a casual sexism in his emphasis on the 'wailing' female performers and in his generalization that 'everyone knows that, in the main, women care for nothing but their own security, and find that in the person of a man' (21 November 1912, p. 66).

8. Edith Craig sat for a portrait by Jacob Kramer. I am grateful to the late Sir Donald Sinden for this information. Craig does not feature in Kramer's biography (Manson 2006).

9. Ezra Pound gave three lectures on medieval poetry in 1912 and was referred to as 'the Modern Troubadour'; Rainey (1998: 15).

10. Apparently written while Ethel Smyth was resting in Egypt and in intense correspondence with Emmeline Pankhurst, *The Boatswain's Mate* (1913–14; produced 1916) allowed Smyth to return to a tale of seafarers and gleefully to challenge conventional ideas about gender and marriage.

11. It was probably a coincidence that at the time when Smyth was writing *The Boatswain's Mate*, Ellen Terry was arranging for James Carew to make a gun available to her at The Farm, presumably as a means of defence during the war (22 September [1915]; *CLET* 6: 1800).

12. As Lesley Ferris notes, Goethe was influenced by seeing an all-male production to write about the undesirability of female performers on stage; Ferris (1990: 58). Craig repeated these two plays for the LAT Skipton Season on 16 February 1925; EC-D201; and at the Everyman Theatre Hampstead on 17 August 1925; EC-D213.

13. Blackwood's novel *A Prisoner in Fairyland* was dramatized by Violet Pearn as *Starlight Express* (1915), a Christmas play directed by Lena Ashwell at the Kingsway Theatre. Blackwood's intriguing title, but not the play, influenced the popular London West End musical *Starlight Express* (1987–).

14. Beatrice Ensor (1885–1974), theosophist and educationalist, was the leading force at the school headed by Isobel King. She had done humanitarian work for children in Hungary in 1922 and her international work on progressive education led her to meet Carl Jung. Both Ensor and King left St Christopher's in 1925 and became involved in the founding of Frensham Heights School, Surrey.

15. Cadbury Research Library, University of Birmingham, Special Collection, XMS38 Theatre Collection, MS38/1950 S. Ansky, *The Dybbuk* collection of reviews.

16. Her involvement was unambiguous and made explicit in the publicity for the production. The programme promoted Edith Craig as director, with a glamorous photograph on its cover; EC-D12.

17. A production of Oscar Wilde's *Salome*, with eighteen-year old Sheila Tomey in the role, attracted press attention. In March 1935 the club was closed as a result of hosting illegal gambling; Steele (1990: 252).

18. Sir Charles Philip Trevelyan (1870–1958) married Mary Bell, half sister of Florence Bell who had enlisted Edith Craig to direct the pageant at Mount Grace. He was President of the Board of Education in the first Labour government led by Ramsay Macdonald in 1924 and Lord Lieutenant of Northumberland (1930–49). 'The Redress of the Past: Historical Pageants in Britain' (1905–2016), briefly features the Pageant of Mount Grace Priory (1927). See www. historicalpageants.ac.uk, accessed 7 August 2016.

19. Lionel Britton's play *Spacetime Inn* (1932) is a futuristic version of the fantasy dinner party theme, bringing Eve, Queen of Sheba, Queen Victoria, Karl Marx and George Bernard Shaw together in a pub. Britton's other play was *Animal Ideas* (1935) and a novel *Hunger and Love* (1931) with an introduction by Bertrand Russell. See interview with Tony Shaw by Gerald Isaaman in 'On the Trail of a Lost Genius', *Camden New Journal*, 23 January 2003; Tony Shaw, 'The Work of Lionel Britton', PhD thesis, The Open University 2007.

20. Edith Craig's involvement in the promotion of Russian drama in London from 1915 was widely known and would have added to her credentials for the production with the MSFG. The programme refers incorrectly to 'the International Workers of the World'. The IWW was founded in 1905 and is still active.

21. Edward Gordon Craig reported in a letter to Count Harry Kessler in 6 April 1931 that he had been invited to give five Shute lectures on the Art of the Theatre at the University of Liverpool in late January or early February 1932, but he apparently withdrew after they had been advertised; Newman (1995: 320).

22. Ivor Brown became the leading drama critic at the *Observer*, and during the 1940s its editor and a renowned Shakespeare critic.

23. I am grateful to Catherine Chorley, Special Collections and Archives, the University of Liverpool for this information.

24. Glen Byam Shaw as Horatio; Andrew Cruickshank as Rosencrantz; Marius Goring as Osric, and Laura Cowie (who had appeared for Edith Craig in *The White Devil* and the nativity play) as Gertrude. Bell's play *The Fog on the Moor* was directed by Craig at both the LAT and St Christopher's Theatre.

25. Such as the Rt Hon. C. P. Hon Trevelyan MP who appeared as Richard II and Lady Richmond as Lady Beauchamp.
26. See Cockin (2011).
27. Film no 5155, Yorkshire Film Archive; http://www.yorkshirefilmarchive. com/film/pageant-mount-grace, accessed 9 October 2016.
28. A keep is a fortification.

# Chapter 8

1. Benjamin's Arcades Project (1927–40). Craig's notes are likely to have been used when she gave talks (EC-M134).
2. The Ballets Russes had used costume designs by Picasso for three productions: *Parade* (1917), *The Tricorne Hat* (1919), *Pulcinella* (1920) and *Cuadro Flemenco* (1921).
3. 'The Higher Court', 17 April 1920, *New Statesman*, pp. 207–10. The play was directed by Edith Craig for the thirty-fifth subscription performance for the Pioneer Players at the Strand Theatre on 11 April 1920 at 8 pm. See Cockin (2001: 125–6, 181–2).
4. These included Robert Donat, Laurence Olivier, John Gielgud, Edith Evans and Sybil Thorndike.
5. For the St George's Day (1945) celebration at the White Rock Pavilion, Hastings, a number of songs and short scenes from plays including *The Merry Wives of Windsor* were performed and in the second half of the programme 'A Parade of Shakespearean Dresses Worn by Dame Ellen Terry' was 'introduced by her daughter Edith Craig'; EC-D164.
6. The Abbey Theatre Dublin by D. R. Hardman, The Old Vic and Sadler's Wells by Clive Carey, Survey of the London Theatre by Ivor Brown, Repertory Theatre by William Armstrong, Experiments in the Art of the Theatre by Norman Marshall, the British Drama League and the National Theatre by Geoffrey Whitworth, Drama in Schools by Laurence Housman, and Spoken English on the Stage by F. G. Blandford (THM 384/14/5).
7. The financial situation at Priest's House was unstable, following the significant loss of income in 1930 for Christopher St John when she lost her regular writing jobs at *Time & Tide* and *The Lady*.
8. Leonard Woolf was trying to secure a production of his own play, 'The Hotel' (Putzel 2012: 65).
9. As women's suffrage veterans, Craig and her partners may have influenced Woolf's 'The Burning of the Vote', a play fragment apparently written in autumn 1935. Putzel overlooks St John's affair with Sackville-West in 1932 and Woolf's reference to it as a continued 'complication' as late as March 1935 (Cockin 1998: 180).

In February 1937 Edith Craig had nearly died of pneumonia.
In September 1938 Vita Sackville-West, Radclyffe Hall and Una
Troubridge attended the garden party at Smallhythe organized by
Craig for the Kent Branch of the English Speaking Union (Cockin
1998: 173). It is not clear whether Craig had invited Virginia Woolf
to the garden party or whether Woolf formally applied to join the
Barn Theatre. Sackville-West suggested that she and Woolf visit
Smallhythe Place; this was only two weeks before Woolf's suicide
(Cockin 1998: 180). An extant photograph shows Woolf in a group
at Smallhythe Place; THM
384/23/11.

10. Florence Locke was a performer who became associated closely
with Shakespeare and as a solo performer of recitals of the poetry
of Amy Lowell as well as Ellen Terry's Shakespeare lectures. She and
her partner, Eleanor Adlard of Postlip House, Winchcombe (Cockin
1998: 186) spent much of 1935 in California and travelling in the
United States. They were honoured with an invitation from Eleanor
Roosevelt to a White House luncheon party at which Locke recited
'Hedge Island' by Amy Lowell. See *Gloucestershire Echo*, 20 March
1935; Florence Locke papers, Folger Library, Washington DC, United
States.

# BIBLIOGRAPHY

## Archival sources

Ellen Terry and Edith Craig Archive, The National Trust (on loan to the British Library, London with some material at Smallhythe Place, Tenterden, Kent; see online guide to the archive for details: AHRC Ellen Terry and Edith Craig Database at <http://www.ellenterryarchive.hull.ac.uk>, accessed 9 October 2016.
Ellen Terry Collection, THM 384, Theatre Collection Victoria & Albert Museum, London.
Folger Library, Washington DC, United States.
John Johnson Collection, Bodleian Library, Oxford.
Katharine Cockin, private collection.
Papers of Vera Holme, 7VJH, The Women's Library, LSE, London.
Scrapbook E.V.6.4 5/5, Ellen Terry's Library, Smallhythe Place, Tenterden, Kent.
Theatre Collection, XMS38/1950, Cadbury Research Library, University of Birmingham.
Yorkshire Film Archive, York St John University, York.

## Primary sources

Adlard, Eleanor (ed.) (1949). *Edy: Recollections of Edith Craig*, London: Frederick Muller.
Craig, Edith (1907). 'Producing a Play', *Munsey's Magazine*, 36, 311–14.
Craig, Edith and St John, Christopher (eds) 1932 (1933). *Ellen Terry's Memoirs*, London: Victor Gollancz.
Craig, Edward Gordon (1931). *Ellen Terry and Her Secret Self*, London: Sampson Low, Marston & Co.
Craig, Edward Gordon (1957). *Index to the Story of My Days Some Memoirs of Edward Gordon Craig 1872–1907*, London: Hulton Press.
Rachlin, Ann (2011). *Edy Was a Lady*, London: Matador.
St John, Christopher (1907). *Ellen Terry*, London: J. Lane.

St John, Christopher (ed.) (1931). *Ellen Terry & Bernard Shaw: A Correspondence*, London: Constable.

St John, Christopher (1932). *Four Lectures on Shakespeare*, London: Martin Hopkinson.

Terry, Ellen (1908). *The Story of My Life*, London: Hutchinson.

Terry, Ellen (1913). *The Russian Ballet*, London: Sidgwick & Jackson.

## Secondary sources

Ackroyd, Peter (1984). *T. S. Eliot*, London: Hamish Hamilton.

Adam, Eve (ed.) (1926). *Mrs J. Comyns Carr's Reminiscences*, London: Hutchinson.

Adlard, Eleanor (1933). 'Remembering Ellen Terry', *Everyman*, 8 August, 173.

Adlard, Eleanor (ed.) (1949). *Edy: Recollections of Edith Craig*, London: Frederick Muller.

Aldington, Richard (1924). *The Mystery of the Nativity*, London: The Medici Society.

An Actress [Jess Dorynne] (1913). *The True Ophelia: And Other Studies of Shakespeare's Women*, London: Sidgwick & Jackson.

Anon. (1921). *The Teaching of English in England*, London: His Majesty's Stationery Office.

Anon. (1944). *Twenty Five Years of the BDL*, Oxford: Alden Press.

Applegate, Debby (2006). *The Most Famous Man in America: Henry Ward Beecher*, New York: Doubleday.

Ardis, Ann (2002). *Modernism and Cultural Conflict 1880–1922*, Cambridge: Cambridge University Press.

Ashley, Mike (2001). *The Starlight Man: Algernon Blackwood*, London: Constable.

Ashwell, Lena (1922). *Modern Troubadours: A Record of the Concerts at the Front*, London: Gyldenhaal.

Asquith, Lady Cynthia (1987).*The Diaries of Lady Cynthia Asquith 1915–18*, London: Century Hutchinson.

Atkinson, Diane (1992). *Mrs Broom's Suffragette Photographs*, London: Nishen.

Atwood, Clare (1949). 'Edy's Ways', in *Edy: Recollections of Edith Craig*, ed. Eleanor Adlard, London: Frederick Muller, 133–43.

Auerbach, Nina (1987). *Ellen Terry: Player in Her Time*, New York: W. W. Norton.

Baker, Michael (1985). *Our Three Selves: A Life of Radclyffe Hall*, London: Hamish Hamilton.

Baldick, Chris (1983). *The Social Mission of English Criticism 1848–1932*, Oxford: Blackwell.

Barker, Clive (2000). 'Theatre and Society: The Edwardian Legacy, the First World War and Inter-war Years', in *British Theatre between the Wars 1918–1939*, ed. Clive Barker and Maggie B. Gale, Cambridge: Cambridge University Press, 4–37.

Barker, Clive and Gale, Maggie (eds) (2000). *British Theatre between the Wars 1918–1939*, Cambridge: Cambridge University Press.

Barranger, Milly S. (2004). *Margaret Webster: A Life in the Theater*, Ann Arbor: University of Michigan Press.

Barthes, Roland (1977) [1968]. 'The Death of the Author' in *Image Music Text*, translated by Stephen Heath, London: Fontana.

Bax, Clifford (ed.) (1941). *Florence Farr, Bernard Shaw, W. B. Yeats*, London: Home & Van Thal.

Beacham, Richard C. (1994). *Adolphe Appia: Artist and Visionary of the Modern Theatre*, London: Routledge.

Beard, Mary (2000). *The Invention of Jane Harrison*, Cambridge: Harvard University Press.

Beasley, Rebecca and Bullock, Philip (eds) (2013). *Russia in Britain 1880–1940: From Melodrama to Modernism*, Oxford: Oxford University Press.

Bentley, Toni (2002). *Sisters of Salome*, New Haven: Yale University Press.

Ben-Zvi, Linda (1992). '"Murder, She Wrote": The Genesis of Susan Glaspell's Trifles', *Theatre Journal*, 44, 2, 141–62.

Blair, Karen J. (1990). 'Pageantry for Women's Rights: The Career of Hazel Mackaye 1913–1923, *Theatre Survey*, 31, 1, 23–46.

Blair, Kirstie (2004). 'Gypsies and Lesbian Desire: Vita Sackville West, Violet Trefusis and Virginia Woolf', *Twentieth Century Literature*, 50, 2, 141–66.

Bland, Lucy (2002 [1995]). *Banishing the Beast: English Feminism and Sexual Morality 1885–1914*, 2nd edition, Harmondsworth: Penguin.

Booth, Michael R. (1986). 'Pictorial Acting and Ellen Terry', in *Shakespeare and the Victorian Stage*, ed. Richard Foulkes, Cambridge: Cambridge University Press, 78–86.

Bowker, Gordon (2011). *James Joyce: A Biography*, London: Weidenfeld & Nicholson.

Brittain, Vera (1968). *Radclyffe Hall: A Case of Obscenity?* London: Femina Books.

Brooker, Peter and Thacker, Andrew (eds) (2005). *Geographies of Modernism: Literature, Cultures, Spaces*, New York: Routledge.

Brown, Ivor (1928). *Parties of the Play*, London: Benn.

Browne, E. Martin (1932). *The Production of Religious Plays*, London: Philip Allan & Co.

Browne, E. Martin (1979). *Fifty Years of Religious Drama: A Lecture Given at Vaughan College, Leicester on 10 November 1978*, ed. Richard Foulkes, Leicester: University of Leicester with RADIUS.

Browne, E. Martin and Browne, Henzie (1981). *Two in One*, Cambridge: Cambridge University Press.

Browne, Henzie (1945). *Pilgrim Story: The Pilgrim Players, 1939–1943*, London: Frederick Muller.

Bush, Julia (2007). *Women against the Vote: Female Anti-suffragism in Britain*, Oxford: Oxford University Press.

Calvert, Louis (1912). *An Actor's Hamlet*, London: Mills and Boon.

Carlson, Susan (2000). 'Comic Militancy: The Politics of Women's Suffrage Drama', in *Women, Theatre and Performance: New Histories, New Historiographies*, ed. Maggie Gale and Viv Gardner, Manchester: Manchester University Press, 198–215.

Carpenter, Humphrey (1985). *OUDS: A Centenary History of the Oxford University Dramatic Society 1885–1985*, Oxford: Oxford University Press.

Carter, Howard and Mace, A. C. [1923] (2014). *The Tomb of Tutankhamun: Volume 1: Search, Discovery and Clearance of the Antechamber*, London: Bloomsbury.

Carter, Huntly (1912). *Women's Suffrage & Militancy*, London: Frank Palmer.

Case, Sue-Ellen (1988). *Feminism and Theatre*, Basingstoke: Macmillan.

Chambers, E. K. (1903). *The Medieval Stage, Volumes I & II*, Oxford: Oxford University Press.

`Chansky, Dorothy (2004). *Composing Ourselves: The Little Theatre Movement and the American Audience*, Carbondale: Southern Illinois University Press.

Chapman, Wayne K. (1989). 'Yeats's "Theatre of Beauty" and the Masque Tradition', *Yeats: An Annual of Critical and Textual Studies*, 7, 42–56.

Chiba, Yoko (1996). 'Kori Torahiko and Edith Craig: A Japanese Playwright in London and Toronto', *Comparative Drama*, 30, 4 (Winter), 431–51.

Chotia, Jean (2008). ' "Henry and 250 Supers": Irving, Robespierre and the Staging of the Revolutionary Crowd', in *Henry Irving: A Re-Evaluation of the Pre-Eminent Victorian Actor-Manager*, ed. Richard Foulkes, Aldershot: Ashgate, 117–34.

Clarsen, Georgine (2011). *Eat My Dust: Early Women Motorists*, Baltimore: Johns Hopkins University Press.

Clay, Catherine (2006). *British Women Writers 1914–1945: Professional Work and Friendship*, London: Routledge.

Clayton, Susan (2010). 'Britomart Quest Anew, Victorians Revive the Elizabethan *Faerie Queene* as Campaigns for Women's Suffrage Intensify', *Cahiers Victoriens et Édouardiens*, 71, 323–38.

Cline, Sally (1997). *Radclyffe Hall: A Woman Called John*, London: John Murray.

Cockin, Katharine (1990). 'Addendum to "British Literary Magazines: The Victorian and Edwardian Age 1837–1913"', *Victorian Periodicals Review*, 23, 2 (Summer), 68.

Cockin, Katharine (1991). 'New Light on Edith Craig', *Theatre Notebook*, 45, 3, 132–43.

Cockin, Katharine (1994). 'The Pioneer Players: Plays of/with Identity', in *Difference in View: Women in Modernism*, ed. Gabriele Griffin, London: Taylor & Francis, 142–54.

Cockin, Katharine (1998a). *Edith Craig (1869–1947): Dramatic Lives*, London: Cassell.

Cockin, Katharine (1998b). 'Women's Suffrage Drama', in *The Women's Suffrage Movement: New Feminist Essays*, ed. Maroula Joannou and June Purvis, Manchester: Manchester University Press, 127–39.

Cockin, Katharine (2000). 'Charlotte Perkins Gilman's "Three Women": Work, Marriage and the Old(er) Woman', in *Charlotte Perkins Gilman: Optimist Reformer*, ed. Gill Rudd and Val Gough, Iowa: University of Iowa Press, 74–92.

Cockin, Katharine (2001). *Women and Theatre in the Age of Suffrage: The Pioneer Players*, Basingstoke: Palgrave.

Cockin, Katharine (2002). 'Ellen Terry, the Ghostwriter and the Laughing Statue: The Victorian Actress, Letters and Life-writing', *Journal of European Studies*, 32, 151–63.

Cockin, Katharine (2004). '"Slinging the Ink About": Ellen Terry and Women's Suffrage Agitation', in *Gender and Politics in the Age of Letter-Writing 1750–2000*, ed. Caroline Bland and Maire Cross, London: Ashgate, 201–12.

Cockin, Katharine (2005). 'Cicely Hamilton's Warriors: Dramatic Reinventions of Militancy in the British Women's Suffrage Movement', *Women's History Review*, 14, 3 527–42.

Cockin, Katharine (2008). 'Ellen Terry and Henry Irving: A Working Relationship', in *Henry Irving: A Re-evaluation of the Pre-eminent Victorian Actor-Manager*, ed. Richard Foulkes, London: Ashgate, 37–48.

Cockin, Katharine (ed.) (2010–15). *Ellen Terry: The Collected Letters Volume 1–6*, London: Pickering & Chatto.

Cockin, Katharine (ed.) (2011). *Ellen Terry, Spheres of Influence*, London: Pickering & Chatto.

Cockin, Katharine (2012). 'Queen Caroline's Pains and Penalties: Silence and Speech in the Dramatic Art of British Women's Suffrage', *Law and Literature*, 24, 1, 40–58.

Cockin, Katharine (2015). 'Edith Craig and the Pioneer Players: London's International Art Theatre in a "Khaki-clad and Khaki-minded World"', in *British Theatre and the Great War 1914–1919: New Perspectives*, ed. A. Maunder, Basingstoke: Palgrave, 121–39.

Cockin, Katharine (2016). 'Bram Stoker, Ellen Terry, Pamela
Colman Smith and the Art of Devilry', in *Bram Stoker and the
Gothic: Formations and Transformations*, ed. Catherine Wynne,
Basingstoke: Palgrave, 159–71.

Cockin, Katharine, Norquay, Glenda and Park, Sowon (eds) (2007a).
*Women's Suffrage Drama: Volume Two, Women's Suffrage Literature*,
London: Routledge.

Cockin, Katharine, Norquay, Glenda and Park, Sowon (eds) (2007b).
*Suffragette Sally and Selected Short Stories: Volume Three, Women's
Suffrage Literature*, London: Routledge.

Coldwell, Joan (1977). 'Pamela Colman Smith and the Yeats Family',
*Canadian Journal of Irish Studies*, 3, 2, 32.

Colmore, Gertrude (1912a). 'The Nun', *Vote*, 26 June, p. 175; reprinted in
Cockin, Norquay and Park, 2, 2007a, 353.

Colmore, Gertrude (1912b). 'The Introduction', *The Suffragette*, 22
November, p. 88; reprinted in Cockin, Norquay and Park, 2, 2007a, 357.

Colmore, Gertrude (1913a). 'George Lloyd', *Votes for Women*, 16 May,
p. 589; reprinted in Cockin, Norquay and Park, 2, 2007a, 365.

Colmore, Gertrude (1913b). 'Oh Richard!', *Votes for Women*, 4 July,
p. 226; reprinted in Cockin, Norquay and Park, 2, 2007a, 367–8.

Comyns Carr, Joseph (1907). *Some Eminent Victorians: Personal
Recollections in the World of Art and Letters*, London: Duckworth.

Cooper Willis, Irene (1928). *England's Holy War: A Study of English
Liberalism During the Great War*, New York: Knopf.

Cooper Willis, Irene (1949). 'The Squares', in *Edy: Recollections of Edith
Craig*, London: Frederick Muller, 107–11.

Corrigan, D. Felicitas (1985). *The Nun, The Infidel and the Superman:
The Remarkable Friendships of Dame Laurentia McLachlan with
Sydney Cockerell, Bernard Shaw, and Others*, Chicago: The University
of Chicago Press.

Craig, Edward (1968). *Gordon Craig: The Story of His Life*, London:
Victor Gollancz.

Craig, Edward Gordon (1911). *On the Art of the Theatre*, London:
William Heinemann.

Crawford, Elizabeth (2003). *The Women's Suffrage Movement
A Reference Guide 1866–1928*, London: Taylor & Francis.

Crawford, Elizabeth (2013). *Campaigning for the Vote: Kate Parry Frye's
Suffrage Diary*, London: Francis Boule.

Croall, Jonathan (2002). *John Gielgud: A Theatrical Life*,
London: Methuen.

Croall, Jonathan (2008). *Sybil Thorndike*, London: Haus Books.

Croft, Susan (2009). *Votes For Women and Other Suffrage Plays*, London:
Aurora Metro.

Cullingford, Elizabeth Butler (1997). 'At the Feet of the Goddess: Yeats's Love Poetry and the Feminist Occult', in *Yeats and Women*, ed. Deirdre Toomey, Basingstoke: Macmillan, 41–72.

Cuthbert, Father (1919). *The Shepherds*, London: Burns & Oates.

Dean, Basil (1970). *Seven Ages: An Autobiography 1888–1927*, London: Hutchinson.

De Bouhélier, Saint-Georges (1949). 'Edith Craig', in *Edy: Recollections of Edith Craig*, ed. Eleanor Adlard, London: Frederick Muller, 59–66.

DeLap, Lucy (2007). *The Feminist Avant-garde: Transatlantic Encounters of the Early Twentieth Century*, Cambridge: Cambridge University Press.

DeLong, Kenneth (2008). 'Arthur Sullivan's Incidental Music to Henry Irving's Production of Macbeth', in *Henry Irving: A Re-Evaluation of the Pre-Eminent Victorian Actor-Manager*, ed. Richard Foulkes, Aldershot: Ashgate 149–84.

De Selincourt, Ernest (1915). *English Poets and the National Ideal: Four Lectures*, London: Oxford University Press.

Dicenzo, Maria (2008). 'Feminism, Theatre Criticism, and the Modern Drama', *South Central Review*, 25, 1 (Spring) 36–55.

Dicenzo, Maria (2011). *Feminist Media History: Suffrage, Periodicals and the Public Sphere*, Basingstoke: Palgrave Macmillan.

D'Monte, Rebecca (2015). *British Theatre and Performance 1900–1950*, London: Bloomsbury.

Doan, Laura (2013). *Disturbing Practices: History Sexuality and Women's Experiences*, Chicago: University of Chicago Press.

Doan, Laura and Bland, Lucy (eds) (1998). *Sexology Uncensored: The Documents of Social Science*, Chicago: University of Chicago Press.

Dobson, Michael (2011). *Shakespeare and Amateur Performance: A Cultural History*, Cambridge: Cambridge University Press.

Dolgin, Ellen Ecker (2015). *Shaw and the Actresses' Franchise League*, New York: Garland.

Donoghue, Emma (1998). *We Are Michael Field*, Bath: Absolute Press.

Donovan, Brian (2005).*White Slave Crusades: Race, Gender and Anti-vice Activism 1887–1917*, Chicago: University of Illinois Press.

Dorney, Kate (2014). 'Excavating Enthoven: Investigating a Life of Stuff', *Studies in Theatre and Performance*, 34, 2, 115–25.

Doyle, Brian (1989). *English and Englishness*, London: Routledge.

Dymkowski, Christine (1992).'Edy Craig and the Pioneer Players', in *The New Woman and Her Sisters*, ed. Viv Gardner and Rutherford, Hemel Hempstead: Harvester Wheatsheaf, 221–33.

Elliott Jr, John R. (1989). *Playing God: Medieval Mysteries on the Modern Stage*, Toronto: University of Toronto Press.

Eltis, Sos (2013). *Acts of Desire: Women and Sex on Stage 1800–1930*, Oxford: Oxford University Press.

Eynat-Confino, Irene (1987). *Beyond the Mask: Gordon Craig, Movement, and the Actor*, Carbondale and Illinoisville: Southern Illinois University Press.

Farfan, Penny (2004). *Women, Modernism and Performance*, Cambridge: Cambridge University Press.

Farr, Florence (1905). *The Mystery of Time: A Masque*, London: The Theosophical Publishing Society.

Farr, Florence (1910). *Modern Woman: Her Intentions*, London: Frank Palmer.

Farr, Florence (n.d.). *The Music of Speech*, London: Elkin Mathews, Vigo Street.

Fernihough, Anne (2013). *Freewomen & Supermen: Edwardian Radicals & Literary Modernism*, Oxford: Oxford University Press.

Ferris, Lesley (1990). *Acting Women: Images of Women in Theatre*, Basingstoke: Macmillan.

Ferris, Lesley (1995). 'The Female Self and Performance: The Case of the First Actress', in *Theatre and Feminist Aesthetic*, ed. Karen Laughlin and Catherine Schuler, Cranbury, New Jersey: Associated University Preses, 242–57.

Finneran, Richard J., Harper, George Mills and Murphy, William M. (eds) (1977). *Letters to W. B. Yeats*, New York: Columbia University Press.

Forbes Robertson, Johnston (1925). *A Player Under Three Reigns*, London: T. Fisher Unwin.

Foster, Roy (1997). *W. B. Yeats: A Life, I: The Apprentice Mage*, Oxford: Oxford University Press.

Franklin, Colin, ed. (1982). *Gordon Craig's Paris Diary 1932–33*, North Hills: Bird & Bull Press.

Gale, Maggie (2000). 'Errant Nymphs: Women and the Inter-war Theatre', *British Theatre between the Wars 1918–1939*, ed. Clive Barker and Maggie B. Gale, Cambridge: Cambridge University Press, 113–34.

Gandolfi. Roberta (2011). 'Edith Craig as Director: Staging Claudel in the War Years', in *Ellen Terry, Spheres of Influence*, ed. Katharine Cockin, London: Pickering & Chatto, 107–18.

Gardner, Viv (1985). *Sketches From the Actresses' Franchise League*, Nottingham: Nottingham Drama Texts.

Glasgow, Joanne (1990). 'What's a Nice Lesbian Like you Doing in the Church of Torquemada', in *Lesbian Texts and Contexts: Radical Revisions*, ed. Karla Jay and Joanne Glasgow, London: Onlywomen Press, 244–54.

Glendinning, Victoria (1984). *Vita: The Life of Vita Sackville-West*, Harmondsworth: Penguin.

Goddard, Leslie (2002). '"Women Know Her to Be a Real Woman": Femininity, Nationalism, and the Suffrage Activism of Lillian Russell', *Theatre History Studies*, 22, 137–54.

Godfrey, Emelyne (2012). *Femininity, Crime and Self-Defence in Victorian Literature*, Basingstoke: Palgrave.

Goebel, Stefan (2006). *The Great War and Medieval Memory: War, Remembrance and Medievalism in Britain and Germany 1914–40*, Cambridge: Cambridge University Press.

Graham, Philip (2013). 'Bernard Shaw's Neglected Role in English Feminism 1880–1914', *Journal of Gender Studies*, 23, 2, 167–83.

Grant Ferguson, Ailsa (2015). 'Performing Commemoration in Wartime: Shakespeare Galas in London 1916–19', in *Celebrating Shakespeare: Commemoration and Cultural Memory*, ed. Clara Calvo and Coppelia Kahn, Cambridge: Cambridge University Press, 202–24.

Gray, Frances (2011). *Meggie Albanesi: A Life in Theatre*, London: Society for Theatre Research.

Green, Barbara (1997). *Spectacular Confessions: Autobiography, Performative Activism and the Sites of Suffrage*, New York: St Martin's Press.

Greer, Mary K. (1995). *Women of the Golden Dawn: Rebels and Priestesses*, Rochester: Park Street Press.

Grime, Helen (2013). *Gwen Ffrangcon-Davies*, London: Pickering & Chatto.

Hallett, Nicky (1999). *Lesbian Lives: Identity and Auto/biography in the Twentieth Century*, London: Pluto.

Hallgren, Sherri (1995). 'The Law Is the Law – and a Bad Stove Is a Bad Stove': Subversive Justice and Layers of Collusion in 'A Jury of Her Peers', in *Violence, Silence and Anger: Women's Writing as Transgression*, ed. Deirdre Lashgari, Charlottesville: University Press of Virginia, 203–18.

Hamilton, Cicely (1909). *Marriage As a Trade*, London: Women's Press.

Hamilton, Cicely (1910). *A Pageant of Great Women*, London: International Suffrage Shop; reprinted in Cockin, Norquay and Park, 3, 2007b: 174–266.

Hamilton, Cicely (1925). The *Child in Flanders: A Nativity Play in A Prologue, Five Tableaux and an Epilogue in One-Act Plays of To-Day*, Second Series, London: George G. Harrap.

Hamilton, Cicely (1935). *Life Errant*, London: J. M Deutsch.

Hamilton, Cicely (1949). 'Triumphant Women', in *Edy: Recollections of Edith Craig*, ed. Eleanor Adlard, London: Frederick Muller, 38–44.

Hamilton, Cicely and St John, Christopher (1913). *How the Vote Was Won*, London: Edith Craig; reprinted in Cockin, Norquay and Park, 3, 2007: 135–73.

Hardie, Ann (1999). 'A letter from Ellen Terry', *Costume: The Journal of the Costume Society*, 33, 110–15.

Hindson, Catherine (2016). *London's West End Actresses and the Origins of Celbrity Charity, 1880–1920*, Iowa: University of Iowa Press.

Hirschfield, Claire (1985). '"The Actresses" Franchise League and the Campaign for Women's Suffrage 1908–1914', *Theatre Research International*, 10, 2, 129–53.

Hirschfield, Claire (1987). 'The Suffragist as Playwright', *Frontiers: A Journal of Women Studies*, 9, 2, 1–6.

Hirschfield, Claire (1991). 'The Suffrage Play in England 1907–13', *Cahiers Victoriens et Édouardiens*, 33, 73–85.

Hoare, Philip (1997). *Wilde's Last Stand: Decadence, Conspiracy and the Most Outrageous Trial of the Century*, London: Duckworth.

Hobson, Florence Edgar (1912). *A Modern Crusader: A Dramatic Pamphlet in Three Acts*, London: A. C. Fifield.

Holderness, Graham (2010). 'Shakespeareland', in *This England, That Shakespeare: New Angles on Englishness and the Bard*, ed. Willy Maley and Margaret Tudeau Clayton, Farnham, 201–20.

Holledge, Julie (1981). *Innocent Flowers: Women in the Edwardian Theatre*, London: Virago.

Holledge, Julie (2008). 'Addressing the Global Phenomenon of *A Doll's House*: An Intercultural Intervention', *Ibsen Studies*, 8, 1, 13–28.

Holroyd, Michael (2008). *A Strange Eventful History: The Dramatic Lives of Ellen Terry, Henry Irving and Their Remarkable Families*, London: Chatto & Windus.

Housman, Laurence (1902). *Bethlehem: A Nativity Play, The Pageant of Our Lady & Other Poems*, London: Macmillan.

Housman, Laurence (1937a). *The Unexpected Years*, London: Jonathan Cape.

Housman, Laurence (1937b). *Victoria Regina*, London: Jonathan Cape.

Howard, Tony (2000). 'Blood on the Bright Young Things: Shakespeare in the 1930s', in *British theatre between the Wars 1918–1939*, ed. Clive Barker and Maggie B. Gale, Cambridge: Cambridge University Press, 135–61.

Howard, Tony (2007). *Women as Hamlet: Performance in Theatre, Film and Fiction*, Cambridge: Cambridge University Press.

Howe, Ellic (1972). *The Magicians of the Golden Dawn: A Documentary History of a Magical Order 1887–1923*, London: Routledge and Kegan Paul.

Innes, Christopher (1998). *Edward Gordon Craig: A Vision of the Theatre*, London: Routledge.

Irving, Laurence (1967). *The Successors*, London: Hart Davis.

John, Angela (1995). *Elizabeth Robins: Staging a Life (1862–1952)*, London: Routledge.

Johnson, Katie N. (2006). *Sisters in Sin: Brothel Drama in America 1900–1920*, Cambridge: Cambridge University Press.

Johnston, Harry (1920). *Mrs Warren's Daughter: A Story of the Woman's Movement*, London: Macmillan.

Kaye-Smith, Sheila (1949). 'More Distant View', in *Edy: Recollections of Edith Craig*, London: Frederick Muller, 126–32.

Kelly, John and Schuchard, Ronald (eds) (1994). *The Collected Letters of W. B. Yeats Volume Three 1901–1904*, Oxford: Clarendon Press.

Kennedy, Matthew (2004). *Edmund Goulding, Hollywood's Bad Boy*, Wisconsin: University of Wisconsin Press.

Kent, Brad (2015). *George Bernard Shaw in Context*, Cambridge: Cambridge University Press.

Kisby, Anna (2014). 'Vera "Jack" Holme: Cross-dressing Actress, Suffragette and Chauffeur, *Women's History Review*, 23, 1, 120–36.

Kohn, Marek (1992). *Dope Girls: The Birth of the British Drug Underground*, London: Lawrence & Wishart.

Laurence, Dan (ed.) (1985). *Bernard Shaw Collected Letters 1911–1925*, Volume 3, London: Max Reinhardt.

Leask, Margaret (2012). *Lena Ashwell: Actress, Patriot, Pioneer*, Hatfield: University of Hertfordshire Press.

Leneman, Leah (1997). 'The Awakened Instinct: Vegetarianism and the Women's Suffrage Movement in Britain', *Women's History Review*, 6, 2, 271–87.

Levi-Strauss, Claude (1962). *The Savage Mind*, Chicago: University of Chicago Press.

Lindsay, Jack (1982 [1958–62]). *Life Rarely Tells: An Autobiography in Three Volumes*, Ringwood, VA: Penguin Books Australia.

Looser, Diana (2011). 'Radical Bodies and Dangerous Ladies: Martial Arts and Women's Performance, 1900–1918', *Theatre Research International*, 36, 1, March 3–19.

Lytton, Lady Constance (1914). *Prisons and Prisoners: Some Personal Experiences by Constance Lytton and Jane Warton*, London: Heinmenna.

MacDermott, Norman (1975). *Everymania: The History of the Everyman Theatre, Hampstead, 1920–26*, London: Society for Theatre Research.

MacNicholas, John (1981). 'The Stage History of "Exiles"', *James Joyce Quarterly*, 19, 1 (Fall), 9–26.

Manson, David (2006). *Jacob Kramer: Creativity and Loss*, Bristol: Sansom.

Mao, Douglas and Walkowitz, Rebecca (2008). 'The New Modernist Studies', *PMLA*, 123, 3, 737–48.

Marcus, Jane (1977). 'Some Sources for between the Acts', *Virginia Woolf Miscellany*, 6 (Winter), 1–3.

Mayhall, Laura E. Nym (1999). 'Domesticating Emmeline: Representing the Suffragette, 1930–1993', *NWSA Journal*, 11, 2 (Summer), 1–24.

Mayhall, Laura E. Nym (2003). *The Militant Suffrage Movement: Citizenship and Resistance in Britain 1860–1930*, Oxford: Oxford University Press.

Mayor, Beatrice (1923). 'Thirty Minutes in a Street', in *Four One-Act Plays*, Oxford: Basil Blackwell, 73–104.

Medd, Jodie (2012). *Lesbian Scandal and the Culture of Modernism*, Cambridge: Cambridge University Press.

Melville, Joy (1987). *Ellen & Edy*, London: Pandora.

Melville, Joy (2006). *Ellen Terry*, London: Haus Books.

Merkin, Ros (2000). 'The Religion of Socialism or a Pleasant Sunday Afternoon?: The ILP Arts Guild', in *British Theatre between the Wars*, ed. Clive Baker and Maggie Gale, Cambridge: Cambridge University Press, 162–89.

Moreton, Andrew (ed.) (2010). *A Chronicle of Small Beer: The Memoirs of Winifred Dolan, Victorian Actress*, London: Society for Theatre Research.

Morosetti, Tiziana (ed.) (2016). *Staging the Other in Nineteenth-Century British Drama*, Bern: Peter Lang.

Morris, William (1876). *The Story of Sigurd the Volsung and the Fall of the Niblungs*. London: Ellis and White.

Neale, Shirley (2001). 'Mrs Beatrice Connell née Adelin Beatrice Cundy (1875–1949)', *History of Photography*, 25, 1, 61–7.

Nelson, Carolyn Christenson (ed.) (2004). *Literature of the Women's Suffrage Campaign in England*, Peterborough, ON: Broadview Press.

Newman, Lindsay Mary (ed.) (1995). *The Correspondence of Edward Gordon Craig and Count Harry Kessler, 1903–1937*, London: MHRA.

Nicholl, Allardyce (1973). *English Drama 1900–1930*, Cambridge: Cambridge University Press.

Nicholson, Harold (1950). (untitled) *The Spectator*, 6 January, 15.

Norquay, Glenda (ed.) (1995). *Voices and Votes: A Literary Anthology of the Women's Suffrage Campaign*, Manchester: Manchester University Press.

Oakley, Elizabeth (2009). *Inseparable Siblings: A Portrait of Clemence and Laurence Housman*. Studley: Brewin Press.

Parsons, Louella O. (1923). 'In and Out of Focus', *The Morning Telegraph*, New York, Sunday, 23 September 1923, 4.

Parsons, Melinda Boyd (1987). 'Mysticism in London: The "Golden
    Dawn": Synaesthesia and "Psychic Automatism"', in *The Spiritual
    Image in Modern Art*, ed. Kathleen J. Regier, London: The
    Theosophical Publishing House, 73–101.
Paxton, Naomi (2013). *The Methuen Drama Book of Suffrage Plays*,
    London: Methuen.
Phelan, Mark (2007). 'Beyond the Pale: Neglected Northern Irish
    Women Playwrights, Alice Miligan, Helen Waddell and Patricia
    O'Connor', in *Women in Irish Drama: A Century of Authorship and
    Representation*,ed. Melissa Sihira, Basingstoke: Palgrave Macmillan,
    109–24.
Pioneer Players Annual Reports; Ellen Terry's Library, Smallhythe Place,
    Tenterden, Kent.
Prescott, Andrew (2003). 'Brother Irving: Sir Henry Irving and
    Freemasonry', *First Knight*, 7, 13–22.
Preston, Kerrison (ed.) (1953). *Letters from Graham Robertson*, London:
    Hamish Hamilton.
Putzel, Stephen (2012). *Woolf and the Theater*, Lanham, MD: Fairleigh
    Dickinson Press.
Raitt, Suzanne (1993). *Vita and Virginia: The Work and Friendship of
    V. Sackville West and Virginia Woolf*, Oxford: Oxford University Press.
Rhys, Ernest (ed.) (1909). *Everyman and Other Interludes*, London:
    J. M. Dent.
Richards, Jeffrey (2005). *Henry Irving: A Victorian Actor and His World*,
    London: Hambledon.
Richards, Jeffrey (2010). *The Age of the Dream Palace: Cinema and
    Society in 1930s Britain*, London: I. B. Tauris.
Rimer, J. Thomas (2015). *Toward a Modern Japanese Theatre: Kishida
    Kunio*, Princeton: Princeton University Press.
Robertson, Graham (1931). *Time Was: The Reminiscences of W. Graham
    Robertson*, London: Hamish Hamilton.
Rogerson, Margaret (2009). *Playing a Part in History: The York Mysteries
    1951–2006*, Toronto: University of Toronto Press.
Rosenfeld, Sybil (2001). *The York Theatre*, London: The Society for
    Theatre Research.
Rowbotham, Sheila (1973). *Hidden From History: 300 Years of Women's
    Oppression and the Fight against It*, London: Pluto Press.
Sackville-West, Vita (1949). 'Triptych', in *Edy: Recollections of Edith
    Craig*, London: Frederick Muller, 118–25.
Saler, Michael T. (1999). *The Avant-Garde in Interwar England: Medieval
    Modernism and the London Underground*, Oxford: Oxford University
    Press.

Savage, Roger (2014). *Masques, Mayings and Music-Dramas Vaughan Williams and the Early Twentieth Century Stage*, Woodbridge: Boydell Press.

Saunders, Graham (2011). 'Modern Literature XIV', *Year's Work in English Studies*, 90, 1, 825.

Schafer, Elizabeth (2006). *Lilian Baylis: A Biography*, Hatfield: University of Hertfordshire.

Schuchard, Ronald (1978). 'W. B. Yeats and the London Theatre Societies 1901–1904', *The Review of English Studies*, 29, 415–46.

Schuchard, Ronald (2008). *The Last Minstrels: Yeats and the Revival of the Bardic Arts*, Oxford: Oxford University Press.

Sharp, Evelyn (1910). 'Shaking Hands With the Middle Ages', in *Rebel Women*, ed. Evelyn Sharp, New York: John Lane, 27–40.

Showalter, Elaine (2009). *A Jury of Her Peers: A History of American Women's Writing from Anne Bradstreet to Annie Proulx*. New York: Alfred A. Knopf.

Sinfield, Alan (1999). *Out on Stage: Lesbian and Gay Theatre*, New Haven and London: Yale University Press.

Smith, Alexandra (2010). 'Nikolai Evreinov and Edith Craig as Mediums of Modernist Sensibility', *New Theatre Quarterly*, 26, 3, August, 203–16.

Smyth, Ethel (1933). *Female Pipings in Eden*, London: Peter Davies.

Sparham, Anna (2015). *Soldiers & Suffragettes: The Photography of Christina Broom*, London: Philip Wilson.

Spender, Dale and Carole, Hayman (1985). *How the Vote Was Won and Other Suffragette Plays*, London: Methuen.

Stage Society Annual Reports; British Library.

St John, Christopher (1923). *The Plays of Roswitha*, New York: B. Blom.

St John, Christopher (1949). 'Close-up', in *Edy: Recollections of Edith Craig*, London: Frederick Muller, 16–34.

Stannard, Martin (2004). 'Nativities: Muriel Spark, Baudelaire and the Quest for Religious Faith', *The Review of English Studies*, 55, 218, February, 91–105.

Steele, Tom (1990). *Alfred Orage and the Leeds Arts Club 1893–1923*, Aldershot: Scolar Press.

Steen, Marguerite (1962). *A Pride of Terry: Family Saga*, London: Longmans.

Stowell, Sheila (1992a). *A Stage of Their Own: Feminist Playwrights of the Suffrage Era*, Manchester: Manchester University Press.

Stowell, Sheila (1992b). 'Rehabilitating Realism', *Journal of Dramatic Theory and Criticism*, Spring, 4, 2, 81–7.

Stowell, Sheila and Kaplan, Joel (1994). *Theatre and Fashion: Oscar Wilde to the Suffragettes*, Cambridge: Cambridge University Press.

Sullivan, Alvin (ed.) (1984). *British Literary Magazines: The Victorian and Edwardian Age*, Westport, CT: Greenwood Press.

Taylor, Clare L. (2003). *Women, Writing and Fetishism 1890–1950: Female Cross-gendering*, Oxford: Oxford University Press.

Taylor, Rosemary (1993). *In Letters of Gold: The Story of Sylvia Pankhurst and the East London Federation of the Suffragettes of Bow*, London: Stepney Books.

Taxidou, Olga (1998). *The Mask: A Periodical Performance by Edward Gordon Craig*, Amsterdam: Harwood.

Templeton, Joan (1997). *Ibsen's Women*, Cambridge: Cambridge University Press.

Tickner, Lisa (1987). *The Spectacle of Women: Imagery of the Suffrage Campaign 1907–14*, London: Chatto & Windus.

Trotter, David (1993). *The English Novel in History 1895–1920*, London: Routledge.

Wallis, Mick (2000). 'Delving the Levels of Memory and Dressing Up the Past, in *British Theatre between the Wars 1918–1939*, ed. Clive Barker and Maggie B. Gale, Cambridge: Cambridge University Press, 190–214.

Walton, J. Michael (ed.) (1991 [1983]). *Craig on Theatre*, London: Methuen.

Warden, Claire (2012). *British Avant Garde Theatre*, Basingstoke: Palgrave Macmillan.

Warrender, Lady Maud (1933). *My First Sixty Years*, London: Cassell.

Waugh, Evelyn [1930 (1996)]. *Vile Bodies*, Harmondsworth: Penguin.

Wawn, Andrew (2000). *The Vikings and the Victorians*, London: D. S. Brewer.

Webster, Margaret (1949). 'Postscript', in *Edy: Recollections of Edith Craig*, London: Frederick Muller, 54–8.

Webster, Margaret (1969). *The Same Only Different: Five Generations of a Great Theatre Family*, London: Gollancz.

Whitelaw, Lis (1990). *The Life & Rebellious Times of Cicely Hamilton*, London: Women's Press.

Winter, Jay (1995). *Sites of Memory, Sites of Mourning: The Great War in European Cultural History*, Cambridge: Cambridge University Press.

Wollaeger, Mark and Eatough, Matt (2012). *The Oxford Handbook of Global Modernisms*, Oxford: Oxford University Press.

Woodfield, James (1984). *English Theatre in Transition 1881–1914*, Beckenham: Croom Helm.

Woodworth, Christine (2012). 'The Company She Kept: The Radical Activism of Actress Kitty Marion', *Theatre History Studies*, 32, 80–92.

Woolf, Virginia (1978). *The Diary of Virginia Woolf, 1920–24*, Volume 2, ed. Andrew McNeillie, London: Harcourt Brace.

Woolf, Virginia (1992) [1941] *Between the Acts*, Harmondsworth: Penguin.

Woolf, Virginia (2000) [1925] *Mrs Dalloway*, Harmondsworth: Penguin.

Woolf, Virginia (2002) [1928]. *A Room of One's Own*, Harmondsworth: Penguin.

Woollacott, Angela (2011). *Race and the Modern Exotic: Three 'Australian' Women on Global Display*, Melbourne: Monash University Publishing.

Zangwill, Israel (1985). 'The Prologue', in *Sketches From the Actresses' Franchise League*, ed. Viv Gardner, Nottingham: Nottingham Drama Texts, 9.

# INDEX

Locators of images in bold